What People Are Saying

"*Big People Don't Pee in the Park: A Mother and Son's Journey with Down Syndrome* is an inspirational and moving story written with great heart and honesty."

-*Richard Paul Evans, #1 New York Times bestselling author*

"*Big People Don't Pee in the Park* is full of honesty, humor, and so much love!"

-*Tiffani Freckleton, NICU RN, bestselling author of My NICU Story: Written with Love and Letters to a Future Nurse*

"Wendy's heartwarming book, *Big People Don't Pee in the Park*, made me laugh and cry and laugh until I cried."

-*Roni S. Miller, mother of three young men, including Remington, who has learning disabilities, librarian, and author of Guy Manzer: The Magician's Reckoning*

"I encourage all individuals that are blessed with a child with different-abled abilities to read this book. The author is authentic, real, and passionate about educating our community concerning special needs children."

-*Jennifer Ann Gillins, author, S.E. paraprofessional*

"This inspiring book is really about being a successful parent and reminding us that all people have value, worth, and are to be respected."

-*Elda Robinson, author of A Simple Cup of Tea and coauthor of Empowering You, Transforming Lives*

"This mother and son journey brilliantly captures the rawest emotions felt when living with someone with Down syndrome."
   -Mikki Anderson, co-owner Anderson Trucking, sister to an adult sibling with Down syndrome

"She has written, with grace and humor, the true magic and wonder of receiving a gift and blessing."
   -Rebecca Taylor, MA, Licensed Psychological Associate, RTC Psychological Associates, PLLC

"Reading about her finding the strength, voice, and purpose, in an extremely difficult situation as a parent, is beyond inspiring. You will laugh and cry at the same time. A must-read!"
   -Todd Schofield, graphic designer

"Uplifting, funny, and inspiring. Fall in love with Wendy as she shares living life fully with Matthew, the gift of special needs, and the love he brings."
   -Maureen Ryan Blake, Maureen Ryan Blake Media

"One of the insights I took away, *was how can I be more inclusive to all*. With this, I believe everyone should have a copy. I know it will be one that I will pick up again and again."
   -Laura A. Phillips, Associates of Graphics Design & Commercial Art UVU, retired, dog mom :)

"I give joyful thanks to Wendy and her son for sharing their story with grace, humor, and truth."
   -Mary Jensen Smith, mom to two, wife, business executive (retired), twenty-six-year MS Warrior

"I loved every minute of this read. It gave me a better understanding of the lives of my students with special needs outside of my classroom, and most of all, I have a new respect for all of the parents of my students. You are truly my heroes."

   -Lena Johnson, Special Education teacher

"This book is a treasure, a delightful and humorous read that I recommend to anyone. It is truly a genre classic that will bless the life of anyone who reads it."

   -Gerald Nebeker, PhD, DBH, President, OrangeSocks.org, father to a daughter with Down syndrome

Big People Don't Pee In The Park

A Mother and Son's Journey with Down Syndrome

WENDY L. HOOTON

BIG PEOPLE DON'T PEE IN THE PARK
A Mother and Son's Journey with Down Syndrome

Inspired Legacy Publishing is a division of (DBA) Inspired Legacy, LLC
P.O. Box 900816
Sandy UT 84090-0816.

Changing Names & Medical Advice
Some names and identifying details have been changed to protect the privacy of individuals.
This book is not intended as a substitute for the medical advice of physicians. The reader
should regularly consult a physician in matters relating to his/her health and particularly
with respect to any symptoms that may require diagnosis or medical attention.

ISBN 979-8-9890842-0-3 (paperback)
ISBN 979-8-9890842-1-0 (hardcover)

Library of Congress Control Number: 2023917394

Printed in the United States of America.

Dedication

To my son, Matthew (aka Star Lord), thank you for giving me stories
to write about, and thank you for making me laugh Every. Single. Day!
YOU are my Son-shine, and YOU are amazing just the way you are!
I am sooooo lucky to be your mom.

Table of Contents

Introduction

To the Reader: In Pursuit of My Purpose

My name is Wendy, and I have special needs. I am blind in one eye, I am overweight, I am impatient, I curse, I am insecure, I can be bossy—or, as I like to call it, I have leadership skills—and I can be temperamental (ewwww, I hate admitting to that one). I am also a mom to a very cool human. His name is Matthew, or Matt, as he prefers being called.

Since the unexpected passing of my parents shortly before I wrote this book, I found myself focusing on my legacy and purpose. After much contemplation, I believe this truly began in my early twenties, when the gifts of compassion and unconditional love were bestowed upon me.

Before I get there, let me tell you a little more about myself.

I'm the only girl in our family, an older sister to two younger brothers. This may be why I carry that nasty, bossy trait. I'm outgoing but shy. I'm loud when I want to be but quiet when I need to be. I love being around a lot of friends, but I also enjoy being alone.

I love to dance! I can bust a move to just about any tune. That's not to say they are good moves, but I can and will do them. I started dancing at age three when my parents put me in a professional class. I vaguely remember tap-dancing to "I'm a Little Teapot" when I was but a little sugar bowl. I wore a white, poofy dress with red polka dots—or was it the other way around? Regardless, I loved twirling in that thing! And I've been dancing through life ever since.

Sadly, my parents divorced when I was in junior high. Because my two little brothers and I never saw them argue, their decision to end their marriage blindsided and hurt us deeply.

Still, I had a lot of my dance enthusiasm and continued to dance at every opportunity. I danced around our house, at my classes in school, and my friends and I went dancing every weekend.

In high school, I desperately wanted to be a cheerleader or belong to any club that might benefit from my loud mouth and killer dance moves—you know, the important qualities in getting a good education. It was the sure way to become popular and get the attention of the cute boys. I'd spent my entire life trying to fit in, and, in some instances, it was like forcing a wildebeest to cohabitate with a pack of lions.

Here's the thing: I had a misconception of what it took to be cool. I thought if you had a lot of friends or were known as one of the popular kids, you were *in*. However, to fit into these categories, in my estimation, you had to be in at least one of the school's coveted clubs.

When I decided to try out, I used the years of dance lessons my parents had invested in as leverage. I wasn't worried about whether I would make it; I had a closet full of tap shoes and tutus to prove I had the skills. I may have won the debate with my parents about going for it, but irrational thoughts began to fill my head. *How will I ever get through tryouts?* I began to doubt my decision, and as I waged this internal battle, I learned something. I suffered from not believing in myself.

The window for tryouts was closing, and after many conversations with my nerves, I finally talked them into it. The one thing I knew was that I would regret it if I didn't, so I decided to go big and try out for all of them! Yup—spirit club, dance club, cheerleading, and drill team. Talk about covering my bases.

After weeks of practice, the time came to showcase my abilities. Tryouts were the same for all of them. We hopefuls waited in the hallway until our names were called. With each audition, I found myself fidgeting as I waited, pretending to adjust my leg warmers while secretly comparing myself to the other girls. They were tall, lean, and very pretty in their new dancewear. My dad was raising us, and we lived on a meager budget. I felt like the other girls could tell money was tight by the looks of my faded tights and leotard.

If that nagging desire to be one of the cool kids hadn't been so important to me, more than likely, I would have backed out.

Instead, I took my insecurities out on my fingernails as I impatiently awaited my opportunity to strut my Ginger Rogers abilities. When they finally called my name, I entered the large, humid room that smelled of sweat and took my place before the judges, mustering the courage to perform my solo. This was painfully new, performing in front of my peers and coaches rather than an audience of strangers.

Here's the problem. I bombed each audition. I'd stifled my spirit and all the skills I possessed. I suppressed my dance energy and, as a result, my name did not appear on a single one of the lists posted. My confidence shattered, I knew there would be no photos of me on the spirit club, dance club, drill team, or cheerleader yearbook pages. Being popular wasn't in the cards. I was just normal—whatever that was. Sadly, I thought this *defined* me. I didn't realize I actually fit in with the majority of the other teenage girls who didn't belong to any of these clubs either.

In 1990, that all changed when I finally became a member, so to speak, of one of these clubs. My son and I joined it together. There were no tryouts to get into this group, its members chosen randomly. Exactly how it should be, right? My son, my beautiful baby boy with his mohawk of blond hair, was born with Down syndrome.

Initially, I thought I was being punished for something I did wrong, and I longed to *not* be one of the chosen but normal. But not long into my journey, I realized this was no punishment. In fact, just the opposite. For some reason, the Universe thought it could trust me with this precious life—a life I needed (maybe more so) as much as he needed me. I now believe this amazing boy came to help me with *my* special needs and make me a better person.

3

I finally became a cheerleader, just not in the sense one thinks of. My uniform didn't include the pom-poms, short skirt, or letterman's jacket. Instead, it consists of thick skin, a strong voice, and strength.

My vocal cords have gotten a lot of use as I've cheered for my baby over the last thirty-plus years. We've had some victories, and we've had some defeats, but we've done our best to be at the top of the pyramid. Doing so requires being able to do a few stunts, like stacking up against the odds. In addition, my son has inherited my killer dance moves. I've watched him dance his way into people's hearts.

Matt is cool and more popular than I could have ever dreamed of being. And I am finally a member of the club best suited to me, exactly where the Universe intended me to be.

I joined this club at twenty-three. Imagine my surprise to learn that we recruit approximately twelve thousand new members each year. Our rally cry is meant to help the world understand our children and see their value. Thank God that in this country, our children are no longer institutionalized for something beyond their control. They are seen for their inherent worth and the value they bring to others and, as a result, are receiving a better education and learning skills to become great contributors to society. They are even working and dating now. And guess what? Their life expectancy has increased as a result.

I will forever be their biggest cheerleader!

I believe my purpose is to help new parents, like you, who may have had a rocky start, just as I did. To help you see the beautiful life you are in for. It is for this purpose I share our story—a story of how I moved past the shock and fear and found peace and joy on my journey of life with an extra chromosome.

I start by outlining the beginning of my journey into motherhood. My narrative then transitions from *me* to *us* as I introduce you to my extraordinary son and the unbelievable miracles he's managed to bring about. Scattered throughout our story are hints of what you can plan for, along with surprising insights I have obtained and feel compelled to share. I'm hoping you will benefit from lessons we learned the hard way and especially from the times that left us laughing hysterically. Overall, it's a story of success and a way of dancing jubilantly through life's challenges. This I know: you can too.

Are you ready? Okay!

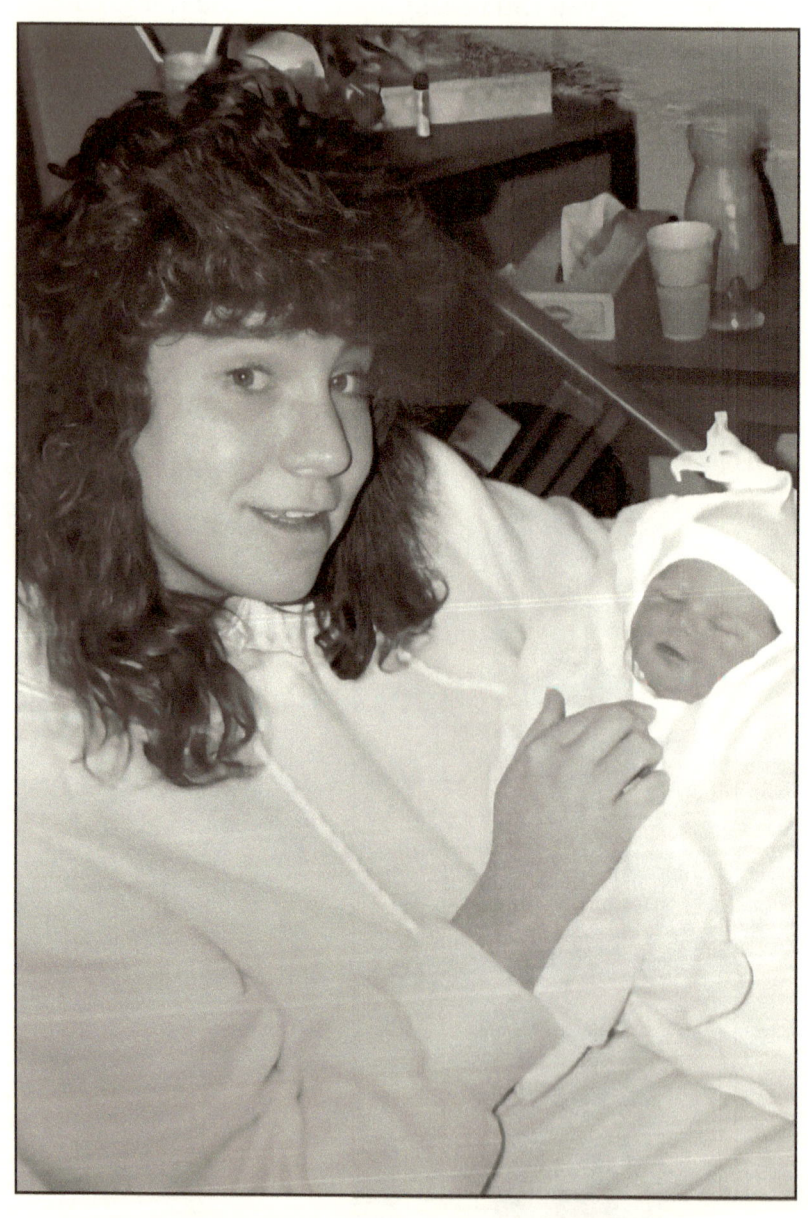

Twenty-four hours into our journey.

CHAPTER 1
Becoming A Mom

What were you eating when you were asked the "big question?" (You know, the one where you decided your entire future.) Was it steak? Lobster? Crème Brûlée? A tuna fish sandwich?

What? You didn't know tuna was the way to go? I didn't mind tuna fish sandwiches, but when it came to being asked to be someone's wife, I did not envision it the way it went for me.

I was four days shy of turning twenty, and Ash and I had dated off and on for only five weeks, give or take. So I didn't see it coming! In fact, I had been dating another guy for over a year, so, if anything, I expected the proposal to come from him—if at all. I was young, and marriage was the last thing on my mind. Still, Ash had made his way into my heart in the short time I knew him. I was falling hard for the tall, dark, handsome guy who sat across from me.

I nearly choked on the tartness of the pickle I had bitten into as he slid the ring box toward me. Speechless, I took a big drink of my soda.

Ash looked at me with his green, Paul McCartney eyes and smiled. "It's just a promise ring," he said, "but a promise that we'll be together and get married one day." To quote my journal, "I was flabbergasted and didn't know what to say."

Six months later, in August of 1987, I became Mrs. Ash Hooton.

We had done everything "right," at least by Utah standards. Ash and I met at a dance club after he returned from serving an eighteen-month mission for The Church of Jesus Christ of Latter-day Saints. Although I had been baptized, I was not a practicing member. He and I dated for a few weeks before he proposed, and after an "appropriate" six-month courtship, we married. Sure, it was a little sooner than I expected, but we were in love—and there was no stopping love. I was twenty. He was twenty-two.

We drifted from the expected standard of the religion by not adding little ones immediately. Still young, we decided to further our education, travel some, and then, almost three years into our marriage and with a little pressure from our parents, we were ready to start a family.

I remember the day I found out I was expecting like it was yesterday. "Aunt Flo" had stood me up for our monthly partee. I didn't miss her by any means. She's got to be every girl's least favorite aunt, but, for me, her visits usually came regularly. So, I took an over-the-counter pregnancy test, and it showed positive. Even then, Ash and I didn't believe it. I had been on birth control our entire marriage, and we had been told it would take a few months before my baby-making system was in full working order.

Because we did not trust the results, we scheduled an appointment with my OBGYN to get a blood test. During the appointment, the nurse, who seemed to be having an off day, asked if we had taken a pregnancy test.

"Yes!" I said, grinning. "That's why we're here. It said positive, but it seems too soon."

"When those tests come back positive, they are almost always accurate," she said brusquely. "If they come back negative, they can be wrong." She seemed irritated, like we were wasting her time. Still, she proceeded to draw my blood and take a urine sample. When she had what she needed, she asked that I wait in the hall while the tests were processed.

I had not walked far when she called me back to the room. "Wendy, not only are you pregnant, but you're *very* pregnant!" she proclaimed, showing me the results. The doctor estimated I was about six weeks along. Apparently, our parents weren't the only ones anxious for a baby: my girl parts were ready to go as well.

It happened sooner than we planned, but this was not Burger King, where you have it your way. While that catchy slogan from the '70s often popped into my head when things were not going my way, this time, I found myself ecstatic that things were not going according to plan.

Ash and I were excited to become first-time parents and thrilled to let our parents know they could stop bugging us. We were finally going to give them a grandchild! They had been anxious for us to make them grandparents from the minute we said "I do."

Of course, our parents deserved to know. We didn't want to tell anyone else until we shared the exciting news with them. As much as we wanted to share it right away, we wanted to do it in a unique fashion, so Ash and I headed off to find the perfect gift for them. We stopped at a local shopping mall, my thoughts racing as reality started to sink in.

As we browsed the shops, it all felt surreal. The little bean in my belly would grow and grow and one day join the world! As enthusiastic as we were, my mind drifted, filled with the details of the process—from creating this life to bringing him or her into existence.

I began to feel a little anxious at the thought of future appointments. I was a modest person,—and now I would have to put my feet up in stirrups! I couldn't imagine showing my hoo-ha to Lord knows how many people. And no thanks to all my friends who shared the unimaginable pain associated with squeezing a watermelon out of "there."

Sure, I had heard you forget about the pain as soon as you hold your baby, but I am an Aquarius. For other Aquarians, 'nuff said. For those who aren't, this means I overanalyze everything.

Fortunately, Ash's reaction to the news helped distract me. He was more excited than I expected, and that made it more special. It was the diversion I needed to fight off those thoughts racing through my head.

"I'm hungry," I said, trying to convince Ash that the cravings had already started, because you *know* that happens at conception. Or at least I let it be so. We made our way to the food court to take care of this important matter for the first time, knowing full well it would not be the last. Glancing at all the menus, we were surprised when we ran into an old friend of Ash's.

As Ash introduced me, he suddenly blurted, "This is my wife, Wendy, and we just found out she's pregnant!"

I stared at him, eyes wide. There we were, standing in front of Hot Dog on a Stick sharing our exciting news about becoming first-time parents with this person I had never met.

To this day, I don't remember the guy's name. What I do remember is staring at this tall, mellow man I had married, with his raven-black hair and green eyes, and feeling the genuine excitement in his tone as he announced the news to the first person he ran into. He was proud he was going to be a daddy. And in that moment of pure joy, he wanted the entire world to know. Since we did not have access to a loudspeaker, it seemed one old friend would have to do.

We finished feeding me and the bean and continued our quest to find the perfect gift for our parents. We landed on large balloons, blown up and filled with pacifiers, onesies, and stuffed animals. We needed three of these fun surprises for the three sets of parents we had between us: my dad, my mom and stepdad, and his mom and dad. Satisfied with our choices, we carefully loaded them into our car and rushed off to make our announcement.

Proudly, we presented the balloons and watched with excitement as each new grandparent peered at the contents. In my mind, it should have been obvious, so imagine my disappointment when, each time, said grandparents were confused.

How can they be confused? The balloons speak for themselves; we're pregnant!

Fortunately, their confusion was short-lived and they showered us with hugs, joy, and laughter. It came as no surprise that our mothers were the most ecstatic.

Over the coming months, I did not experience morning sickness, and I knew I was fortunate to be able to say that. I had friends who were extremely sick during their first trimester, and I never took my experience for granted. One of my biggest challenges was gaining weight . . . properly. I found myself putting on ten pounds one month but then nothing the next, then ten again, then nothing again! Crazy.

My doctor did not sugarcoat it when he told me I was doing it all wrong. I needed to gain the baby weight *gradually*, and if I continued doing it this way, I could have problems. His lectures irritated me As if I had chosen to gain my baby weight this way!

Pregnancy is a beautiful thing, or so they say. You see all those photographs of women's silhouettes clutching their baby bumps or pictures of expectant mothers standing in meadows in long flowy dresses as the sun sets on the bouquets of daisies they hold.

Then there was me, Wendy the wooly mammoth, just making my way through my expectant state. I did not feel beautiful or like I belonged in a dress in any meadow—unless it was to graze.

I really wanted my first baby to be a girl. I had visions of pink frills and bows in what would likely be a beautiful shade somewhere between my medium-length brown hair and Ash's raven black. I wanted a daughter who grew up to be my best friend. I also wanted the makeup of our family to follow that of my childhood. I'd loved being big sister to two younger brothers. As a mom, I wanted to have one girl and two boys and in that order—my daughter protecting her younger brothers just as I had.

I had plans.

But again, this baby had plans for me. Throughout the pregnancy, there was no having it my way. I began craving hot dogs, chocolate peanut butter cups, and Pepsi—all things I didn't normally eat. This made me wonder if the babe growing within my womb would be a son. If so, this meant there would be no pink frills or bows.

While my instincts said I might actually be creating a little boy, I was sure these cravings meant he or she would one day be a baseball player. When we had the ultrasound revealing the gender, Ash and I pretended we didn't want to know what we were having—that we wanted to be surprised—but it was a lie, and the baby knew it! Highly active that day under the ultrasound, with one swift move of the warm, jelly-covered wand across my belly, the baby rolled over, legs spread wide open. And, people, we were NOT looking at the umbilical cord! Our first child was going to be a boy. Food suspicions confirmed.

To be truthful, it disappointed me a wee bit that my first baby would not be the daughter I had hoped for. That said, it did not take long for me to start mentally preparing for a son. In fact, I realized, a future with cute denim overalls and miniature baseball caps and all things blue would be just as fun! As my belly grew, so did our excitement for our soon-to-be son, and we chose what we thought would be the perfect, masculine name: Brock.

Everything was going to be okay. I would get the frills and bows the next time around.

Ash and I celebrated our third anniversary when I was six months pregnant by going to a Mexican restaurant a friend recommended. I ordered my favorite dish, a delicious chimichanga platter, of which I enjoyed every bite.

A few hours later, however, it was clear the food did not agree with me. In fact, it did not agree with me all night and the next day. It turns out some bad chimi was making my bowels changa.

I became dehydrated from all the bathroom activity, and at the advice of my doctor, I went to the hospital, where I spent the next day getting IV hydrated. We were supposed to attend my five-year high school reunion later that night, and I lay there thinking about it. Although I had looked forward to seeing my friends from the past, I wasn't anxious to see them in my wooly-mammoth state.

It was supposed to be an eventful anniversary-reunion weekend for us, and it was, but not in the way we had planned. In twenty-four hours, I had gone from a restaurant booth to the porcelain throne to a hospital bed—from celebrating to medicating. When all was said and done, I didn't even receive the traditional third-anniversary gift of leather—unless you counted my poor leathery bottom, but we won't go there. Instead, I received the gift of food poisoning. But seriously, Ash had not overlooked our anniversary and surprised me with flowers and a gift to celebrate our three years of wedded bliss.

The entertainment did not stop there. About a month later, after surviving my bout of food poisoning, the Universe had another eventful evening planned for us.

Refusing to let a little thing like pregnancy slow me down, I continued to work for a service-award company where my job was to assemble samples of our products to ship to clients. These items were often needed on short notice, so it was perfectly acceptable to utilize my skill of "Let's get this done!" as I rushed around from department to department like the speed walker my family always accused me of being. If you're exercising or in a hurry to get somewhere, it can be a good thing, but not so great when shopping with family that can't keep up. I can't help it if we women take our shopping seriously and cannot be bogged down by those who can't keep pace. Being a fast walker can also cause problems if you are at work, trying to get to the company warehouse . . . under extenuating circumstances.

Picture this: A young woman, seven months pregnant, lost in thought (daydreaming about what to make for dinner later, or the new maternity top she hoped for, or zebras running through the Serengeti, or all three because she just happens to be able to multitask when it comes to daydreaming). Yep. That's me.

As it's almost lunchtime and I don't want to miss the macaroni-and-cheese special at the cafeteria, I quickly stride across the foyer, not registering the change in the surface of the normally carpeted floor and that fresh layer of carpet glue.

In the blink of an eye, this young, pregnant brunette finds herself flat on her back and staring at the ceiling while people who witness from afar run to rescue both mother and unborn child. Stunned and out of breath from getting the wind knocked out of me, I lie there while one rescuer angrily shouts, "She's pregnant!" at the contractors who appear as if from nowhere.

Suddenly, I find my voice and blurt, "No, I'm not!" as I try not to be humiliated and navigate this sticky situation with humor, even as my belly screams the bald-faced truth. The embarrassed contractors quickly rope off the area.

Fortunately, my rescuers carefully help me to my feet and whisk me off to a nearby women's restroom, where they grab tissues to wipe away the glue covering my backside.

Should I need to explain, tissue and carpet glue—well, they do not go together.

As I look up in the mirror and see the reflection of my peers trying to help me, I start to laugh. The person in the mirror looks rather tarred and feathered! Between the yellowish glue and millions of small pieces of tissue shredded into feathers, my embarrassed laughter turns into tears of shock and then gratitude. I feel so loved at this moment. What a team! Now they are not only trying to wipe the glue away but also picking off an infinite amount of shredded tissue they realize has become one with me. As I watch, I can see and feel their genuine concern for me and my unborn babe.

Word about the incident spreads quickly. My employer, worried about me and my baby's safety, instructs me to head home and call my doctor. But that's the next challenge—getting me home! My sweet friend Cathy offers to drive me. I graciously accept.

As Cathy and I leave the bathroom to get my things, we note that the area where I've just made my skate-in-the-glue debut had been properly marked off with yellow caution tape and safety cones. *Thanks, guys!* I think. *With no macaroni cheddar cheese for lunch, baby is not going to be happy with you.* Our next dilemma? How will I sit in Cathy's car without getting the wet glue all over her seats? The stuff does not dry quickly. Bubble wrap! We are proud of our clever plan, sure it'll work. We spread a layer we confiscate from our shipping department over the seat. On the drive home, you can hear an occasional (and maybe intentional) pop here and there, but we've protected her seats and I have cush under my tush all the way home.

Twenty minutes later, Cathy pulls into our designated parking spot, and when I try to get out of the car, we realize the humor of this situation has not ended. In that short commute, the bubble wrap has adhered securely to my backside. *Of all days to wear my brand-new outfit!*

I chuckle at the thought of how ridiculous I must look getting out of her car with my swollen belly in front and bubble wrap stuck to my backside. Our brilliant solution gives a whole new meaning to the phrase "bubble butt."

Through our laughter, my friend pulls and tugs, trying to remove the wrap, to no avail. She makes one last attempt by putting one foot on the car and yanking with all her might. Only then does my relationship with those bubbles finally end. I'm free! We laugh so hard I might have peed a little, which, thankfully, is acceptable when you are pregnant.

When I call my doctor to let him know what's happened, he feels there's nothing to be concerned about but instructs me to lie down and take it easy for a while. Before I can rest, however, I need to remove my ruined clothing. Every item I've put on that day has to be thrown out, as the glue has seeped through each layer.

I still have one final issue to deal with—and to me, it's a big one—my hair. I feel reassured that both my baby and I are not in any physical danger, but I suspect my hair is a different story. If you visualize strings of the most badly tangled Christmas lights you've ever seen, just know my hair was worse. My shoulder-length, permed brown locks are completely stuck to the back of my head, looking like a rat's nest. I can't even get a comb or brush through them!

It feels like hours before my husband finally walks through the door. Instead of "Hi, honey, how was your day?" he finds his hormonal wife crying, worried sick over the thought of losing most or all her hair.

He becomes my hero that night. After I get him caught up on the events of the day, we begin the uncomfortable process of ridding my head of my not-so-attractive mess. I lie back on the bathroom counter, my mountain of a belly pointed to the sky, my hair soaking in warm water as he takes a tiny comb and slowly cleans each strand. It's a lengthy process, but it works.

In my mind, we looked like a couple of monkeys in the wild, my mate grooming me. It may not have been an ideal date night, but we would never forget it. I loved him for helping ensure my head would not match our baby's as I brought him into the world. Although I now realize that losing my hair was hardly the worst-case scenario.

My due date neared, which meant the baby's lease was almost up. I had my first doctor's appointment in the third trimester, with a full exam to check my progress. The physician said everything looked fine and predicted I would go *past* my due date. Okay.

I had *plenty* of time. I had not had my baby shower yet, and we didn't have the baby's crib set up. Why rush? According to my math, which is not my strong suit, if I wasn't due until November 28th, and if my doctor predicted another week, I technically had until December 2nd to get everything ready. I took my doctor's word as gospel, counting on him to know when the baby would come. I did not count on my body and baby making that decision for us.

I felt great and continued to work full-time. Early one chilly Thursday morning, I went to the department where we made custom rings. The manager and I often bantered back and forth. On this day, he sat at his desk just behind me as I looked up the information on an order I had been working on. As I bent down to pull some examples out of a cabinet, I felt a gush of water.

Oh no. What just happened? I stood up quickly. Had the manager seen anything? Could he or anyone else see that my pants were wet?

Something told me this was not right, so I rushed back to my desk, praying nobody saw me, and mentioned it to a good friend, Stacey, whom I felt comfortable enough to tell the truth.

"I think I peed my pants!" I whispered.

She laughed. Fortunately, she had been through this scenario three times.

"It may be your time. Call your doctor."

I stared at her, hesitant because I was not due for three or four more weeks. And I was not ready.

No way! No way! This is not going to work with my schedule.

My dad often joked that I would be late to my own funeral, but I have found I do my best work when under pressure to meet deadlines. However, this deadline was being moved up by almost a month, or more, if my doctor could be counted on, which he obviously couldn't. I wasn't ready to become a mom. I still had so much to prepare, not just physically but emotionally.

Sinking into the realization that it was nobody's fault but mine and Ash's, I phoned my OBGYN. Though it had only been two days since my appointment, the nurse advised me to come in right away. The butterfly feeling in my belly was not the baby moving—and it wasn't gas. It was fear, and I needed emotional support.

Ash's place of employment was close to mine, so I stopped by to pick him up. Flustered, It didn't even register that I was driving as we made our way to my doctor's office.

On this early November day, tiny snowflakes teased us as they fell from the sky, just enough to wet the ground but not enough to need the windshield wipers. Thank goodness. A heavier snowfall would have made it difficult to drive up the steep hills in the avenues and me more nervous. I already had a million thoughts running through my mind. I was scared and not ready for what my body would soon endure. But would that be today?

I hoped we still had time. Ash bounced in the passenger seat like a small child, exclaiming, "We're going to have a baby! We're going to have a baby!"

Would you be reacting the same if you had to push this baby out of your man part? I thought huffily. *And why aren't you worried about everything we have not done to get ready?*

His behavior initially irritated me, but as I glanced over at him, I couldn't help but feel happy at his eagerness to become a daddy.

Because traffic was light, we arrived sooner than I wanted to. The doctor found a hole in my amniotic sac that was slowly draining, which meant they were going to have to induce me or my baby would no longer be happily bouncing around in his watery little sanctuary. His life would be in danger.

Today was the day.

My doctor instructed us to get to the hospital, just across the street and conveniently within walking distance from his office. Not only had I driven myself and Ash to the appointment in my wooly-mammoth state, I also waddled through the light snowfall, right on over to the maternity ward, where they were expecting us. Once I checked in and dressed up for the event in my new, backless gown, we contacted all our family, who quickly joined us. It was about to become a joyous day.

My dad's reaction surprised me the most. He was a military guy, and I rarely saw the soft side of him. At one point, he left the room, I assumed to have a cigarette, a habit of which I did not approve. But he surprised me when he returned a short time later with a bouquet of beautiful flowers, an "It's a boy!" balloon, and a proud grin from ear to ear.

With a trickle of a tear, I felt honored to be making him a grandpa. I could not wait for him to meet his grandson. A nurse commented sarcastically that she had never seen gifts like this *before* the baby came. I frowned, but I wouldn't let it ruin my joy. The tough guy who had raised me had shown a side others rarely saw.

Baby boy took his time to arrive. It had been about seven hours with no progress. One by one, family members left, heading home to get dinner and be with their families—except for the grandmas, who were too excited and were not going to miss the long-awaited moment.

A few more hours passed. Thanks to the miracle injection I'd received in my spine, I felt great. We were watching an episode of the old western *Bonanza* when a nurse came to evaluate things. To our surprise, it was time. When the doctor arrived, the grandmas were asked to leave the room as he prepared to bring my son into the world. This was it. As terrified as I

18

was, my body did what it was supposed to and was pretty darn good at it, if I say so myself. Fifteen minutes later, our child was here.

Just like that, I became a mommy, and the little life I had been creating, the babe who'd often had the hiccups and relentlessly kicked inside me, was now in our arms. Our family of two had just become three. Our baby was born at 11:15 p.m. to the *Bonanza* theme song playing in the background, but all I could think about was the beautiful being we had created.

Focused on inspecting my sweet boy to see if he had hair and whether the name Brock fit him, I didn't notice what others might have called imperfections. I didn't know what was not "normal." I didn't notice his protruding, longer tongue, almond-shaped eyes, tiny ears, or low muscle tone. All I saw was a perfect baby with his little mohawk of blond hair, and, to me, the name we had chosen fit him perfectly.

Because he'd arrived three weeks early and was jaundiced, along with other issues neither I or Ash picked up on, they whisked him off to the NICU, with my husband in tow, so they could get him cleaned up and into light therapy. Ash was to have that new daddy experience of giving Brock his first bath.

As I lay there, I felt high—not on drugs but on motherhood. My baby was perfect!

The doctor hummed along with the *Bonanza* theme song as he finished up with me. I could feel the epidural wearing off, and while the doc obviously felt comfortable humming into my enlarged lady part, I said, "Umm, Doc, you may want to hurry and finish up as I am starting to feel things." He gave me a nod and picked up the pace. Finally, he rose, took off his gloves, and congratulated me, sharing that he would be back in the morning.

The grandmas had left when baby Brock went off for his bath. They hugged me before leaving, but because I was tired, I did not notice anything different in their hugs or see the concerned looks on their faces. Several years later, I learned of their solemn ride in the elevator as they made their way down to the parking garage. Both had given birth to a few children, and they saw what I did not.

Alone with my thoughts, I wondered if I would miss the familiar punching and kicking I had grown so used to. Would I miss the small flutters that came every time baby had the hiccups or miss watching and feeling him move as I playfully placed a bowl of ice cream on my swollen belly? After almost nine months, I was alone again.

Ash returned from bath time to join me in the room I had been moved to. It had been a long day. Because I was exhausted, I didn't notice the change in his demeanor.

It was not until later, when the pediatrician walked in with my infant in her arms, that I realized Ash was more than tired. He held something back from me. He knew our world was about to change, and he didn't know what to say. In those early hours, as the *Bonanza* theme song replayed through my head, little did I know that my entire world was about to change.

✳✳✳

Imagine with me, if you will, a breathtakingly beautiful autumn day and driving through the majestic Wasatch Mountains of Utah, enjoying the purr of a cherry-red convertible as you make your way up the windy roads amongst a colorful patchwork of reds, oranges, and yellows. While the sun showers the earth with warmth, there is a perfect, cool breeze, making the aspens waver and whisper to one another, their sweet smell adding to the scent of pine permeating the crisp air.

Suddenly and without warning, an unexpected sharp curve in the road causes the convertible to fishtail and spin out of control. It careens toward the steep edge, and you are filled with overwhelming panic. At that moment, time freezes and the car comes to an abrupt stop. Your heart races, and your tears cannot decide if they should flow or not. In an instant, your feelings of peace and joy turn to shock and fear.

This was how I felt the moment I heard, "We think your baby has Down syndrome."

Brock was only three hours old, and becoming a new mom had quickly gone from being on the most beautiful ride to feeling like I was spinning out of control. I couldn't contain the many emotions I experienced. My heart stopped, and the tears flowed.

At that moment, I allowed myself to experience that heartbreak, gave myself permission to grieve the child I thought we would have and the life I thought we would share.

But with each passing day, I grew a little stronger. The more I looked into my son's precious face, the more I realized I would have to summon every ounce of strength to be his mom. That's when my engine restarted and I slowly started my journey away from the rocky cliff and into the unknown.

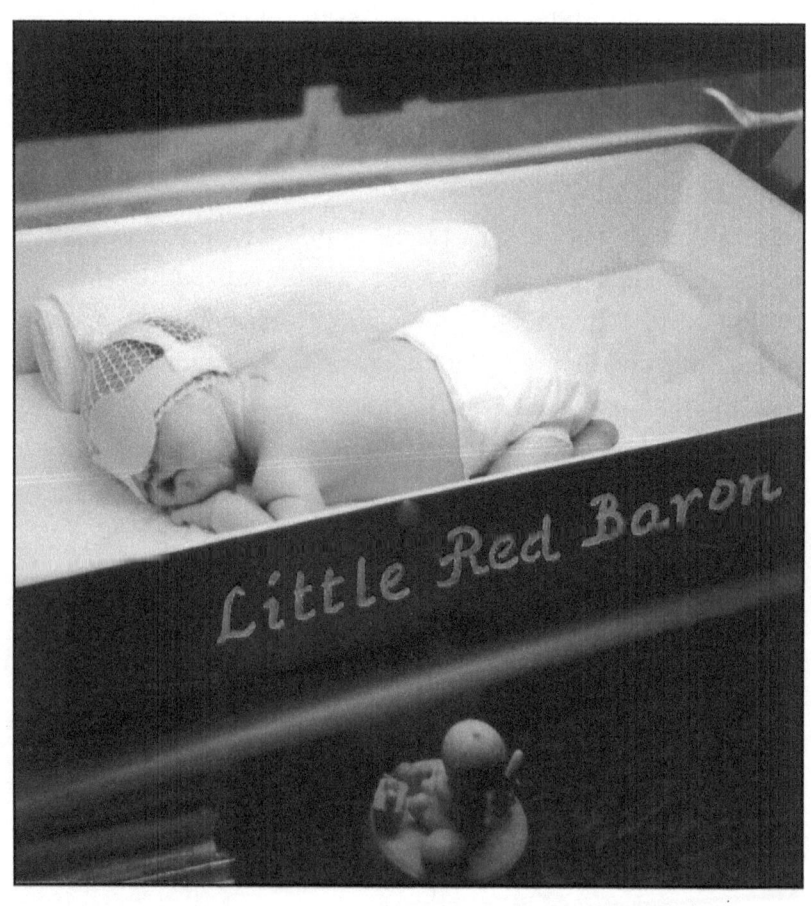

Getting some much-needed rays.

CHAPTER 2

Delivering—This Time, the Doctor's Turn

I'm curious. Are there any hospital rooms that compare to a five-star hotel room? At least one that takes my insurance?

Apart from the occasional murmur from the nurses in the hall, the maternity floor was quieter than it had been earlier that day. Ash and I were trying to get some rest—that is, as much as one can ever rest in a hospital room. The thin mattress on my bed and the bars of the frame jabbing me in the back made it almost impossible to get comfortable.

Ash slept restlessly in a chair next to me. Just inside the doorway, a second chair sat against the wall, empty. Both chairs were worn, having seen better days. I imagined they held as many secrets as they had visitors.

It was around two in the morning, which meant baby Brock was barely three hours old. Our room was quiet, the lights dim, as I dozed in and out of sleep, smiling often, sweet thoughts of my new babe filling my mind as I tried to recall every detail of his tiny face.

I heard a gentle knock on our door before it opened slowly. I roused myself enough to see the on-call pediatrician asking to come in. She had short blonde hair, was of medium height, and appeared to be in her early thirties. She wore yellow scrubs, and in her arms lay our new bundle of joy. Immediately I scooted up in my bed, excited to be reunited with my son.

"May I sit with you?" she asked as she lowered herself into the chair against the wall. I nodded as she did so but secretly hoped she wouldn't stay long. I was anxious to shower my little boy with the abundance of love that had built up in the last several months.

The woman smiled kindly at me and Ash, who was awake by now. I smiled back, waiting impatiently for her to hand Brock to me. She then said quietly, "You have a very beautiful baby boy here."

My smile faded, and I began to feel uncomfortable. Something about this sentence did not feel right. I began to assess the scene. The hour was late, or early, depending on how you looked at it, and this person was not a nurse but a doctor. She held our newborn swaddled tightly in his blanket. She had not wheeled him into us in his hospital bassinet.

I don't know if it was women's intuition or my new-mommy instinct, but I had a feeling we were about to receive bad news. I fell back onto the bed, wanting the mattress to swallow me so I couldn't hear what came next.

My eyes darted from her to the little bundle peacefully still in her arms. The world went on outside my room, but from where I sat, time stood still. And then it happened.

"We think your baby has Down syndrome," she said.

And there it was. The news hit me like a wrecking ball. My heart sank, and my entire body began to tremble.

And then the silent screams crowded my mind. *NO! NO!*

I had not had much exposure to people with Down syndrome, but I did know it affected their appearance and that they were intellectually impaired—enough information for me to pray that her suspicions were false. As a young mother who had just given birth to my first child, I did not want this for me or him. I didn't want us to be a "different" family. My head filled with fog, and I began to weep. I was devastated!

Then, suddenly, from my left, I heard, "What is Down syndrome?" I looked over to see the confused expression on Ash's face.

Before the doctor had a chance to answer, I said through tears, "It's all those retarded people in the McDonald's commercials."

Flashes of the commercials raced through my mind: an older man or teenage girl wiping down tables or emptying trash as the food chain advertised their Big Mac special. I didn't remember their smiles or realize how tremendous of McDonald's it was to offer job opportunities to those with Down syndrome. All my young mind could see was how these types of jobs were valued. I'd had big dreams for my baby before he even took his first breath, and cleaning up after people was not one of them.

The room felt dark, and it had nothing to do with the time of day. I could barely see the doctor or Ash's emotionless face through my tear-filled eyes. The awkward silence felt like it lasted an eternity. And then my husband and I simultaneously found our voices.

"What makes you think he has Down syndrome?" we asked in unison. I desperately needed to know because my baby looked so "normal" to me. I'm the one who argued as she answered our question.

"Well, he has low muscle tone," she said softly.

"He's brand-new!" I responded defensively. "He will develop muscles."

"He has a thicker neck."

"So? I'm a little thicker everywhere."

"He has a gap between his first two toes," she said gently.

"My second toe is longer than my big toe."

Her head tilted to the side, and she patiently went on. "He has smaller ears."

"I have small thumbs," I said as I held up my thumbs to show her.

"He has almond-shaped eyes."

"My husband has Paul McCartney eyes." I began to feel defeated.

"He has the simian crease," she added, stumping me with this one.

"What's a simian crease?" Ash joined in this time.

"It is a horizontal crease in his palms."

I studied the lines in my own hands, thinking they were just lines; we all had them. *In fact, they tell a story. Just ask any palm reader.*

She calmly proceeded with, "He has a longer tongue," but at this point, her words were just white noise. The symptoms she had listed felt like insignificant descriptions of my baby's features. I mean, really, how did one know a person's intellectual abilities based on a line in their hands and a gap between their toes?

I finally came back to myself as she shared that the medical team was 95 percent positive of the diagnosis. Still, they had drawn his blood to confirm it through genetic testing. The results were expected back in a week. I did not know it at the time, but for the next several days, I would pray harder than ever that we would be in the 5 percent that proved her team wrong.

The silence in the room became almost deafening as two new parents tried to absorb the news they had just received. The pediatrician sat patiently with us, still holding our precious newborn, ready to answer any additional questions.

Then it hit me. What had we done wrong? What had *I* done to make this happen? Was this because I had fallen in the carpet glue at work? Had the food poisoning from our anniversary dinner caused this? Had I screwed up with my weight gain during pregnancy? We had done everything right by Utah standards, so why had this happened to us?

The emotional distress caused me to lose my voice, but I managed to find the strength to whisper, "How did I fail my pregnancy? What did I do to cause my son to be born this way?"

"Oh, Wendy," she responded quickly, "it wasn't anything you did or experienced during your pregnancy. Down syndrome is genetic and happens at conception."

I looked at her. If this was true, it meant our baby had been different from the moment we learned we were pregnant. The moment we were having those balloons stuffed with prizes. The moment we shared the news with friends and family. The moment I had the bad chimi. The moment I landed myself in that sticky situation. My baby had an extra chromosome with every hiccup and kick and with all the love I felt for him as he grew within me.

After what felt like hours, the doctor stood to leave so she could give us some privacy. "Would you like your son?" she asked.

26

"No," I said without hesitation. "Please take him back to the nursery." As much as I longed to hold him, I wasn't prepared to see his flaws.

As she turned to walk away, I suddenly realized that this stranger was leaving with my baby. *My* baby. That's when my heart screamed that he belonged in that room—with us.

"Wait!" I called through sobs. "Please bring him to me."

I felt her compassion as she laid him gently in my arms. He slept so peacefully. Still, I could not resist as I gazed into his perfect face. I held him up to kiss him, hoping not to awaken him as my lips and warm tears met his soft cheek. Our son was just three hours old, and this was the first time we needed each other as a family.

I looked up just in time to see the doctor exiting our room in her yellow scrubs. As I watched her leave, my thoughts went back to those golden arches.

In a matter of three hours, I'd realized how valuable time was. I'd gone from the high of that beautiful new-mommy feeling to feeling cheated of the experience others delivering that day were having. So many questions ambushed my young mind.

What did we do now? What did this mean for my baby? For me? For our family? How would the future play out? In a time meant to be joyful, I found myself in a whirlwind of unexpected thoughts and emotions, my head and heart battling with one another. In my head, that tiny extra chromosome took over my entire world, wreaking havoc on all the dreams I had for this little life we had created. In my heart, there was a whole new beat as my baby danced his way into it.

I've had years to relive that night—time to think back on the events of that gloomy hospital room. There are things I wish I could change. My heart still feels heavy when I recall how I responded to Ash when he asked what Down syndrome was. On multiple occasions, I have tried to put myself in his shoes, tried to understand how it must have felt to have his wife answer that question in such a hurtful way, to not only hear that his son was "retarded" but to hear it from the person who had just brought his baby into the world, the person who was supposed to love their son no matter what.

I cringed as I wrote this sacred part of my story for you. I have shared this intimate detail with very few people. In fact, I considered omitting it, but after much thought, I decided to be vulnerable and real because my goal in writing this is to reassure new parents that any similar thoughts or feelings are valid.

To this day, I ache to my core when I allow myself to relive that moment. I am ashamed of those words, of how *that* word, *retarded,* even crossed my lips. But this was proof of how naïve and uneducated I was. I'm sure it would've still been hard to accept what we were being told, but if only I had had more exposure or known at the time what my world would be like, I don't think I would have been so reactive.

Over the years, my thoughts have often gone to the doctor who had the task of delivering this news. Was it hard on her? And how did it affect her in those early hours on that November morning? What did she have to do to prepare herself before walking through my door? How long did it take before she felt ready to face us? What did she think about my reaction? Did she think I was insensitive? Ignorant? Naïve? Or was my reaction normal? Does she even remember me?

My hope is that wherever she is now, she may one day read this because I want her to know how much I appreciate her and the gentle, compassionate influence she had on our family. Her job as a doctor was to share the unexpected clinical findings, yet she did so much more. She made a difficult experience more personal. She lovingly carried our little boy into our room, treating him like a human and not a diagnosis. She brought love and kindness with her soft approach. At times I can be easily swayed, so, had she handled this differently, my journey could have been a different one. The impact of her small but intimate gesture gave me and my baby a chance.

I've heard many stories of other parents who experienced something much different. They received no compassion or comforting words and, as a result, felt shame and desolation. Despite our fast-paced world, circumstances such as these deserve extra time. If only all medical professionals would take the time to take off their scrubs (okay, not literally) and become people for a few minutes, sharing a shocking prognosis would be a different experience for those about to undergo a range of emotions and significant life change. It could be the difference between a new mom telling the doctor to take her baby to the nursery because she cannot bear to look at him and choosing to keep him with her so she can bond with him and give him the unconditional love he deserves. This I know: the words and actions of the doctor who delivered our news will be felt for years to come.

I hope my book reaches any medical professionals who might benefit from hearing how meaningful my experience was.

It's the two of us against the world.

CHAPTER 3
When Love Changes

I believe in honesty, so here goes. To those parents who just received a Down syndrome diagnosis, your life just got hard. Now that I have answered any questions you had about that, let me follow up with this: the wonderful experiences you are about to have will be worth it. I promise.

AND you are not alone.

As a parent of a child with Down syndrome, you will be met with unthinkable challenges. You will endure endless emotions. You will compare your child to others. You will be in uncomfortable situations. But you will also discover how creative you are as you devise solutions for yourself, your family, and your child. You will feel a great, encompassing love you didn't know existed. You will be reminded that all babies grow and develop at their own pace. You will be in uncomfortable situations. You will laugh . . . *a lot.* Your skin will get thicker, and your heart will get bigger. You are no longer just a parent—you are now a teacher, an advocate, and a mentor. You are a warrior.

"It takes a village to raise a child," the saying goes. That is an understatement for those of us in the special needs community. My village became more like a small city populated with citizens who were excited to play a part in my child's upbringing. They included friends, family members, and Down syndrome advocates, all of whom were willing to help if I let them in. That, however, was the hardest part for me.

The Down syndrome community has grown since I first joined it over thirty years ago. It continues to grow and, as a result, plenty of rich resources are now available, such as online support groups, podcasts, personal websites, and sites for national and nonprofit organizations.

In many areas, groups schedule in-person get-togethers. These groups are led by individuals who are living the story and understand the position you're in. They not only assist you emotionally but celebrate with you and provide an outlet where you can be around others who relate to you.

It may be hard to reach out at first, as it was for me. I was in denial. Seeking help meant admitting my truth, my baby's truth. I wanted to stay in my quiet little bubble where I felt safe from the stares and uncomfortable conversations. Yet I had so many questions, like when would my baby hold his bottle by himself? When would he start crawling? And why did I have these feelings? By hiding, I did myself and my baby a disservice. I was not getting answers. I was living in the dark.

When Matt (aka Brock, details on this great story in my next chapter) was about eighteen months old, I decided I needed to shut down my pity party. Nobody could help me if they didn't know I was suffering. So I faced my fears, put on my big-girl panties, and made some calls. I contacted a local organization and, after speaking with the president, thought this may be my answer.

Afraid that I would lose my courage, I made it a priority and followed through immediately. They had weekly meetings for both parents and children and happened to be having one in the next few days. While Ash worked, Matt and I went for the first time.

I did not know how to socialize with the other parents, and, honestly, I did not want to . . . yet. They were strangers, and the circumstances were still so awkward for me. But I wanted Matt to interact with their children. I wanted this playtime for him. For now, I chose to take things cautiously, sitting off to the side, careful not to make eye contact with anyone. I feared doing so would be misunderstood as an invitation to chat.

I took mental notes as I observed the others in the room. They seemed at peace with their children. I expected to find comfort in watching my little boy play with toddlers like him, but I didn't. Instead, I experienced the opposite. The scene brought the sadness I felt for my child to the surface. But why? I'd finally found a group where my child fit in, and it was the perfect setting.

In this room, various toys had been pulled from their shelves and lay scattered across the floor. The walls were decorated with pictures colored by these little artists. A small table with chairs attached sat in the corner next to a tiny sink stained with paint washed from little hands. In this room, my child was not different. But as I looked out the window, watching those who passed by, I was reminded he *was*. The exact reason why I had not reached out. I wished this room had no windows.

After the first meeting, I sat in my car and sobbed.

"How am I going to do this? Why me?" I yelled through my tears while pounding my steering wheel.

I was drowning in self-pity when I heard a sweet jabbering behind me. I turned to see two beautiful blue eyes gazing at me from my son's car seat. My meltdown happened because of him, and yet he radiated nothing but unconditional love for me.

Feeling unbearable guilt, I looked toward the sky and whispered, "Why would you send him to me? He deserves so much more." I could not take these thoughts home. I didn't want Ash to know. As the chatter behind me continued, I began to feel selfish for my meltdown. I wiped my tears and put my key in the ignition, anxious to get back to my safe place.

These meetings were supposed to help, but they highlighted my reality. I did not want to go back, and my resistance won out. I sunk back into denial. In my heart, I knew things would get better with time. I had made promises to my baby but, so far, I sucked at keeping them. After a six-week hiatus, I mustered the courage to return.

Ash rarely went with me. He either had to work or did not want to go. Eventually, I made friends, friends who understood me, my fears, and my concerns. And my sweet little boy made friends. He "hung out" with other toddlers all at the same level—behind—yet growing together.

As a mom who found not only huge relief but benefited tremendously from this group, I encourage those impacted to use these resources. Ideally, both parents should be involved. That is my strong suggestion.

Having a child with special needs can affect who you are as a couple. It can affect other family members. Relationships require work, and if a differently abled child comes into the family, your work just doubled, possibly even tripled, depending on the diagnosis and severity. Though not intentional, as parents, your focus may be more on baby than each other. These children have medical needs, therapy, and other appointments that will consume your time. Even playtime and feedings will require therapy and education. You may find yourself giving your child additional love as you overcompensate for any guilt or remorse you empathetically experience because of the difficult life they've been born into.

Because it can be exhausting, this is the time to unite as parents and push forward, to be a team. If one spouse feels they carry the majority of the burden, this can cause bitterness, frustration, and even resentment.

Divorce rates are higher when a child with special needs is born. You put so much of yourself into your child that it is easy to overlook the love that created that child. Seeking assistance is not only beneficial individually but as partners. Can I share some wisdom I learned?

Don't lose each other. Remember, you are the same two people who were excited to welcome your new baby. The diagnosis may have been unplanned, but your child is still a product of your love. Take breaks and leave him with a person you trust so you can date each other. Refill your tank so you have the energy to face each day. Talk through the things to which you need answers. Work together to be your child's warriors. Collaborate and problem-solve to protect her, keep her safe, and help her become the best she can be.

As you adjust to your new life, don't overlook how this will affect the entire family, which includes any siblings. Because you and baby will be getting a lot of attention, it's crucial to include brothers and sisters as you create a strong foundation. Your roller coaster of emotions may be confusing because they may not comprehend the details of the situation.

Continue to show your other children the love and attention they have come to know. They are also adjusting to this big life change. Include them in conversations. Be transparent with them. They have special roles as big brother or sister. They are not only his siblings but his teachers and protectors for the rest of his life. Just like you, they can benefit from being around those who understand their family dynamic.

Remember, you are not alone! Surround yourselves with those who have walked your path. Fight for your love. Fight for your family. Whether you have a child with special needs or you are dealing with a physical or mental illness, loss, or any other life-altering experience, there is comfort in being around those who relate to you.

Sadly, my marriage to Ash did not survive. Not long after our son was born, I felt like I carried the burden alone. Once I accepted my reality and could openly talk about it, those around me could understand my pain. Ash did not express himself as I did. This did not mean he did not grieve; I believe he did. He just did it differently. Any grief he experienced, he internalized. Our baby was born different. The dreams we had for him shifted. We did not stay united, instead allowing our sorrows, denial, and lack of sharing emotions to put a wedge between us, eventually tearing us apart.

We fought, but we did not fight for *us*. We lost each other. So, my wisdom comes from what I wish I had known and could have put into practice.

Our son was just three when I became a single mother. And my journey went from hard to harder.

I did not want a divorce. Next to the birth of my son, it was one of the hardest things I have ever been through. For almost ten years, I raised my son by myself. Ash took him every other weekend, which was my only break. Those were hard years. I spent countless hours crying over the loss of my marriage, feeling overwhelmed with all my son's appointments, and frustrated by the everyday challenges I faced. I should not have had to go to war to get him the education he deserved.

I should not have had to justify why he required extra speech therapy. I should not have had to fight to have him in classrooms with typical children his age. It was exhausting!

But this sad and lonely chapter of my life eventually passed. In time, I found an amazing guy. And the second time around has been my success story. Partly because I learned where I'd failed with Ash, partly because I had several years to focus on me and my son, and partly because of this special man who found us. I've learned that good things are worth the wait. He sure was!

I had been afraid to date and could not put myself out there because of my "baggage." (Note: I do not like that term, but if my son were baggage, he would be Louis Vuitton!)

Seven years after my divorce, my knight in shining armor came into our lives. I met John on AOL.com. (For those who are familiar, did the AOL dial-up just sound in your head?) His username? Sir Jonathon. I was never going to date anyone online. I did not trust those "weirdos" and did not want to bring one into my son's life. John and I talked through Instant messaging for four months before we met in person.

I will never forget that day. My computer had crashed, and John came over to help fix it. Because we talked daily, I had forgotten that, technically, we were still strangers. When I opened the door, I did not expect the butter-flies in my stomach to arrive with him. I tried not to notice how handsome he was as he stood there in his denim shorts and red shirt.

At five feet eleven inches, he was taller than I expected. He was soft-spoken compared to my boisterous voice box. His smile was pleasing to the eye. Since we were just going to be "friends," I needed to banish the bugs from my belly. I reminded myself that I would never kiss his 'stache-covered lips or hold his manly hands—hands that looked like they were not afraid of hard work.

But Cupid had other plans. He hit us with that damn arrow and ignited a spark. And John and I fell in love. Still, we dated for three years before committing to a partnership.

I welcomed the companionship and relief John provided.

John did share with me years later that his choice to be with me came with a few hesitations. Being with me meant so much more than just a man and woman growing old together. It meant knowing we would not be a couple but a trio and that he was choosing to spend the rest of his life with not only me but my son.

John knew there was a strong possibility my child would not marry or move away. To be with us meant his future would change. John, too, would have to become a warrior. He would have to learn to advocate and help my son become a man. Unlike me, John CHOSE this. He chose to take on a responsibility that required day-to-day care.

Despite how much I loved this man, a dark cloud hovered over our relationship. I lived in fear that this would become too much for him and, one day, he, too, would leave us. Fortunately, after three years, I realized that not only had he chosen us, but the ring he'd placed on my finger symbolized full commitment.

I believe wholeheartedly that God sent John to our family. We are lucky to have him. Matt scored, for he has two dads who love and support him.

Though I longed for them, I did not have any other children. I yearned to make my son a brother, a sibling who would look out for him at school and protect him from those who would even consider bullying him. My hopes were for him to have a best friend who helped him learn as he grew. I could not give him that. But Ash did.

At the age of fifteen, Matt became a brother to an adorable baby sister. Although I am on good terms with Ash and I love Matt's sister, who is now a teenager, I do not get to enjoy the day-to-day interactions between the two.

There is no question about the sibling love they share; however, I wish I could watch how they get along, fight, and get on each other's nerves. Do they share the same interests? Do they like to eat the same things and watch the same shows?

During the years Matt is not with me, I find myself wondering what Christmas mornings are like between brother and sister. Do they get up early and sneak in to take a peek at the gifts, like I did with my brothers? Do they steal the chocolate from each other's stockings?

Ash and I both miss out on the life Matt lives when he's with one or the other of us. We miss out on amazing people we may never meet. Even though Ash and I communicate openly, I will never have these experiences with Matt. And yet, I am happy Matt gets to experience them.

I have chosen to share these intimate thoughts as something to consider if you're ever working on relationship challenges. I am not anti-divorce; I understand there are circumstances under which it is the answer. My point is to provide a perspective that may prove helpful should you and your partner find yourselves on a path to divorce.

Well, that was heavy, wasn't it? I am writing this as if I have a degree in marital counseling. I do not. I have only personal experiences—but real experiences a degree cannot prepare you for.

Receiving a Down syndrome diagnosis does not mean you are doomed as a couple. I would like to share that many of the friends I've made along the way survived the strains. They fought and won.

Up to this point, a lot of my story has been heavy. But now that I have shared those difficulties and you know a little about me, I'd like to introduce you to Matt, who really is the star of the show, the person responsible for making me a better human. I am so grateful to this beautiful human for giving me a life I could have never imagined and for showing me how to appreciate my abilities and find joy in every little thing. I hope our stories help to dry your tears, provide you comfort, and get you excited about what lies ahead. If love changes—between you and your baby or in a relationship—I hope you feel the successes.

And with that, ladies and gentlemen, I would like to introduce you to . . . Matt!

He goes by many.

CHAPTER 4

What's In A Name? A LOT

What you can plan for:
Your child may change his identity.

Have I confused you? I just introduced you to baby Matt when until now I've been calling him Brock. So, about that. Let me tell you what happened.

The babe within my womb needed a rugged and masculine name, but Ash and I struggled to agree on one. We were a unique couple—a little crass, funny, and Mormon—so a common name was out of the question. Once I learned we were having a boy, I racked my brain trying to remember all the hunks I'd crushed on in high school. Isn't that what girls do? There were many, but the right one had to be someone who hadn't treated my heart like the cafeteria meatloaf. Perhaps equally important, Ash had attended the same school, so I had to be careful not to give away the guys I'd had the hots for.

Soap operas were another great resource for names and, for me, a sweet escape from daily life. Ash did not share this same addiction, so I did not have to be cautious when proposing the manly options therefrom. Bo and Luke were two of my favorites. Ironically, these were also the names of the hot Duke brothers. Unfortunately, neither made the final cut.

Ash's dad hoped we would name our baby after him and Ash, giving him a third-generation name. I loved his dad, but I could not agree with this. We already experienced mail mix-ups—packages or letters intended for the one ending up at the other's house. I certainly didn't want to cause further confusion by adding a third.

Our list of names wasn't long, though, and one by one, we found reasons to cross off the options we had come up with before we finally agreed on Brock. It screamed "stud" and flowed well with our last name. (Plus, it really was the name of one of the guys I'd had a crush on in school.)

My mom hated the name. In fact, she one day sarcastically asked if his middle name would be Lee. She followed this by asking if we ever had a girl would we name her Calli with the middle name Flower? She worried she would have a vegetable garden of grandchildren. But her complaints had no effect. If Ash's dad couldn't change my mind, neither could she. Brock sounded solid yet slightly preppy, and the more we referred to our soon-to-be son by the name, the more it grew on everyone. My baby, a stud before birth.

And then everything changed.

Our room at the hospital started to brighten as the sun rose, although there was still darkness around my heart after our visit with the pediatrician. Around 6 a.m., approximately seven hours after we became parents, Ash and I decided to make the dreaded call to our parents. We could not put off sharing our devastating news any longer; we just didn't know how to do it. It pained us to have to tell them that something might be wrong with the grandson they had waited for.

Our voices quivered as we tried to say the words aloud. Each family member could tell we desperately needed them, and one by one, they quickly arrived. When my parents entered our hospital room, I felt like a little girl again, lost in the embrace of Mommy and Daddy, who held me tightly as I let my sadness flow. We all wept. Our room was small but large enough to contain the sorrow and grief each family member bore. I could see it in the pinched and devastated faces and hunched and shaking shoulders that matched mine.

In a nursery down the hall lay a sweet baby under bright-blue lights. He weighed seven pounds three ounces light but heavy with the entrance he'd made into our world.

Around 9 a.m., Dr. Nelson, in his white coat and clipboard in his hand, opened the door and stepped into my room whistling a cheerful tune. How could he be happy in my moment of despair? His smile faded and his tune changed when he saw Ash somberly sitting on my bed, consoling me as I sobbed, and family members around us sniffling.

"What's with all the tears?" he asked as he looked at each of us with a confused expression.

At first, I just stared at him. What a strange question. Was our reaction somehow abnormal? It didn't seem like it could be, but still, I couldn't speak. Suddenly, it dawned on me: he didn't know how drastically our lives had changed since he last saw me in labor and delivery.

Waiting for an answer, Dr. Nelson continued to look at each of us.

"They . . . they think the baby has Down syndrome," Ash finally mustered the strength to say.

For a moment, the doctor looked as shocked as we were. Then, as he relaxed against the wall, his stunned expression faded. He hugged the clipboard to his chest and said, "I am sorry. I was not aware of this."

I felt his sincerity. Even when he gave us a reassuring smile, I realized he wasn't apologizing for my baby; he was apologizing for not being aware of our circumstances. I felt a flash of compassion, realizing how it must have been for him to walk into this unexpected scenario. Still, I could only watch as he stood quietly and sympathetically gazing at me and Ash.

"What do you plan to name him?" he asked, his face showing sincere interest.

My brow furrowed. *We've just been told our baby may be "different," and you want to know what we are going to name him?* Of all the things I had been thinking about in the last few hours, a name was certainly not one of them.

In unison, Ash and I quietly said, "Brock."

He nodded as if he approved and said, "Might I suggest you name him Brock Matthew or Matthew Brock?"

In my head, I answered quickly and angrily. *No way! Why would I name him Matthew? Every family in Utah has a Matthew! I want a studly and unique name, and this is neither.* Even though I knew he spoke with compassion, internally, I lashed out even more furiously. *And why is he worried about his name right now? Can't he tell we're devastated?*

As if reading my thoughts, Dr. Nelson continued in a soothing voice. "Matthew means 'gift from God.' I understand this may be overwhelming and may not feel like it right now, but I believe you will find this baby you have been given is a gift, a gift who will bring you much joy, each and every day. I can see you're afraid, but you're going to be okay." He paused but was careful to look first at me and then Ash, right in the eyes. "Just love him like the baby you were expecting. You're a special couple to be given this special little boy."

That captured everyone's attention, and all went quiet except for an occasional sniffle.

He then asked, "How is the baby's health?"

"He is jaundiced from being born more than three weeks early," Ash answered quietly, "and he's having some challenges with eating. Also, he has a small hole in his heart, but they believe it will close."

"That's good. I'm glad to hear that," Dr. Nelson replied. He talked with us a little longer, sharing more words of encouragement and softly apologizing again for not knowing of our situation prior to coming to see us.

Like a Tilt-a-Whirl, my head spun with all the information I had received in such a short time. I had gone from feeling like I was being punished to being told I was special. *What exactly did it mean to be special? And why me? What made me special?*

I didn't want to be special. At this moment, I wanted to be normal.

I hadn't thought to ask the doctor why we hadn't caught this diagnosis during my pregnancy. I just appreciated that I had been given the gift of his time that morning, something a lot of doctors don't have. He'd treated me as if I were his only patient that day.

Dr. Nelson then completed his assessment of me—the initial purpose for his visit—determining that, physically, I was okay to be released from the hospital. He gave me a loving nod, then excused himself.

As he did so, he took hold of my mother's arm, escorting her out of my room and shutting the door behind him for our privacy. She later shared with me that he'd marched to the nurse's station with her in tow, then slammed his clipboard on the counter, getting the attention of all seated on the other side. He then bellowed, "I should have *never* walked into that room without knowing what I was walking into! Why wasn't I told about this baby?"

He never explained why he took my mom with him to reprimand those on duty. Perhaps it was to show them the pain on my mother's face—the same pain he'd witnessed as he'd whistled that happy tune.

While Dr. Nelson addressed the awkward situation he had been put in, we engaged in small talk with our family, all expressing gratitude for him. He'd managed to say all the right things in the time he visited with us, positive words of encouragement a grieving family needed to hear. His words offered comfort and hope—real hope—for the life ahead.

I still needed time, however. My emotions were playing a game of ping-pong. I was so grateful for my family's support, which I needed more than words could say. Still, I wanted to be alone.

And I was not the only one. Ash excused himself and went into the bathroom inside my room. A few moments later, I heard a strange sound coming from the other side of the door, a deep moaning. I quickly ambled over and opened the door to find my husband on the floor, sobbing. My heart winced as I closed the door behind me and ran to him. My giant of a husband, the man I had only seen cry one other time when his beloved grandad passed away, could hold back no longer. He had succumbed to the grief. I dropped to the floor and hugged him tightly, consoling him just as he had consoled me—a sacred moment between a young husband and wife.

The following day, Ash and I were in a better mindset as the initial shock wore off. When he went home to shower and pack an overnight bag for us, I was left alone with our baby for the first time. I had been released from the hospital, but we opted to rent the room to stay near Brock, who still needed to be in the NICU under the bili light and getting extra observation for his safety.

Where the events of the day prior had been so overwhelming, we had not had the opportunity to discuss whether we were going to change our baby's name. I was sitting up in bed, my sweet little boy lying between my legs as I carefully looked for the identifiers that had been pointed out. I located the simian crease on his small, soft hands, and noticed the gap between his cute little toes. I looked forward to the day I would teach him these were his piggies and how one of them liked roast beef. We stared lovingly into each other's eyes, me searching for that almond shape, unsure as they were still covered in new-baby goop.

Do you see my tears? Is that trust I'm seeing? I hope I can be the mom you're going to need.

My door opened . . . again. There had been so many people coming and going that I no longer paid attention unless they needed me. This time was different when I heard a combination of squeaky wheels and a scuffling of shoes making their way across my room.

I looked up to see a silver-haired elderly woman wheeling in a small desk with a typewriter on it. I didn't know if it was the desk or her shoes, but the screeching ended when she stopped in front of my bed. Breathing heavily, she carefully lowered herself into the old chair attached to the desk. That seemed to take forever. Her crooked fingers, manicured with pale-pink polish, shook as she put a piece of blue paper into the typewriter and turned the knob. (Yes, this was back in the days before computers.)

"Hello," she said, all businesslike. "I'm here to generate the birth certificate for your baby. So, what's his name?"

I stared at her blankly. Ash hadn't returned, and we had not discussed this important topic. However, with all the effort it had taken her to get into position, I didn't dare ask her to come back. I wasn't sure her heart could manage the exertion of getting up to leave already.

I looked at my little guy, who clutched my finger tightly. *Are you Brock?* I wondered as I studied his face. I had become attached to his name, but Dr. Nelson's words came back to me. Matthew wasn't a name I had given an ounce of consideration to prior to yesterday, and somehow, it didn't feel right to link it to Brock. I suddenly felt that if I were going to give him a name like Matthew, it should be the name he went by.

As I stared at him, a warm, beautiful feeling came over me. This precious baby *was* a gift, and this name suited him. Matt suddenly felt studly. He was my little stud with an extra chromosome, and we were going to conquer the world together!

I decided at that moment. "Matthew Ash," I declared. A gift from God for his dad from me. *The best name ever,* I thought proudly.

By the time Ash returned to the hospital, our baby had a name. He didn't argue with my decision, so I knew I had done okay. My father-in-law sort of got his way, too, as his grandson now had a piece of his name. And my mom got her way in that her grandson had not been named after a vegetable.

And that's how Brock became Matthew. Then Matt grew up and began changing his name. Every. Single. Day. Seriously.

Over the last thirty years, I've shared with him on numerous occasions the beautiful story of how he became Matthew. But he is rarely wowed by hearing he is a gift to us. You see, from the time Matt was about twenty, he would rather be known as a superhero from another universe or a dark lord from a different galaxy. He's strategically planned these identities during his nightly routine and every morning, still surprises me with a new alias for the day. Of all things, this is the topic that causes the most conflict in our home.

My office has a view that is out of this world, at least in the form of 100 percent cotton. Every morning after Matt showers and dresses, he emerges from the bathroom with his chest puffed out like a rooster in a henhouse—his way of calling my attention to the character on his shirt, usually one from another dimension.

He stands before me long enough that I can see what I'm expected to call him for that day. If that were all, I could rise to the challenge. The real difficulty is when he decides he's going by the actor's name instead of the character's. So I lose this game most days, in fact, several times within each twenty-four-hour timeframe. He despises it when I forget and call him Matt and will pace his room from end to end, cursing me as if I'm the villain.

"Don't call me Matt. I don't like it! I'm [so and so] today," he hisses through his teeth as if I can't hear him. I've contemplated sharing that if he were to slam the door while telling me off it would add a more dramatic effect, but why should the doorframe be punished too?

If I'm having a particularly off day, I may hiss back that I grew him in my belly and therefore get to call him the special name I gave him! Every other time, however, I beg for his forgiveness, explaining that his mother is old and cannot keep up with these things.

It happens almost daily. On a positive note, at least he's getting his steps in.

I may find myself in the doghouse when I call him Matt, but calling him Matthew really causes issues. Understandably so, as he only hears it when he's being disciplined. To be fair, the only time I ever heard my full name was when I was growing up and got in trouble. Still, more than once, I've thought, *Is it sacrilegious to use a name that means "gift from God" when he's in trouble?* Darth Matt does make a more appropriate "Uh-oh, you're in trouble" name. If only I could remember.

Speaking of Matt's identity, this is an excellent opportunity to sneak in a loving teaching moment.

Whether it's Super Matt, Darth Matt, Lord Matt, magic genie, Mr. Smith, Mr. Black, or whatever he happens to be going by, I have always referred to my son as a *person* first. My handsome boy has never been my Down syndrome son or my Down's kid. He has always just been my son whose name is Matt, and if the situation is one where I need or want to share, I may follow with, "He has Down syndrome."

48

It has never felt forced or like I'm attempting to make a point when I introduce him the way I do. It has always just come naturally. In fact, when Matt was around five or six years old, we were at a park playing. I had made small talk with a few of the other moms whose kids were also on the playground.

As Matt and I were about to leave, a woman approached. She had overheard me talking to the other mothers and now introduced herself as a journalist for the *Salt Lake Tribune.* She said she heard me introduce Matt and was impressed that I had introduced him as a person first. Could she do a short blurb on me in her next article? she wondered.

I was pleasantly surprised when the woman told me she felt this was an important topic—this treating him as a person first. She shared how she appreciated being acknowledged as a person first. Oh, did I mention she was in a wheelchair? Of course, I gave her my permission to write about her experience with us, and the article was printed not long after. That day, I learned that people are listening. Something as simple as your choice of words may land you in a newspaper article—and may educate someone else.

Changing word placement recognizes our loved ones as people first. For example, rather than saying "My neighbor has a Downs kid" or "Those Downs kids are always so happy and loving" can be reworded to "My neighbor's son has Down syndrome" or "Kids who have Down syndrome are always so happy and loving."

Oh, and speaking of people with Down syndrome always being happy and loving . . . Guess what. You may be surprised to hear this, but it isn't always so. Shocking, right? And guess what else. They have the same emotions we do! Our kids have bad days too.

My son gets grouchy and bossy and irritable, and some days he's a pain, just like his mom. The difference is that, unlike me, it's easy to snap him out of it. Also, unlike me, he doesn't hold grudges. (I'm working on it) He doesn't care if anyone sees him dancing or hears him singing. And he's not afraid to show affection. Since people with Down syndrome dare to live freely, when they are happy, *everybody* knows it. How would that be?

Good or bad days, I love him exactly the way he is.

My son is Matthew Ash aka Matt aka Star Lord. He has Down syndrome. Today, he is happy.

Lesson Learned

My doctor was right. My son is the greatest gift I have received—a gift that keeps on giving!

Thank you, Dr. Nelson.

Our first experience with the Special Olympics,
and we took the gold.

CHAPTER 5

Waterfalls On My Face

What you can plan for:
You'll want to take out stock in tissues.

"You will probably cry every day of his life," Matt's pediatrician said to us as we sat in his office shortly after Matthew's birth. Confused by this remark, I clenched my fists as I fought the urge to make his words true yet again. This may have been the first day I had not cried . . . yet.

Matt's original physician declined him as a patient upon learning of his diagnosis—not because of prejudice but the other way around. He referred us to Dr. Durham, a colleague who practiced in the same office, because Dr. Durham was a specialist of a different sort. He had a daughter with Down syndrome.

Ash and I were elated and relieved by this doctor's suggestion as it meant we would have an expert who not only had medical but personal experience. We did not have to think twice about making the change.

The fact that Matt's bilirubin levels were still quite high meant visits to the doctor's office every other day to monitor his jaundice. I hated these trips. My baby's adorable, tiny feet were now bruised purple from the millions of pinpricks the mean ol' nurses made when taking his blood. His squeals of anguish bruised my heart. I could hardly wait to snatch him up so I could cradle him and make it all better.

We rarely left our home in the beginning, limiting Matt's outings to visit our parents or the doctor's office. Preparing for these outings took skills, new mommy skills I learned quickly. Grandma and I got a little carried away shopping for darling baby outfits in bright primary colors and softer hues of light blue, along with coordinating fluffy blankets. Matt's closet looked like he had his own department store. In addition to making sure he looked adorable every day, I also made sure the cold of his first winter didn't stand a chance of getting to him.

Today was an important day. They would be doing more than drawing blood. We were finally going to meet Matt's new doctor. I had to decide which outfit he would make cute that day. After bundling him in his first warm layer, I added more warmth by putting him in his soft bear-eared, fleece snowsuit. The most important step came next—softly kissing each cheek as I inhaled his sweet baby scent before delicately placing him in his car carrier. Once I had him strapped in, I snuggly tucked a matching blanket around him, along with all the straps. Satisfied that he looked warm and safe, I placed a nice thick blanket over the carrier. This extra barrier was my way of fending off any wind or snow that might try to get to him on the short trip to the already warmed-up car.

Deep in the winter months now, we faced concerns about our newborn getting sick, and the constant fear of SIDS plagued my mind.

Ash and I were eager to meet Dr. Durham. As we patiently sat in the exam room, waiting for him to make his grand entrance, the strong smells of rubbing alcohol and disinfectant made their way up my nostrils. I imagined they sanitized the rooms after each patient so as not to spread the icky germs of winter from one child to another. Still, I kept my baby safely covered in his carrier.

I found myself drawn to laminated images of the human body that hung on the wall. They actually looked kind of gross with their colorful, detailed depictions of muscles, tendons, and veins. On the wall next to this, I noticed a more appealing image—a poster of a darling baby girl with the saying, "A person's a person no matter how small." I looked toward the carrier that held my sweet bundle of joy and thought, *And they matter even if they have an extra chromosome.*

The turning of the doorknob caught my attention. Anxious to meet the man who would care for my baby, I had so many questions! He welcomed me and Ash with a warm smile and strong handshake that felt as if he were saying, "I've got you."

"Hello! I'm Dr. Durham," he said enthusiastically, his comforting greeting putting my mind at ease. I knew we were in good hands and that Matt was in the best of hands.

Dr. Durham's light-brown hair was parted to one side and fit the profile of your typical middle-aged man of the nineties. He had kind eyes that lit up when he talked and a calm voice, one that provided needed reassurance to new parents who were unsure of the life ahead of them. His easygoing demeanor made him approachable anytime we had concerns.

Ash had placed the car seat on the only chair in the exam room. On the exam table, Dr. Durham laid a manilla folder, empty now but soon to be filled with my son's life history. "Is this Matthew?" the doctor asked as he approached. He appeared excited to meet our little guy.

I watched proudly as he removed the colorful circus-print blanket I had draped over Matt. He gazed into the carrier and grinned wide enough to expose his teeth. *Is this taking him back to his own experience?* I wondered as he caught his first glimpse of the little life we'd brought into the world. I tried to look over his shoulder to see if Matt had awakened, but the doctor had positioned himself to where his broad shoulders blocked my view. Perfect baby, great doctor—a match made in heaven.

I bonded with Dr. Durham almost immediately, solidifying our decision for him to care for our baby.

Turning to me, he asked an odd question. "Wendy, are you hot?" I had on a sweater but had taken my coat off and draped it over the chair.

Bewildered, I glanced at Ash and then over at him. "No, I'm fine. The temperature in this room is perfect."

Dr. Durham's lips formed a sheepish grin. "I can already tell you're going to be protective."

I smiled and nodded.

"I'm glad to see you're taking care to keep Matthew warm."

Oh, good. I'm not doing so bad for not knowing how to do this mom thing.

His voice softened as he went on. "But even though babies are small, they are just like us. If you're hot, he's hot. If you're cold, he's cold." Confused, I looked at Matt all snuggled in his carrier. "In other words," Dr. Durham went on, "it isn't necessary to cover him up with all this warmth. We don't want to overheat him."

Suddenly, the only things getting warmer in that room were my cheeks. Embarrassed, I asked "Too many blankets?" Dr. Durham smiled and nodded.

"I'm sorry," I whispered, disappointed in myself.

"Wendy, you're doing great! Matthew is lucky to have you for his mom," the doctor reassured me as if he could see I felt like I'd already failed my baby.

I left that appointment walking slowly behind Ash, watching as he carried our son to the car. Diaper bag in one hand and one of Matt's extra layers in the other, I made a mental note of what I'd learned that day. I certainly did not want to roast my little one—who, I noticed, might or might not have rosy cheeks.

In addition to the fact that I had been overheating my infant, Dr. Durham had shared the big news.

"You will probably cry every day of his life."

At the time, we didn't have a clear understanding of what he meant. Naturally, I interpreted this as we were going to be sad every day—yet Dr. Durham seemed so proud of his daughter. So why would he tell us this? My emotions were delicate and all over the place, which I'm sure he knew. I did not know how to accept that this would be my life, that it would not get better as I dreamed it would, and that I would cry every day.

While at the time I did not understand why he made this comment, I later did. It took years of ups and downs, frustrations, and celebrations for it to make sense.

During my journey, my experience has been that the majority of people believe that being a mom to a child with Down syndrome comes with a lot of love, hugs, and joy. And they are right! However, if I'm being completely honest, it also comes with many frustrations that lead to many tears. Both have been brought on by the challenges I've faced, dealing with people who don't understand, and simply trying to do my best to give my son a productive and meaningful life.

There are the obvious obstacles that come with parenting a child with extra needs: struggles with potty training, speech/communication, schoolwork, and inclusion—and hearing again and again the things your child might never be able to do. Ironically, many of these limitations were imposed on my child by the professionals and specialists I encountered. I quickly learned to advocate for Matt, and as long as I was realistic but not limited in my vision for him, I had a secret weapon that allowed him to grow in areas others didn't believe he could.

Then there are the not-so-obvious obstacles not discussed in any of the books I read or meetings I attended—obstacles that amplify the emotions associated with raising a child who has special needs, occasionally bringing Matt and me to tears and making me want to scream "I give up!" and throw my hands in the air. However, giving up has never been an option.

In my hope to help other parents avoid these unknowns, I thought I would share some of the daily challenges I encountered where I had no resources to turn to in overcoming and understanding them.

Nutritional "Advice" for Sanity

Let's start with something you would assume comes naturally: eating. My son has now mastered this skill, but that's not how it started. When choosing to breastfeed, the hope is the baby will latch on with ease and begin to suckle. Some babies struggle to get the hang of it. For babies who have Down syndrome, it can take longer.

My baby's larger tongue and struggle to breathe through his nose while eating made this task difficult for him. Most of the time he stopped breathing while sucking. Starving and frustrated, he would cry and cry. Then I would become upset because I knew he needed to eat but doing so almost choked him. The entire process became physically and emotionally exhausting for both of us.

As a new mommy, I felt an obligation to nurse Matt. I wanted him to get the natural nutrition he needed, along with the antibodies that come with breastfeeding to help fight off the gunk he could be exposed to. After a few months of pools of tears and dedication to making it work, Dr. Durham explained that my baby could sense my frustration, which added to his anxiety during feeding. I had given it my best with no improvement, so he advised me to start bottle feeding. It may also have been his gentle way of saying, "Stop starving your kid!" As much as I wanted to naturally give my baby his nutrients, it didn't work for us. I grabbed the towel and threw that sucker in, my boobs and I surrendering!

Off to the store I went to buy their replacements, including several different bottle styles, before finally finding the one where Matt could eat and breathe at the same time. Finally! My baby could now have a meal in peace. I appreciated the formula option because, without it, my poor child would have starved. (Thank you, Similac!)

From that moment on, mealtime became a much better and more treasured experience for us and the beginning of assuaging Matt's very healthy appetite.

Babies and toddlers are naturally messy eaters. It's part of the process, but I did not understand why my child looked like he was at war with his food well past his toddler years! I had no idea eating could be difficult for some when consuming foods with more than one texture. Heck, I never even realized foods had different textures (e.g., in chicken noodle soup, you have the noodle, the broth, and the gross little meat chunks, and when Matt was learning to eat those three textures simultaneously, it just made a mess!) Anything I tried to feed him with more than one texture ended up everywhere, especially where his extra-long tongue struggled to ingest it. All I know is when *I'm* eating and it tastes good, I have no problem filling my piehole regardless of how many different types of ingredients are in it. Not so with all babies.

Before Matt arrived, I complained (if only slightly) about my mom's addiction to buying baby clothes because his closet shrunk so fast. I used to tease her that she needed to attend BSA (Baby Shopping Anonymous). However, once Matt started eating foods beyond the bottle, the complaining stopped. His department-store closet of clothing came in handy as I had to change him at least three times a day—that is until I got tired of doing so many loads of laundry!

One day, by accident, I found how well a heavy-duty dishcloth doubles as a bib. *Imagine that.* I created something new. *Just like in the olden days when Mom and Grandma safety-pinned towels around our necks.*

My baby certainly did not look as cute wrapped in an oversized mirage of blue and mauve geese, but his designer day-of-the-week bibs weren't doing their job. At least by the end, he no longer looked like he'd gone swimming in his meal, and laundry was minimized mostly to those easily foldable towels I found to be a godsend.

Taking Medications—The Bitter Pill

Teaching Matt to swallow pills pained me—which I find ironic since meds are usually taken to relieve pain. Remember the more-than-one-texture thing? There were countless nights with Matt gagging and sobbing as I tried to get his medication in him.

"Crush them up and put them in apple sauce," they said . . . which worked perfectly if you wanted to fight about eating nasty-tasting apple-sauce and end up with a whole different type of mess to clean! It would be great if pharmaceutical companies understood the need for medications to come in a liquid, decent-tasting chewable, or even dissolvable form and created something for people who have difficulty swallowing. This could put an end to resistance and help eliminate some of the mess they obviously don't realize parents have to deal with.

Clothing and Learning

How difficult could it be to teach my child to put his socks on? After all, you just slip your foot in and pull it up, right?

Wrong! Those darn pinky toes make amazing escape artists as they venture off on their own. I'm not sure if you're aware, but you kind of need all toes tucked in to be able to pull up your sock. Rather than joining the little piggy family, this smallest member of the group managed to take the sock with it as it sought independence. It shouldn't be so frustrating or take so long to clothe your feet. Then there were other clothing atrocities to address.

If I had a dollar for every time Matt came out of the bathroom with his pants undone, I would own a villa somewhere on a tropical island. Heck, I may even own that island! I regularly had to come to his rescue because his chubby little fingers couldn't get his button through the holes in his jeans! Why in the world do manufacturers insist on making them so narrow and tight? Sometimes I have a hard time getting my own pants done up. Naturally, anyone who may be differently abled will struggle. I hope those companies figure it out and implement some quality control focusing solely on the buttonhole, stretching it out, double-checking that it's wide enough—anything. Just fix it!

Some suggested buying pants with an elastic waistband, but I insisted Matt look stylish and that he fit in where possible, so those pants were not an option. Vanity versus practicality? Not even!

How could I teach my child to button his pants or tie his shoes when he could barely pick up a Cheerio? And zippers! Everything had zippers—pants, jackets, and coats. You know how it is when they get stuck—that is, if you are able to get zipper and teeth aligned to even get to the stuck part.

Cleanliness Is Next to Godliness

When it came to showering, you would have thought we were supplying the shampoo for an entire boys' locker room and not just one kid. I happened to catch Matt one day treating it like hand soap, lathering up so well hardly anything made it to his hair. When I realized this, I wondered how many days his hair actually got washed. At least his hands were clean.

Phew! Now that we're dressed, let's get to school.

Cutting the Learning Curve: School

Yay for homework! Did you know how confusing the English language is? Have you ever tried to explain why the *a* in *cat* sounds different than the *a* in *rain* or why the *f* in *foot* sounds the same as the *ph* in *telephone?* It's a wonder my son learned to read at all with me at the head of his residential classroom. As we read together, Matt would get confused, and as much as I'd always wanted to teach for a career, I had something different in mind—you know, like helping thirty easy kids instead of one. I learned quickly that maybe a teaching career would not have suited me. The wavy pages of our books and Matt's schoolwork were evidence of the many tears shed in this department. Oh! What I really mean is that our dog made a mess of anything paper in our home. *wink, wink* Just don't tell the teacher.

Speaking of not telling the teacher and other important adults, let's tackle another bodily function.

Toileting! 'Nuff Said

Toileting is still an ongoing issue.

I know potty training is not easy for any family, but for me, it took sooooooooooooooooo long. Before Matt arrived, Ash and I thought we were being smart by buying diapers every payday so we were well stocked when baby got here. Originally, we thought our child would be an overachiever; instead, we underestimated by about two years. We could have never anticipated our baby would be in diapers for the first four years of his life! You'll need to prepare for that too. Needless to say, we were a little short on inventory. Back then, I had an

61

extremely difficult time finding diapers or Pull-Ups for a four-year-old. Fortunately for you, that need has been filled!

To whoever it is that came up with the idea of family restrooms in public places, thank you! I can't tell you how many times Matt and I were out in public and I was faced with the dilemma of how to help him go potty. Being the overprotective single mother I was, I never sent him into the men's bathroom alone. This became especially challenging as he got older. He began to recognize that he shouldn't be in the women's bathroom, and little girls were sure to call out to their moms when they saw a boy.

Each time, I did my best to scope out the surroundings. If the coast was clear, I rushed him into the handicapped stall, but I didn't always manage to go unnoticed. If the women's bathroom had a line of customers, I would holler into the men's room because, for some reason, men don't pee as often as women. If nobody answered, I stepped in (again, if the coast was clear), commandeered the space, and stood guard while Matt did his business. For just a minute, no men were allowed in the men's restroom.

As Matt got older and bigger, I planned my outings based on when he had his last meal or bio dump and the bathroom availability at our destination. Now you understand my celebration of those family restrooms! Fortunately, as our friend circle grew, there were often adult males in our group. They had the fun task of standing guard so nobody dared to touch or even look at my son, as well as monitor social hour with Matt whenever he peed with strangers since he will start a conversation anywhere. My male friends were, and still are, my lifesavers.

Speaking of toileting, how in the world do you get these kids to understand that just because you're having fun in the pool doesn't mean you can poop in your swim trunks! (Enter foul language here.) Sure, little kids do it all the time, but what happens when that kid is a teenager? I don't know if it's better that he did it in a friend's pool—or if it would have been less embarrassing to have him do it in a public pool where we didn't know anyone. I contemplated never telling them about the "incident," as I like to call it. After all, isn't there enough chlorine in the pool to kill poop? He was old enough that the poo was good and solid, but my conscience got the best of me. Unlike my boy's swimsuit, I came clean.

We were never invited back. Something tells me they didn't appreciate Matt using the corner of their pool as an outhouse.

To this day, I have to remind Matt to pee. He's like a camel. Only instead of storing water, he stores his urine. He'd make a good truck driver! I'm still trying to figure out if he doesn't feel this sensation. (Sometimes I wish my body was designed that way, especially at two and five in the morning—yay for getting older!) In an effort to avoid bladder infections, I learned to set an alarm on Matt's phone to remind him to use the restroom. I'm just thankful those who may be around don't ask him what it's for. "I need pee!" I can easily see him announcing unashamedly.

Stranger Danger

"Don't talk to strangers." We pound this statement into our children's little heads but fail to abide by the rules ourselves. How many times have we struck up conversations in hotel lobbies, elevators, or while waiting for a table at a restaurant? Do our children notice? I can't help but laugh every time I order an Uber because this is definitely getting in a car with a stranger.

But what happens when an unknown visitor comes to your front door and asks for you by name? First of all, you reiterate the rule about opening the door at all and getting a parent instead. Then you make an example of said stranger, who's acted as if he knows you. After all, he's asked for it.

"Mom, you's friend is here," I heard Matt call out as I fed my washing machine another meal of dirty laundry. Since I had no plans with any of my friends, I continued with my task of sorting the pile of clothing that had taken over the floor of my dark basement. Imagine my surprise when I turned to see an intruder standing behind me. Yes, I jumped, possibly even screamed, and I'm pretty sure I piddled like a puppy does when people come to visit.

This "friend" had managed to walk through my living room, kitchen, and down two flights of stairs to get to me. He wanted to try to sell me some cable or other stupid service. Horrified that I did not hear him walk through my house, I scolded him as if he were my own child.

"Just WHAT are you doing in my home?" I hollered as I scooted him up my stairs. He appeared to be in his early twenties and tried to blame it on Matt.

"He let me in and told me you were downstairs" he responded, his voice cracking as he spoke.

"So you make a habit of trespassing to make a sale?" I snapped back, livid and terrified all at once. We had made it back to my living room, but I blocked the front door so he could not leave. Before he had a chance to respond, I turned to Matt

"Do you know this man?" I asked sternly.

Matt smiled and cheerfully said, "Yep."

"Oh yeah? What's his name?" I asked, my tongue sharp as a knife.

Matt hesitated, responding with a blank stare.

"What is his name?" I asked again.

"I don't know," he said, his smile disappearing.

"Matthew, this is a stranger, and you let him in our home!"

"And you!" I continued, turning back to the young man. "I'm sorry to make an example of you to teach my son a lesson, but you should never, ever, *ever* go inside a person's home to make a sale unless you are invited by someone capable of extending the invite."

"I'm sorry, ma'am," he said as I opened the door and allowed him to escape, which he did quickly. (I'm surprised he hit the stairs at all as he ran down the porch.)

I slammed my door shut, locking it. I turned toward Matt, intending to reprimand him, but I could see the confusion on his face. *Oh, my gosh. When will he understand that not everyone is nice?* I sat him down on our sofa, and we had yet another conversation about stranger danger.

I had been so upset I didn't consider any of the repercussions that might come from making an example of this young salesperson. Thankfully, he never came back to show his appreciation by egging our home.

Next up: Other duties equally as important as keeping the household safe and sound—"sound" having everything to do with sanity.

Chores and Responsibilities

When Matt was eight or nine, I gave him simple tasks around the house. Sometimes it was to test the water on which responsibilities he could handle. But I soon discovered I needed to do some appliance 101 before assigning him certain tasks. After I described the functions of the washing machine, dryer, stove, and oven, and the distinction between a refrigerator and a freezer, I screwed up by not staying consistent with what I called them. For instance, it's either a washer or washing machine or a fridge or refrigerator. Instead of asking me what I meant when I used a different name, Matt made his own decision on how to complete my request. Needless to say, I ended up with ice cream in the vegetable crisper and dirty clothes mixed in with my clean clothes in the dryer. At least he tried—and I learned along with him.

So here we are, thirty years in, and it has definitely been a life of frustration and tears, just as Dr. Durham promised.

But you know what? With each of these challenges has come celebrations. And we have celebrated A LOT!

When my son finally captured his pinky toe in his sock, we celebrated! When he got that darn button through the hole in his pants—and consistently—we celebrated. We sang Matt's praises when he learned to pick up a Cheerio and when he learned to tie his shoe. We celebrated when he brought his spelling tests home and his score was circled in red with a big smiley face next to it. We did the happy dance when he finally learned to swallow his medicine—and boy did I whoop and holler over that one!

65

We celebrated when Matt got out of the pool to poop. Who knew this would be cause for celebration? We definitely celebrated when his hair began smelling cleaner. We've celebrated every Special Olympic event, every belt he's earned in karate, his amazing performance with his dance group, when he runs fast and works hard at his soccer games, and when he spoke at his school graduation. I especially give him kudos when he does kind things for others, such as when he helps older and younger family members. This family celebrates!

It's more than holidays, birthdays, and other obvious celebratory moments. The most heartfelt have been recognizing each and every achievement. These accomplishments are not more significant than those of other children, but because it takes a child with extra needs two to three times longer to complete them, for their parents, the accomplishment often has more meaning.

For me, no true celebration is complete without tears. I'm talking Niagara Falls on your face. Waterfalls of pride. Tears of "We did it!"

There have been many times I've wanted to give up, but it had to be complete defeat before I threw in the towel. For Matt to accomplish all the things he has, I needed to stay in the fight. Each challenge gave me the opportunity to grow stronger and appreciate my abilities. I have learned what I have taken for granted.

I get it now. Those tears Dr. Durham told me I would shed every day of Matt's life weren't going to be limited to tears of sadness and frustration. They have mostly been tears of overwhelming pride and unimaginable happiness over the great blessings that have come our way!

Lesson Learned

Life is a celebration, so let's party! Oh, and dishtowels not only make for great bibs but do a great job of soaking up tears as well.

Thank you, Dr. Durham.

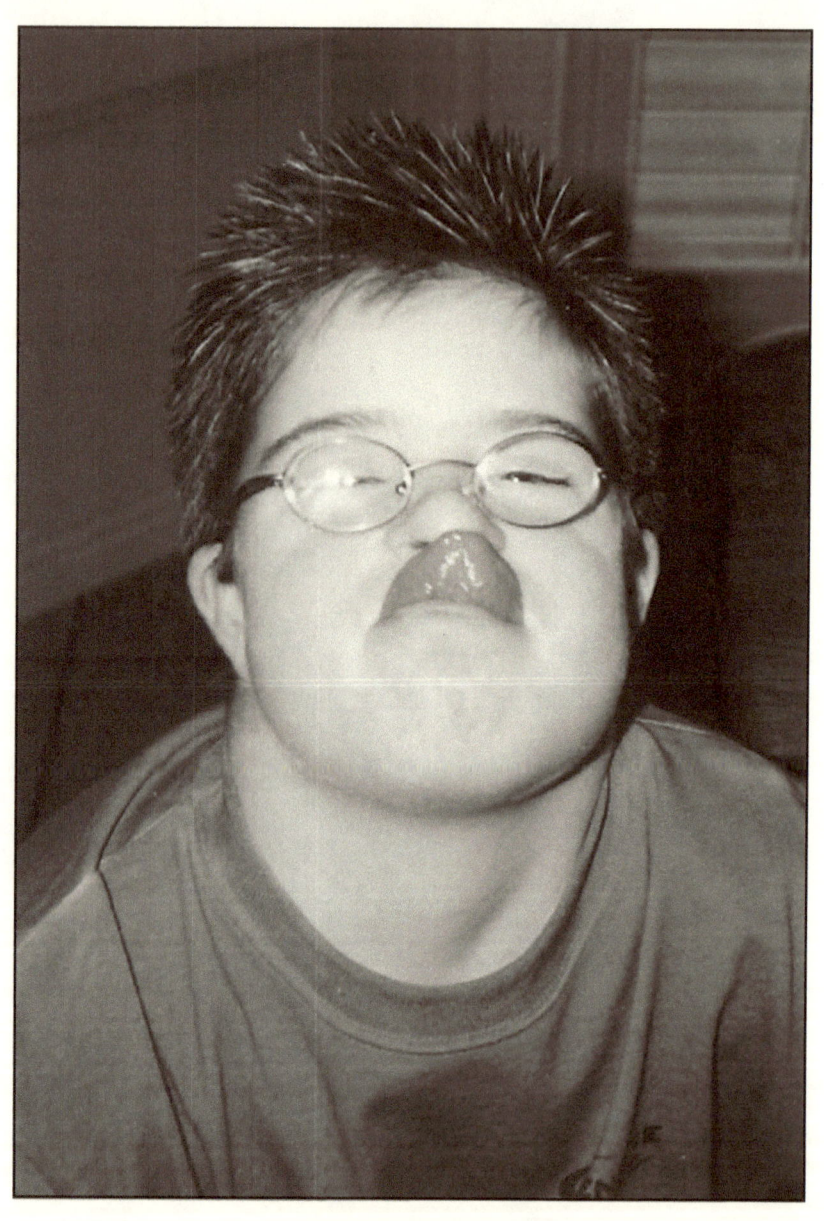

"I bet you can't do this!"

CHAPTER 6

That Darn Tongue

What you can plan for:
**Making difficult and not always the best decisions
and arming yourself to make better ones as you go**

It's discouraging to hear all the things your baby will never do, especially when your baby is young and you may still be grieving, so to speak.

When my son was just a few months old, his occupational therapist, or OT, stuck another knife in my heart when she nonchalantly said, "You're going to want to teach him sign language because he may never talk."

Because she sat with her back to me, she couldn't see me fighting to keep the tears from escaping my eyes. On her previous visit, she had shared that Matt might never walk, and now he might never have a voice to express himself?

I wondered how she would feel about her insensitive delivery if she were in my position. With her professional opinion, she was draining what little joy I felt about motherhood. How had I, an upbeat, fun, and crazy young lady, ended up with a child who might never walk or talk? The idea was unfathomable.

As I observed her every movement with my little boy, memories of other people I had seen with Down syndrome argued against her comments. My thoughts went to actor Chris Burke, the young man who starred in the hit television series *Life Goes On*. Chris also had an extra chromosome, and he not only spoke but memorized scripts! He had a distinct tone in his voice, the same tone I didn't know Matt would grow to have, but Chris possibly spoke more clearly than others. Try as I might, I had no personal recollection of anyone with Down syndrome not speaking at all.

I stared at the brown ponytail on the back of the therapist's head and thought, *Lady, you have underestimated me and my baby!*

Clueless to my internal tongue-lashing, this OT had encouraged Ash and me to teach our son sign language should he not be able to communicate verbally.

I could not wait for the appointment to end and for her to be on her merry way, sprinkling sunshine wherever she went! I'm pretty sure she didn't make it completely out the door before I closed it on her. I rushed back to my baby, who lay peacefully on the floor, then picked him up and smothered him with kisses. "She's wrong. You're going to talk. I just know it," I whispered into his sweet face.

When Ash got home from work that afternoon, I couldn't hold back the tears as I shared the conversation with him. I began to detest the person whose purpose was supposed to be to help us. For me, she'd created more emotional harm.

It felt like hours passed as Ash and I discussed this sensitive topic. We created a pros and cons list and concluded that our focus would be to help Matt learn to use his voice instead of depending on sign language as his primary means of communication. We made this choice because we wanted to be sure he could communicate with his family and the other people he would engage with throughout his life. We did not want to burden anyone or put expectations on them by asking that they learn to sign, especially when we weren't sure it would be necessary.

Admittedly, her comment stuck like gum on the bottom of my shoe. Were we making the right decision? But if Matt used sign language, would he try as hard to use his voice? I had already decided that no matter what, he would speak, and that, by darn, I would make it happen.

To be fair, before that session with our OT, I had no idea that our tongues were the muscle largely responsible for speech. Sure, I may have been taught this in a health class in school, but I'd either doodled my way through that day or skipped it altogether. Had I known this, I think I would have understood the reason for her comment.

That said, it did not justify the way she'd delivered the information. My sensitivity and pride often got in my way when professionals gave their expert opinions.

Since then, I've done a lot of research and learned that people with Down syndrome are often born with larger tongues—or average tongues but smaller mouths. Both can contribute to difficulties with speech. It is also why parents must do exercises to teach babies and toddlers who have Down syndrome to tuck in their mighty mouth muscles. It's kind of like trying to get a semi-truck into a single-car garage.

In time, I became more familiar with trisomy 21, and I believe what this therapist meant that day was that my baby's long tongue might contribute to communication challenges. But difficult is one thing; not speaking at all is another. I refused to give up on my child before I knew what he was capable of, and communication became my main priority. It's also been the most challenging.

Although Ash and I may not have strongly pursued teaching Matt to sign, the early intervention program he attended taught our toddler some of the basics. Matt caught on quickly and did well using the motions for *cookie* and *more*. I couldn't resist giving in to either request when he brought his chubby little hands together in the "more" gesture. He looked so cute as he stared at me with his pleading eyes and toothless grin. How could I say no to one more cracker or cookie?

Sign language was fattening him up. All the extra crackers and cookies I gave him due to his cuteness were turning his fingers into little sausages, and he began to get a muffin top before it was a thing. According to one of my closest friends who was from Taiwan, I had the cutest little Buddha baby. She nicknamed him this because she loved all his rolls. It fit him perfectly.

Still, Matt needed to communicate much more than "more" if he was going to survive. Speech therapy was costly, and our son definitely needed more than I could do with him at home. His entire future depended on the decisions we made for him, and I felt this one may have come with a negative result. If you were to ask me today, we may have done him an injustice by not teaching him to fully sign.

In my defense, I might have made a different choice if I had known I would have problems getting him the speech therapy he needed. I battled with the school on this every year in IEP meetings. Children who were differently abled were given access to additional speech therapy, but it wasn't enough. When I asked for more, the response was always, "If we give your son more time, it will take from the other children. Do you feel okay about that?"

"Of course not!" I would reply. "But my priority is my son. Those parents should be here advocating for their kids too!" Twenty minutes a week was all the time given to our children to help them communicate. I questioned the educators again and again about how they thought this was adequate for when these children got older and were out in society. They felt that was enough—seriously?

Fortunately, Matt did well with reading and writing. He struggled and still struggles with math, but speech continues to be his biggest challenge. That darn tongue!

When you think about it, the tongue is an odd organ. It's like a strange creature that hides out in a dark cave. While mostly hidden, it occasionally makes an appearance. I think most of us have caught unexpected sightings in photographs and have been flashed by one when provoked. Some have the power of becoming wind instruments if one has the talent to curl them perfectly, but not mine. Some can climb to higher summits, aka the nose, another talent I lack. And believe me, just like you, I've tried.

Matt is another story. Not only can he reach higher ground, but I'm sure if he tried, he could lick the sweat from his forehead. Ewwww! Give him a margarita to go with that salt. His strange-looking saliva snake is the trusty sidekick in a one-man show as he entertains others. However, it's so long that when he starts showing off, I have to make sure he's not fighting a cold, otherwise he may get a salty snack.

My son definitely uses his big ol' mouth muncher to entertain others. Anyone who knows Matt and has been flashed by his tongue would agree that he could be a member of the rock band KISS. He's an expert when it comes to mimicking Gene Simmons.

The size of the tongue isn't the only difference associated with the extra chromosome. The tongue itself may have a different appearance. Matt's looks like a dry, cracked lakebed.

When I first noticed all the crevices, I panicked because it looked like it had been attacked by a fork or knife.

At one of his appointments, his doctor reassured me this was normal and no need for concern. He did not call it by any name, so I had no idea it had one—until Matt had surgery earlier this year.

We were at the hospital's preoperative room, waiting for Matt to be prepped for cochlear-bone-implant surgery. A friendly, younger male nurse introduced himself. To distract Matt, he made small talk as he hooked up his IV. He told Matt a joke, and Matt laughed, which, of course, exposed the monster in his mouth. The nurse caught a glimpse of it. "Hey! You have a geographic tongue just like my wife's." I had been looking the other way because, you know, me and needles, but my ears perked up. I risked a look in his direction.

"What did you just call it?" I asked.

He repeated himself as he swabbed Matt's hand with an alcohol wipe. "He has a geographic tongue; my wife's looks like his."

"Really? I had no idea it had a name. I thought only people with Down syndrome had this."

"No," he responded, and I quickly looked away at the sight of the needle going in for the kill. "It's actually pretty common."

Curious, I pulled out my phone, looked up the name, and BAM, I saw several images of my son's holy ham hock. *Well, what do you know!*

He continued to poke and prod my boy while I educated myself. It had been named a geographic tongue because of the map-like pattern. In my opinion, the patterns on Matt's tongue look more like potholes, but I guess "pothole tongue" isn't an appealing medical term. Regardless, it's fitting it's named after something having to do with a road.

However, he had piqued my curiosity, and when we got home, I did more research. And as happens when you start clicking away on the internet, I ended up down a rabbit hole. I also found some interesting information on fissured tongues. Both conditions were harmless, and Matt's tongue resembled both images. At least I knew it was one of the two. It had been a mystery to me for years, and within minutes of meeting this young man, mystery solved. Perhaps I have educated others as well. If so, you're welcome.

So, Matt grew up and can speak. Yay! That said, understanding him can at times be difficult, even for me. It's almost like trying to understand someone from another country, possibly another planet. Unfortunately, there have been conversations between us where I felt like I failed him—after all, a mother should be able to comprehend what her child is saying, right?

Matt doesn't always clearly enunciate each letter. Some words he says well, others not so much. For instance, the word *suck*. This has always been a word he pronounces perfectly. Just recently, I had to laugh when I overheard him suddenly say from the other room, "Well, that sucks!" as he watched a game show on TV and the team he was rooting for lost.

When we hear young children blurt out inappropriate words, we usually find it amusing (unless it's our child in an inappropriate setting). It's the same with Matt—at least I think it is. Maybe it's the innocence of the mouth from which these words spew.

One evening I had to turn my back so he didn't see me laughing when he yelled, "Well, that pisses me off!" as he stomped up the stairs to his room to get ready for bed. Apparently, he did not like me waking him up to put his pajamas on after he had fallen asleep on the couch.

I can't really get mad at him when he reacts like this. After all, he's heard it somewhere, (it wasn't me!). When he expresses himself, which I encourage, boy, does he do it well. Yes, we may have a few things we still need to work on.

For those occasions when I am having a harder time understanding him, we've devised creative solutions. For instance, he loves to write, and for the most part, he does well with his spelling. If we are having a conversation and I don't know what he's saying, I will give us three chances and then ask him to spell the word I am hung up on. The majority of the time, he's willing to do this, and it works.

Technology has also helped. He's pretty proficient on his phone— better than me, in fact. If he's talking about a certain character, telling me he wants to go somewhere, or if there's an item he would like and I'm not quite getting it, I'll ask him to show me a picture on the internet. Within moments, he pulls it up, and after my aha, we carry on with our conversation.

I've always tried my best to be sure he knows that what he has to say is important; however, there have been a few heartbreakingly frustrating moments. No mother wants her child to give up on her. Hearing him say, "Oh, never mind" and then go on with his day because it's easier than to trying to help me understand sucks! (See, I use that word pretty well too.)

In these circumstances, the tables are turned and he has to be patient with me.

I will never give up on him, and I don't want him to give up on me, so it is important we have these solutions to work through our communication barriers. For the most part, the solutions work. However, not all of our friends, and definitely not strangers, know the tricks.

I'll be honest. Some days I still struggle with resentment toward the school system. They really fought me over this one issue, and now that Matt is an adult, we are dealing with what I feared. It's a challenge when Matt is having a conversation with others, especially new friends, and I have to step in and save them from an awkward moment. I know the signs. A polite smile and a nod of the head but no words spoken translates to they have no idea what Matt's just said. If the moment feels right, I usually step in and help lead the witness. "Yes, we did watch that show last night, didn't we?" I then see a look of relief that translates to "Ahh, I'm with him now," and the conversation takes off.

I understand this may be difficult or uncomfortable, so I appreciate it whenever people don't give up, especially because his conversations usually revolve around movies, superheroes, or Disney—all favorite topics. I must admit I have a limit to how much time I can devote to these subjects before he loses me.

When we decided against sign language as a backup, I admit I had second thoughts. Ironically, around age twenty, Matt took matters into his own hands. Literally. He took it upon himself to learn this skill by watching YouTube and reading books from the library. The more he learned and tried to use it to communicate with us, the more remorse I felt that our family hadn't learned it when he was a child. Yet I am so proud of him!

As with most anything, it's never too late, and we're trying to work through it now. That said, it's extremely frustrating when *I* sign "more" but I don't get another cracker or cookie. Whatever happened to "You scratch my back, and I'll scratch yours"?

If I could offer any advice, if you're even questioning it, learn sign language, at least the basics, to avoid the guilt I've had to deal with. Even though a large part of me has struggled with this, there have been some amusing times as a result of his speech problems, if that's okay to admit.

I hope I never tire of "car-aoke." Matt's quick to turn up the volume and perform as if in front of a sold-out concert at the Hollywood Bowl. He sings most of the lyrics wrong, which I feel comfortable making fun of because he's not the only family member with mondegreen talents. (Made you look that up, didn't I?)

76

As an adult, I learned I had been singing the classic "Brick House" wrong most of my life. Don't you agree that "my tomato" sounds a lot like "mighty-mighty"? "She's my tomato, she's . . ."

Matt has a lot of "my tomato" examples; in fact, they're in every song. If you try to correct him, he shrugs you off or tells you to stop, annoyed you've interrupted his performance! If the song has fast lyrics, rather than trying to keep up, he has a tongue-rolling technique he does that works for him and entertains us. Again with the tongue.

My son is a great performer, and his schedule is fairly clear for anyone who would like to book his next gig.

Lesson Learned

Don't believe predictions about what your child won't do. It's a farce! Not only does my son talk, he never stops.

"Hi, I'm Fireball."

CHAPTER 7
Turning A Split Into A Strike

What you can plan for:
Making space for Olympic medals

I have never given much thought to how pretty a bowling ball is with its swirls of well-blended colors or galactic sparkles. I have definitely never wondered what's on the inside of one. When I go bowling, I have one thing in mind as I pick up my weapon of pink, gold, and blue, and that is to take out the ten white victims taunting me from the dark end of the alley. I try desperately to defeat them all at once, but as much as I would like to brag that I do, it isn't always so. At times, those buggers fight back, sometimes in dirty ways, leaving two of their guys standing at each side of the alley's edge knowing full well that I have lost the battle. They call this move a split, and when this happens, my ego goes splat.

Matt has participated in various categories of the Special Olympics since he was ten years old. At age twelve, he picked up bowling, which ended up being his favorite, and he's a better bowler than anyone in the family. He's won numerous medals and ribbons in this event—too many to count but enough to bow the special rack a friend made for him to show them off. Every one of these awards symbolizes hard work and dedication to the sport, a testament to Matt's success.

When Matt first began bowling, my younger brother nicknamed him Fireball because he threw the ball with so much force you almost expected it to ignite a spark and catch the lane on fire!

This nickname fit him perfectly. Once he put on his bowling shoes and picked up his ball, he was no longer Matt. He became the one, the only . . . Fireball!

Matt had been saving his money and surprised us by announcing just how he wanted to spend it—on his own bowling ball and shoes. We supported his decision when it became obvious his bowling was going to be a routine activity for him and our family. His thirteen-year-old mind was made up, and he was excited.

Because he thought his nickname was cool, we agreed it would be fun to go with a fire theme. Now he couldn't wait to go shopping.

The following week after practice, we stopped by the shop inside the bowling alley. It didn't take long for Matt to make his selection, for as soon as we walked through the door, sitting on display just in front of us sat a shiny red-and-black ball, its colors swirled together like flames.

This caught Matt's eye as if it called out, "BUY ME! BUY ME!" Next to this taunting sphere of fire was a pair of white shoes with black flames down the sides. They could not have been more perfect.

Matt got the salesman's attention. After showing him what he'd picked out, he went for his wallet, and the gentleman rang up his selection. As I watched the process, my mama heart felt as though it might burst with happiness. To witness my son emptying his wallet of birthday money for one single purchase made me feel like the luckiest mom on the planet. I watched him bouncing from one foot to the other, his excitement noticeable as he was eager to start breaking in his purchases.

About ten or so months after Matt bought his beloved pin crusher, his class took a field trip to a bowling alley, something they did often. Since Matt has small, plump thumbs and extra-wide feet, I allowed him to take his personal gear so he could bowl comfortably. Turns out, Fireball caused a ruckus, a real game-stopper, literally.

Upon seeing what I saw when I got home, I imagined that afternoon's event went something like this:

The crowd sat patiently on the benches, each waiting for their turn to bowl. Fireball's name appeared on the screen, letting him know he was up. He stood quickly and marched over to pick up his ball, a cocky "I'm going to get a strike" expression on his face. Ball in hand, he carefully eyed the pins at the end of the lane, swung his arm back, did a slight skip forward, then let his ball fly. It flew fast; however, instead of rolling down the lane to smash the pins waiting to be obliterated, it snagged the corner of the lane, and when it made contact, there was a split, only not in the pins but in his ball, and right in half. The crowd went quiet as Fireball and his teacher stood in shock, eyes as big as hockey pucks, watching two pieces of what used to be a ball teeter to a stop.

Now, to be fair to me, the email I received from the school was vague and did not provide any details; it said only that Matt's ball was broken. They noted nothing about it being in two pieces, a detail you would think one might elaborate on! So, as I read the email, it didn't concern me. It just so happened I bowled in a league at the time, and some of the balls available to the public had gouges in them. I assumed this to be normal due to the beatings they took from the many hands that used them. I envisioned a fresh gouge in my son's ball, possibly a large one. Like many mom issues, I planned to deal with it when I got home from work.

I had barely walked in the door when Matt impatiently handed me his bowling bag. I did not expect what I saw when I unzipped the zipper. Before my eyes lay my son's prized possession. Holy cow! My eyes must have been as big as hockey pucks. A million thoughts ran through my mind. *Is what I'm seeing real? Is that two halves? Geeze, Fireball! How hard did you throw this thing?* Perplexed, I looked closer. I had never seen the inside of a bowling ball, and it had my undivided attention. It was barely a year old and didn't have a lot of strikes on it.

Matt stood and watched, heartbroken. Unable to communicate his emotions verbally, he cried as I examined it, I mean *them*. I had no idea about the warranty on bowling balls, but surely they should last longer than a year, especially when used by one owner. My twelve-pounder held up like a real champ, and I used her weekly. While I couldn't tell why this had happened, I knew that neither mom nor duct tape would be able to fix this baby, and those two things can fix most anything. A hug would have to do for now.

John and I wanted to take care of this immediately, and, fortunately, I found the receipt. The three of us packed up our injured pin crusher and headed to the shop at the bowling alley, anxious to share with them the evidence of the day's event. Secretly, I couldn't wait to see their faces. We hoped that once the shock wore off, they would reach out to the manufacturer for assistance with the situation. Given that this place was roughly a forty-minute journey from our home, we hoped for the best. I consoled myself with the fact that visiting this shop, which was located inside a family fun center that also had an adjoining pizza parlor, meant we would surely stop in and pick up some of their amazing breadsticks, the best I'd ever had. Each was a foot long and thick and chewy, with the perfect amount of salt and garlic butter. This delicious treat alone would be worth the trip. *Not the dinner I had planned but much better!*

When we arrived, we were met with the sounds of Skee-Ball machines and other arcade games. In the distance, we could hear the noise of pins crashing against each other as they met their fate. The shop was located just inside the main doors. Matt, who was emotionally charged, marched right in and presented the remnants of what used to be a ball to the employees on duty. They were astounded. We engaged in small talk as they studied each piece as curiously as I had.

After a few minutes of deliberation amongst themselves, we were approached by an older gentleman in the group, a man with salt-and-pepper hair and a weathered, round, unsympathetic face. The manager.

His polite customer service must have been on a break because rather than greeting us with a friendly hello, he skipped right to "You're going to have to work with the location where the ball broke." According to this ray of sunshine, the bowling alley where the incident happened would have to help us with our unfortunate situation. If it weren't for the snacks our stomachs patiently awaited, we may have been upset for having driven so far. Instead of letting this get the best of

82

us, however, we grabbed our bag of disappointment and picked up an order of three satisfying treats, which we quietly devoured on our way back to the crime scene.

Half an hour later, we arrived at our destination and, with breath that could fend off any vampire, asked to speak to the manager. A middle-aged man approached us to see how he could help. When we opened Matt's bag to show him the reason for our visit, his eyes bulged like the breadstick in my intestines. Evidently, the contents shocked him just as much as they had us. Honestly, I was surprised his staff hadn't shared the excitement of what had happened earlier that day. Seemed like good gossip to me.

He carefully examined each piece and then excused himself to inspect the lane Matt's class had used that afternoon. We didn't wait long. He'd concluded there were no issues with the lane. He did, however, find a chip in Matt's ball, which he pointed out. Sure enough, a chunk in the shape of Ohio taunted me from near one of the finger holes. The manager went on to explain that if this were to make contact with something hard, it was enough to break the ball. At his next words, I felt my internal temperature rise.

"I think the ball is defective. You will need to return this to the shop where you purchased it." *UGH! You gotta be kidding me!*

Above Matt's head, I gave John a look of sheer frustration, which he returned. I pursed my lips as I shook my head and looked upward in disbelief. Now it really felt like we were getting the runaround.

"I can't believe this," I muttered quietly to John on our way out to the parking lot. "Neither location seems to feel any sort of obligation." We had to go to work the next day, and all the back and forth had started to get the best of me. We felt we needed to address this now, while the parties involved were still available.

We were no longer hungry, so the bad news was that the emotional pain we were dealing with could not be healed with thoughts of breadsticks.

Reluctantly, we headed back to the original shop. The older gentleman was not happy to see us again. His weathered face scrunched up before he turned his back on us as we walked into his store, his way of accentuating that this was not their responsibility.

This would be no easy task. All I wanted was for my boy to have his ball, and nobody was willing to help! This was ridiculous. After a few minutes of back and forth, some pleading on my part, and some insincere apologies on his, the mama bear in me emerged from her cave. The heat made its way to my face, and my heart pounded wildly while my mind filled with about every four-letter word there is.

Unfortunately, when I get this worked up about being treated unjustly, the tears take over. So big, bad, mama bear fought back cry-baby mama bear while keeping completely irrational mama bear from throwing herself over the counter and strangling the insensitive jerk.

Suddenly, Matt stepped in and saved the day. I swear, in circumstances like these, he's magic!

Oblivious to what was happening, he had no idea how greatly the odds were against us. What he did recognize was that his mom was upset—as manifested by her split personalities. My boy, my Super Matt, walked right up to the guy who had upset his mom and unexpectedly grabbed his hand and looked him in the eyes. He shook that hand and said, "I Matt," which caught my new frenemy off guard. The man hesitated at first but then returned the handshake and introduced himself to Matt.

Matt's face broke out in a grin. "Hi, you a smart man."

We all stood there in awkward silence. After a few moments, Mr. Cranky Pants, with his salt-and-pepper hair and now-fading scowl, looked right at Matt and asked, "Do you like to bowl?"

"Yes. I like a lot. I bowl in Special Olympics. Have lots gold medals."

The man nodded as he listened, looking as if he were drifting off in thought.

The tension that had filled the room started to lift. This person who had been agitated just moments ago looked at my husband and me for a moment, then took the receipt and asked if he could keep Matt's busted sidekick. He could not promise us anything but agreed to give the manufacturer a call.

My protective emotions subsided, and John and I expressed our appreciation. We were just about to walk out of the shop when Matt turned back to the guy and hugged him.

"Thank you, thank you, thank you!"

I watched as the man's leathery face softened.

And his wasn't the only one. My emotions got the best of me. My son had changed the mood in that room in a matter of seconds—and he had no idea what he had done. Filled with pride, I tried hard to keep from bawling like a baby. But as proud as I may have felt, I didn't feel confident we would get Matt's beloved ball fixed. In fact, my gut told me we would be buying him a new ball.

A week later, Matt's friend from the bowling alley called. I recognized his voice immediately, his tone much more pleasant this time. Unfortunately, just as I suspected, the manufacturer refused to cooperate. This perplexed me—it had been less than a year since we made the purchase. As a customer service representative, I spent my days doing everything possible to give our customers a great experience. It disappointed me that this company was falling so short. Before I had a chance to express my extreme unhappiness, his next words stopped my mouth from making a fool of me.

"Ms. Hooton, I'm sorry about your son's ball, but I have to tell you that this situation touched me in a way I've never experienced." He paused, gulping back an emotion very different from the outrage I'd felt just a moment before, and I chose to listen. "After your family left that night," he continued, "I found myself in the back room, crying. Crying because I had been so harsh—and in a matter of minutes, your son helped me understand the things in life that are most important to us.

85

He made me think of everything that gets me upset, and I realized they are trivial things—things that just don't matter. For your son, his ball is important to him."

He paused again, and I swore I heard the touch of a smile on his lips. "I am glad I met your son. I have ordered him a new ball and taken care of the expense."

Do you feel it? Do you feel what I felt that day? I sat there speechless. Knots the size of tennis balls formed in my throat and chest. I could feel my eyes beginning to sweat. I knew I needed tissues—and fast. This man had a change of heart all because Matt had stepped forward, said hello, and introduced himself.

The man and I shared a few more kind words and talked about the things that make Matt special, and I thanked him repeatedly for taking care of my son. Had I been in the shop, I would have hugged him just as Matt had done the night we first met.

When I hung up, I could not hold back. My face fell into my hands as I cried tears of happiness. It felt so incredible to have a son with the ability to create magical moments.

A few weeks later, we received the call that Matt's ball was ready. This time when we arrived, there were no scowls. Instead, we received a warm welcome, and Matt exchanged high fives with our new friend, who led Matt to the counter to receive his new/old gift.

Pleased, Matt cried out "Woo-hoo!"—his go-to cheer—as he admired his new long-lost bowling buddy. But when he turned it over, something caught my eye and John's. We leaned in to get a closer look and were surprised by what we saw. It had been engraved with one special word: Fireball.

No words were needed when we locked eyes with this gentleman. What had started as an unpleasant circumstance that first day had been transformed into one of love and admiration when this man took customer service to the next level. All because of a boy called Fireball.

In March 2009, shortly after this incident, my son's team took the gold in the Special Olympics, which sent them to the state competition. A few weeks later, they bowled their hearts out, and it paid off. They took the gold at state. What a momentous year!

Matt still has that ball and uses it weekly when he bowls with friends. I usually stay and support him from a distance. I love it when he gets a strike, and so does he. The whole place knows as he turns to his friends and shouts "Wahoo! I'm awesome!" while throwing his hands in the air and dancing his way back to his seat.

If only he were as humble as he is magic.

I think of that man often as I watch my son. It is hard not to see him when I look at that ball.

Lesson Learned

There are things my son has broken that I have not. There are things my son can fix that I cannot.

"I'm lost."

CHAPTER 8

Mr. Katy Perry: His Teenage Dream

What you can plan for:
**Your child will find love. Now, whether it's real
or fantasy is to be determined.**

Two. The number of love interests it took before Matt finally picked the woman he decided to spend the rest of his life with—the woman he calls his wife. He's been married to her for thirteen years now. It's a solid marriage, and he loves her as much today as when they first got together.

Just one small detail separates their nuptials from most. They've never met.

Just like with any real relationship, Matt had to date before making his final decision on who he would commit to—although the girls in his dating pool were as realistic as his wife.

The truth is, Matt has not had any real girlfriends. That said, I'm not giving up on that dream for him just yet. After all, several people his age have not had serious relationships, Down syndrome or not.

While his list of girlfriends may be nonexistent, he has dated quite a bit. If I exclude all the dates he went on with his grandma and mom, however, that narrows it down to one actual date. That's right, one date in thirty-two years. Not exactly my dream for him when we left the hospital after his birth, but, again, I'm not giving up hope.

Amazingly, one date can equate to many when the girl is unique in her own right. This girl didn't just give Matt a wonderful experience; his entire family was impacted. Everyone was excited, and everyone cried. We never dreamed our sweet boy would one day be asked to prom.

A sweet, cute young lady, Dana happened to be a senior at Matt's high school when she asked him to senior prom his sophomore year!

When I learned he had been asked, my heart imploded into small shards of love and gratitude over something I never imagined would happen.

However, as excited as I felt when I first heard about it, my "momdar" went up. This sort of thing never happened in my day. Why would a cute senior ask someone with special needs to her last prom? I found myself asking, *What are her intentions?* My emotions warred between excitement and suspicion. I had to put my mind at ease, so I reached out to see if she would meet with us. I was surprised when she politely agreed. I wanted to interrogate—er, I mean, get to know her.

Dana arrived right on time for our visit. As I opened the door, she flashed me a warm smile. "Hi, Mrs. Hooton, I'm Dana." Her teeth were perfectly straight and white, showing no signs of teenage soda addiction. Her dark hair hung to her shoulders in a simple style.

I had just welcomed her into our home when Matt, excited to see his friend from school, leaped up from our sofa and rushed over to give her a side hug. I breathed a short sigh of relief. *Oh, good, he's listening to me after all.* When it came to girls, I had been teaching him to give side hugs since I believed it more appropriate. He towered over Dana's petite figure. *Cute girl,* I thought, and invited her to sit down in our front room. She exuded an air of confidence. If she was nervous, I couldn't tell.

John heard the commotion and joined Matt and me as we sat across from her. I asked Dana to tell us a little about her, which she did without hesitation. She looked forward to graduation as she had plans to go to college. And she had been saving her paychecks from her part-time after-school job to help with those expenses. I nodded in approval.

Okay, that's enough of the idle chitchat. I need to address the elephant in the room. I sent Matt off to do something so I could have the next part of the conversation with just Dana. John nodded, signaling me the moment Matt was out of earshot.

"To be candid," I said, "I'm having a hard time understanding why a cute girl like you would ask my son to your last school dance. Could you share with us why you chose him?"

Dana smiled. "I'm an aide in his classroom, and I love working with him. He's a good kid and has a fun personality." I smiled at the thought of the joy my son brought to his fellow students. She went on. "I also have a family member who has special needs, so I know how important it is to be kind to and befriend these kids."

At these words, my protective-mama heart softened.

"There's so much drama at school, and I want to have fun at my last dance, and I know I will with Matt." *Ah, the drama. I remember those days all too well,* I thought as certain cliques came to mind.

Those were the words I needed to hear. She'd won me over. I felt I could trust her with my son. John and I looked at each other, and I could see the approval in his overprotective eyes. The date for prom was on.

So many things had changed since I went to school. Proms no longer consisted of just dinner and the dance—they were an all-day event. They often took place in group settings, so it would be the first time I let Matt go off alone with a bunch of teenagers I didn't know. Even though we had taken the time to meet Dana and liked her, I still had reservations. *What if Matt innocently does something that embarrasses her? What if the other kids in the group are not as accepting?* Would any of them make fun of my son? I had to trust that Dana would treat him like the family member she told us about.

Since this was Matt's first official date, John and I decided to send him on a mock date with his sweet Aunt K so he could practice.

First, we did some Gentleman 101 training. We taught him about opening and closing the car door for her, and we reminded him to hold any doors for her when they went in and out of a building. We taught him as best we could about tipping the waitress at the end of the meal. We stressed the importance that all bodily eruptions must be held in, but if that burst of air from either end should slip out, it must quickly be followed by an "Excuse me!"

When Aunt K arrived for the date, I stood on the porch and watched proudly as Matt walked her to the car. She didn't realize he had followed her to her side and was caught off guard when he reached around and opened the door. For just a moment, she stepped out of the role of his date and into the role of aunt and gave him a big hug. He then walked around to his side to get in. So far so good.

The entire time they were gone, I fidgeted as I puttered around the house, checking my phone often. You know, just in case they called. I stayed close to the front window, where I could occasionally sneak a peek to see if they were back.

After two long hours, they finally returned, all smiles. Aunt K tried to fill me in but could barely get in a word as Matt ignored my rule of not interrupting. *Well, we need to work on that one,* I thought as he burst with emotion, sharing his side of their evening together. His aunt had made sure he'd followed through with all my expectations while they were out and reported that he had been the perfect gentleman. Before heading back to her own children, she gave him her blessing. "My nephew is going to do just fine," she beamed. Passing grade.

I went to bed that evening, grateful for Matt's sweet aunt and proud and excited for the experience my young man would soon be having.

On the big day, Matt woke early and without an alarm. I checked in on him to see if he needed any help getting ready only to find he needed none. He had taken extra time with his hair, using his gel to spike it perfectly. His face showed no sign of scruff, meaning he'd actually paid attention as he shaved that morning. He had on his favorite superhero shirt and some jeans. I watched him brush his teeth, noting he spent more time than usual, no nagging needed from Mom. All the extra effort and he still got ready in record-setting time. *Wow! This boy needs to get asked out more often.*

My nerves danced to the surface of my skin as Matt paced and watched anxiously out the front window for her to pull into our driveway. "Finally!" he exclaimed when her car pulled in. He nearly plowed me over trying to get to the door before she even had a chance to knock. This startled Dana.

"He's a little excited," I said, as we both chuckled.

"I ready. Let's go," Matt ordered as he led her down from the porch to leave for OUR first date. My mom heart forced its way to my throat as I attempted to holler after them to have fun. I watched my handsome young man walk her to her little red Honda. He quickly squeezed in between her and the door, catching her by surprise, just as he had his aunt. When she realized he wanted to open the door for her, she appeared impressed. She shot me a quick glance over the top of her car and smiled as she waved and got in. He then scurried over to his side, belted himself in, shot me that big, beautiful smile of his, and waved as they drove off.

I imagined the scene in her car: Matt making himself at home, fumbling with the radio, looking for a good tune as he went on about all the animals waiting to see him. They were spending the first part of their date at the zoo. *Take care of my boy, Dana,* I thought as I tried to distract myself with the small projects I'd planned out for my day. It worked; I got lost in my cleaning, which kept me from overthinking things.

Several hours later, Matt rushed in to change into his clothes for the dance. I couldn't wait to hear about his day, but there was no time for idle chat. "I have get ready, Mom," he said, annoyed with me. How dare I interrupt him right now! I did at least get out of him that he had a great time at the zoo with his new friends.

Prom was informal, so Matt and Dana wore matching T-shirts Dana had let Matt choose and then bought. They may have been in casual dress, but for his big night, I wanted him to smell formal and not like he had spent the day living among the apes. I made sure he washed up well and put on extra deodorant, and, of course, a splash of cologne. Then, they were off again for round two. Their next stop, dinner, and then finally to boogie the night away. My insides boogied as I waited impatiently for this wonderful day to be over. How could I be so selfish and wish for this dream I had for my son to end? I couldn't help it! The helicopter in me wanted my boy back home. We were done now, thank you very much.

Around ten that night, her car pulled into our driveway, and it was my turn. Finally! After a long day and night for this mama bear, her cub had made it back to the den. Dana could barely keep up with Matt as he rushed to the porch, excited to tell me all about his day. John and I stood ready and waiting. Dana thanked Matt for the fun date and me and John for allowing her to spend the day with him. And she confirmed that he'd used his Manners 101 skills. Phew!

Due to our communication challenges, I will never know the full details of how Matt spent that day. While I still had so many questions, I reassured myself that, based on his actions and Dana's smile, all had gone well. He talked about the date for days, so he obviously had an amazing time.

Matt only went to one prom. But that's one more than I expected. And who knows what other miracles might happen? I hope he will have more dating opportunities. My dream is for him to experience love from a companion. I often have to remind myself that while my heart knows what he is missing, his does not. He's fine. This could be partly due to the fact that in his mind, he has had three serious girlfriends, all famous, and he boasts about them to anyone who will listen.

I would hope this disclaimer is not needed, but I'm putting it out there just in case:

This next section is not based on actual experiences.

Now that we're clear...

The cute blonde who first stole Matt's heart when he was sixteen had a pair of healthy lungs. How do I know this? You may know her; she goes by Britney Spears. Yep, you read that right. He believed wholeheartedly she was *his* girl. To tell him otherwise was like trying to convince him Santa didn't exist.

His "relationship" with Britney consisted of talking to her in his room as he danced and sang along to her songs—if you can call it singing.

When it comes to dancing, my boy has the moves; I'm told he got them from me. He has this way of squatting to a perfect level as he swings his hips left and right to the beat of the music, a move I CANNOT do.

His booming voice, on the other hand? Well, it can't quite maneuver like his hips do! His singing is indescribable, and, sadly, it overpowered Britney's as he performed for himself and anyone in the vicinity. I'm told he also inherited my vocal cords. And, just like his mom, he doesn't care what others think. Nothing stops him from slandering a great song. Luckily, Britney's music has easy-to-understand lyrics, which makes it easier to sing along. Matt's "Baby One More Time" is off the charts, although Simon Cowell would say "It's just dreadful."

My son's relationship with Britney fizzled out when she disappeared from the media to deal with personal struggles. It's not like he wouldn't support her through difficult times, but she went cold on him. Like a number-two pencil, he wrote her off as her eraser got dark and worn.

It didn't take long for him to put himself out there again. Before we knew it, another blonde entered the picture. Girlfriend number two was a *rare* find. Her name? Stephanie, but you might recognize her as Lady Gaga. My boy seemed to be drawn to blondes. In this case, I believe what attracted him most was the fact that she was different. Ironic, right? Her unique looks lured him in like a moth drawn to bright light. Anytime she came on TV, he admired her one-of-a-kind outfit, oohing and ahhing as if at a firework show.

Of course, Matt loved her music just as much. What can I say? He knows talent when he hears it. Anytime one of his favorites comes on in the car, the volume goes up ten decibels—at least. It cracks me up when he belts out "Poker Face," or, as he calls it, "Poka My Face." "My, my, my poka face, ma-ma-my poka face." Anytime he sings it, John and I can't resist doing as he says. We poke at his cheeks, chin, and forehead. He doesn't understand what we're doing, even when we sing along, barely able to get the words out through our laughter.

Matt's relationship with Lady Gaga terminated a few months after it began when another woman came into his life. I can honestly say my heart wasn't too broken up over this breakup. I may really enjoy Lady Gaga's music, and I'm impressed that she dares to be herself, but her out-of-this-world costumes are a little too much for this mama's taste. I couldn't imagine this "girlfriend" sitting at my Thanksgiving table in a dress made of raw meat.

I thought his next girlfriend would be a phase like the others, but Matt promoted her to wife almost immediately.

This daughter-in-law is special. She's beautiful and talented, and not that we've ever discussed it, but I think she may be rich. She's also a mom and is married to another. There's a good chance you know of her. Her name is Katy, and she makes my son *roar!*

They've been going strong for thirteen years now, or at least Matt has been. It's surprising how a nonexistent relationship can be stronger than most existing ones. Her chaotic schedule makes it difficult for them to actually date, so the fact that she's his wife is a miracle. They've managed to go on two dates in the last thirteen years—sort of. There were several thousand people who tagged along. Still, he enjoyed her company as she sang to him for two hours as if there were not another soul in the room.

Matt has visited her on many occasions; however, his chats have been somewhat one-sided and less than discreet. At first, I wasn't aware of these visits until I overheard him from the shampoo aisle at Target. "There she is!" he exclaimed with a satisfied chuckle. *There who is?* I wondered as I followed the sound of his thunderous voice (because Matt and quiet don't go together). I found him chatting with images of Katy in the Cover Girl section. The way he talked with her, you would think she actually stood in front of him. I could only smile and shake my head. Who else would feel so at ease speaking to an advertisement?

What an amazing feeling it must be to pick a famous person to be your spouse and believe it to be true. If it were that easy, I know exactly who my second husband would be, but I'll never tell.

Matt's Katy phase started around age eighteen. I have a hunch it's because of her popular song "I Kissed a Girl," since nothing could stop him from chiming in anytime he heard it. But that was not the end of her influence.

When Matt completed his high school courses, we began the process of getting services to help him transition into adulthood. In one instance, we were in a meeting with a state worker who, given his gray hair and the lines beneath his eyes, I assumed was in his sixties. His button-down shirt hugged his round belly, over which hung a dark tie, slightly askew, triggering my OCD. I allowed Matt to answer his basic questions while I fought the urge to reach over the table and straighten the guy's crooked accessory.

"What's your name? What's your birthdate? What's your address?" he asked Matt when he noticed I'd allowed him to speak for himself. I beamed. I really appreciate it when people speak directly to Matt.

Unlike his tie, his next question straightened me up.

"Are you married?"

And here we go, I thought as I watched his pen hover over the No box on the questionnaire, about to make its mark.

"Yep!" my son replied proudly.

The gentleman raised his caterpillar-like eyebrows, surprised, and glanced over at me. I smiled as I watched him mark the Yes box. He shook his head slightly; I wondered if he couldn't believe Matt was married because he had Down syndrome or because he was just barely out of high school.

He moved his pen to the Spouse Name field. "What's your wife's name?"

"Katy Perry!" Matt proclaimed as he sat up in his chair, excited to be sharing the news with someone.

The pen stopped midair again. "What was that?"

"Katy Perry."

"Katy Perry . . . as in the singer?"

"Yep!"

"You're lucky; she's hot!" he said as he smiled and laid the pen down.

"Duh!" Matt exclaimed. He then followed up with, "And my mom's boyfriend is Thor." This piece of information shocked even me. The whole room filled with laughter as we enjoyed the moment.

That's my boy. Unpredictable to others and always making them smile.

Matt challenged my supermom status when he informed me in his early twenties that he wanted a Katy Perry–themed party. How in the world did one accommodate this tall request? It would have been cool to have her actually RSVP since he added her to his guest list, but we all knew that wouldn't happen. I put some thought into what I wanted to do and came up with what I believed was a brilliant idea. *Karaoke KP style.* I made several calls and found a local bar that had exactly what I was looking for. Small and quaint, it was one of those places where regulars hung out. The manager shared that his patrons were fun and understanding and could tolerate hearing Katy Perry songs all night; they might even join in.

I had a cake made with a photoshopped image of Matt and Katy standing together. It was so well done that when I picked it up, the girl at the counter exclaimed how lucky we were to have met her. I teetered on whether I should tell her the truth.

With Katy's photos printed, framed, and placed on the tables in the pub and the DJ informed on how the night would go, friends began to arrive to get their KP on. The staff treated Matt amazingly well, and the customers went along with our shenanigans, just as the manager predicted. That cozy little bar really rocked that night, and Matt loved being the center of attention. His performance was lively and did not disappoint. The evening was "funtastic." As we drove home, the soft snores from the back seat whispered, *Great job, Mom!*

For Christmas one year, Matt wrote a letter to Mr. Claus asking for wedding stuff from Zurcher's for him and his wife. This confused me since, according to Matt, they were already married. But when he sets his mind on an idea, sometimes we just have to go with it. Mr. Claus received his letter and chuckled at the creativity of the specific details. However, come Christmas morning, Mr. C disappointed a certain young man by not making that trip to Zurcher's. Mrs. Claus could not believe her husband had laughed off this young man's wish, and she scolded him for doing so. Maybe his thoughts were aligned with mine, meaning the gift was unnecessary since they were already man and wife. The following year, he got a second chance when the same request showed up in Matt's Christmas letter. Santa knew he best not mess up this time because Matt had been especially good that year.

Christmas morning brought squeals of joy when Matt saw the gift addressed to him and his wife. The nicely wrapped package held a groom's glass, a cake topper with a couple that looked similar to Mr. and Mrs. Perry, and invitations for when they were ready to make it official. These items are still on display in Matt's room.

I knew there would come a day when Katy came to Salt Lake City in concert, and when that time came, I would do anything to get Matt tickets. In preparation, I recruited friends who were just as determined.

In 2014, we were faced with the challenge to make this happen. The minute tickets went on sale, all my friends and work colleagues turned into a small call center. My heart raced with excitement when, thirty minutes later, a woman finally answered. And then my heart stopped when she muttered those horrible words: "We're sold out." I couldn't believe it! I had waited months for tickets to go on sale. Ticked off, I thought *How is that possible? NONE of us were able to get in!*

This mom is not one to be defeated. I emailed local radio stations and Katy's people—or so I thought. I even wrote a letter to Ellen DeGeneres. Tail between my legs, I succumbed to pleas on social media. I did everything except sell my soul. I did not want a handout, just someone to help make it possible for me to take Matt to see his wife. In the end, I had no choice but to buy three tickets from a reseller, and I paid heavily. It felt like I had sold my soul, but being a part of this experience with Matt was 100 percent worth it!

Before the big day, I made Matt a one-of-a-kind shirt with the photoshopped image of the two on the front (a huge attention-getter when we arrived at the concert hall). I created a design on the back stating that she was his firework. He loved it and couldn't wait to wear it.

To this day, I choke up when I think of that special evening. Matt stood all night, and for him, that's huge because he struggles to stand long for anything. This night, however, he was preoccupied as he sang along with his whole heart and soul. In between the singing, he yelled how much he loved her. Our seats were so close he had a perfect view.

At the end of the concert, dripping with sweat from all his dancing, Matt begged me to take him to the stage to see his wife. I had to explain that all the men around her were protecting her so we couldn't. Thankfully, he handled the disappointment well. He talked about that night for so long I knew I had done the right thing. We had fulfilled a "teenage dream". The love I felt for him and from him that night was indescribable. As much as it pained my wallet to get us there, through Matt, I have come to discover the heartwarming feeling that comes with doing something magical for someone else. My heart still swells, and my eyes sweat when I think of the memories we made that glorious evening.

I thought for sure that one day Matt would break yet another girl's heart, but nope. In the most random moments, Matt will say he needs to go to Vegas to get his wife, Katy. He blasts his music in his room, and when "Roar" comes on, I fear his roar is going to blow out his vocal cords. He has asked for a Katy Perry tattoo on his forearm (I had to explain that real tattoos are done with needles and not just "lick-and-sticks," like all the temporary ones he gets). He even surprised me on Valentine's Day one year when he walked downstairs from his room, plopped down on one knee while holding an oversized fake diamond ring, and begged her to marry him, "Please, please, Katy! Please be my wife!" The whole thing was so tender I didn't have the heart to tease him that a proposal wasn't needed if they were already married. It may be that he's now recognizing that the joyous part of getting married, the "I do's," and the party, never happened. Uh-oh. Has this mom been defeated?

It would make me so happy to see my son in a real relationship, but it makes it kind of hard when the times I bring it up, his response is always, "Mom, don't be silly, I have wife."

I don't argue. It's been fun living this crush with Mr. Katy Perry.

Lessons Learned
- Imaginary or authentic, love is love!
- I'm not giving up hope. There is a special girl out there waiting for Matt.

He's not so "bad."

CHAPTER 9

Smooth Criminal

What you can plan for:
Your child will steal.

Decorations: check. Cake: check. Good food and music: check! One more day before the big celebration, the end of fulfilling my motherly duties—I mean, Matt's high school graduation.

I looked forward to the day Matt finally finished high school. Rumor had it this meant he no longer needed me and I no longer needed to support him. He would get a job, move out on his own, and go to college. Right? I'd worked hard caring for him for the last eighteen years—packing school lunches, helping with homework, supporting school activities and fundraisers—and now payday had come. As soon as they threw their caps in the air and we got their graduation pictures, we could cut the apron strings and celebrate our accomplishments.

Had I missed something? Do you mean that's not how it ended for me?

Nope. A mother's job never ends. It's true for any of us. After Matt got his high school certificate of completion, he attended a program in our area that provided additional education. This meant more school lunches, more homework, and more activities, but the three to four additional years of peace of mind were worth it. This wonderful program is available for those who are differently abled until they reach age twenty-two. I was thrilled.

The decision to use this program was made via Matt's Individualized Education Plan (IEP), which we followed with teachers and school officials from kindergarten through high school. Matt may have been of age, but because I feared the big, bad world would eat him up, I welcomed anything that postponed the inevitable.

Matt loved his years at South Valley. On the days he and his classmates were on campus, they continued with basic classes such as English and math and also learned how to cook and do laundry. Two to three days a week, they spent time in the community, learning how to use public transit, grocery shop, find items on a list and price match, and visiting local businesses that provided work for kids with special needs. These businesses gave them simple tasks intended to help them decide what types of jobs they might want to pursue.

In the early days of the program, I worried about Matt losing friendships; however, several of Matt's childhood friends also continued on to South Valley. During registration, he even reconnected with pals he hadn't seen for years.

"Hey! I 'member you!" he'd exclaim whenever he saw a familiar face. Due to district boundaries, these relationships had been put on pause during the transition to middle and high school.

As I watched their reunion, it took me back to my own youth and reconnecting with friends I hadn't seen for the same reason. I could relate to that giddy feeling in your belly when you see a familiar face from your past. The kids' hugs, smiles, and squeals of joy made me happy. Unfortunately, Matt's feelings of excitement toward his friends were short-lived.

The instructors at South Valley were fun, nice, smart, cool, and cute—and the reason Matt lost interest in most of his peers! As he became more comfortable, he gravitated toward the staff instead of the students.

If they were young and male, he looked up to them and wanted to be their bud. He talked about them nonstop at home. If they were young, female, and blonde, he crushed on them, talking about them even more than the males. And these innocent women succumbed to his cunning charms as he weaseled his way into their hearts. My Casanova had the ability to make them fall in love with him. Okay, not literally, although I often heard they favored him. How could I not be flattered? Truth be told, I'm sure they said that to all the parents. His ability to play the ladies' man worked to Matt's advantage anytime he required disciplinary action. He would use his charm and handsome features (okay, so I may be a little biased) to get him off the hook. Fortunately, there have been few instances of needed discipline, but when they happen, I have no difficulty doing my job as a mom.

By this time in our story, Matt had stolen the payday I thought I had coming when he graduated from high school. He'd stolen the attention of his teachers and my evenings of lounging around. Instead, I helped with more homework and continued to take him to school functions. Those were his small robberies.

And that's not even close to his biggest heist.

What started as a normal Wednesday morphed into something unrecognizable.

The annoying buzzing of my alarm clock interrupted the silence of a perfectly good slumber, so I did something about it. I hit snooze again. *Last time, I swear,* I promised, although I'm not sure with whom I made this particular pact. Being the reasonable person I am, I allowed myself only two to three snoozes before I forced myself to roll out of bed, still half asleep even with the extra z's, hating mornings as much as I hate peas (ick!). I never actually went back to sleep, so I'm not sure of my method to this madness, other than I love mornings as much as I love peas. By the way, in case you haven't heard, I hate peas.

As usual, I felt like a big slug trying to roll myself out of bed. The morning's first sounds reached my ears—movement in the next room and Matt whispering to himself.

"Good morning, bud!" I hollered in his direction, hoping to help get him up and moving even as I tried to stand on my own morning legs.

"Hi, Mom," he replied groggily. I listened for a minute and heard the familiar sound of his closet opening. Satisfied we were both awake, or at least pretending to be, I began my morning grooming ritual.

On this specific day, my hair and I were getting along, I had no problems selecting my outfit, and I felt energized, considering. *Okay,*

Wednesday, let's see what you have in store for me, I challenged as I grabbed my earrings and headed to the kitchen.

The smell of toothpaste and freshly washed hair lingered as I made my way past Matt's bathroom. I peeked in on him and found him shaving. *Hmmm . . . he's further along than I expected.*

"You're sure hairy, just like your dad."

He giggled as I teased.

Happy with his progress, I smiled and asked what he wanted for breakfast.

"Bagel, please."

Of course. Stupid question, I thought as I descended the stairs. I couldn't wait for the day he surprised me and changed things up. For now, I scurried about, making his plain bagel with plain cream cheese and a tall glass of milk. A creature of habit, Matt plopped himself into his seat at the counter and took a big bite out of his bagel, just as I finished pouring his milk. He seemed to be enjoying the breakfast I'd put so little effort into, although I'd added an extra dash of "Mom's love" to spice it up. In case you want the recipe for Mom's love, it's easy. You lick the cream cheese off your fingers (the mess you made when making the first half) and proceed to spread cheese on the second half without washing. Enjoy!

Noticing we were almost out of milk, I started to write a grocery list as I watched him eat. "Mmmm. Good, Mom," he said as if he didn't eat the same thing at least ninety-two mornings in a row.

"I'm glad you like it, bud," I responded with a hint of sarcasm, suggesting I had never made this for him. I continued with my list as he ate. After he consumed his last bite, I handed him a napkin to wipe away the cream-cheese smile he'd managed to give himself.

How in the world do you get this stuff from ear to ear? I wondered as I watched him wipe the napkin down the sides of his face, taking the mess with it. Bagel and schmear. So much for cleaning up.

I checked my watch: 7:00 am; we were right on time.

106

Mornings are hectic but smooth unless something unexpected happens, like Matt selecting socks that don't match or filling his pockets with toys he tries to sneak to school. These situations seriously disrupt our schedule. When this happens, "Hurry up" and "Down syndrome" don't play well together in our home. So why not just get up earlier? Honestly, I'm just not a morning person, so let's add that phrase to those that don't play well together.

This day, I first helped him do a better job with his face, erasing the evidence of his morning meal. Then I scooted him into the next room to put on his shoes while I quickly cleaned up the breakfast mess. Moments later, we both plopped ourselves on the couch and watched out our large front window for Matt's big yellow taxi, aka school bus, to arrive. After the hustle and bustle of the morning, I welcomed any extra minutes we had to relax and enjoy each other's company. If time allowed, we would review his spelling words for the week or discuss his class plans for the day. Sometimes we just poked fun at each other, telling knock-knock jokes or silly stories. It never got old.

"Hey, Matt," I said, scaring him from whatever thoughts he was having.

He tried not to laugh. "What, Mom?"

"Knock, knock."

"Who's there?" he said, sounding annoyed.

"Boo."

"Boo who?"

Now I could tell he was really annoyed.

"Aww, don't cry bud. We'll see each other again this afternoon!" I laughed, proud I even remembered a joke.

"Yeah, right," he said while shaking his head as if I'd just said the dumbest thing, which I kind of had.

When his taxi arrived, I sent him off with my usual, "I love you, bud. Have a good day," as he yelled back while running to the bus, "Love you too, Mom." After finding his seat, he flashed me the sign for "I love you" with his chubby hand. I returned it and waved as they drove away. Little did I know that just hours after we'd laughed at my knock-knock joke and signaled each other with our loving gangster signs, I would be tempted to give him away.

On this specific Wednesday, Matt's class was taking its weekly afternoon trip to the grocery store to do mock shopping. Imagine how surprised I was when, several hours later, Matt's teacher called me at work.

"Ms. Hooton, I need to talk to you about what happened with Matt today." I heard a hint of embarrassment in her voice.

"Sure, what's going on?" I asked.

"The class had some free time after shopping," she went on, "so we allowed them to browse through the books and magazine section."

"Umm-hmm," I responded as I multitasked between work and listening to her. This was nothing new.

"Well, Matt found a magazine that had Michael Jackson on the cover."

Of course he did, I thought. *He loves Michael and spots him anywhere.*

"Well," she went on, "thrilled with his finding, he began skimming through it. He got more excited and quite animated as he turned each page. I never get this excited over a magazine, so I enjoyed watching him. I think he really likes him."

I nodded, visualizing the scene.

"He asked to purchase the magazine, but he didn't have enough money with him."

"Yeah, I know," I said, acknowledging that he only had a few dollars that day.

"No biggie. But when it was time for us to leave, I instructed him to put it back and advised him to talk to you about possibly coming back to buy it later. I had to turn my attention to the class to start rounding up all the students." She hesitated. "Matt's usually pretty good at following my instructions, so I'm surprised by what he did today."

Uh-oh. What did she mean? He is usually pretty good at following instructions . . . usually. Suddenly, it dawned on me. *No. He didn't.*

Have you ever wondered why the pockets on cargo shorts are so big? I mean, really, do the designers of these shorts really think they need to be big enough to carry a picnic lunch or one's collection of superhero action figures? Or did they intend for them to be used to sneak drinks and snacks into movie theaters? Or, even better, did they make them to hold stolen goods?

Yep, that's where Michael ended up, in that magazine-sized pocket on my son's shorts, pocketed by a "smooth criminal," my son, who had done something "bad."

Well, crap, I thought as my focus turned solely to the call.

By this late in the day, the teacher could not take Matt back to the store for the walk of shame to return the stolen item. "I don't expect this of you. I'll take care of it when we get home," I told her.

She asked if it would be okay if she threw it away. I said yes and requested she have Matt watch, as I knew this would devastate him. Here's the thing: when living with a person who has Down syndrome, or at least my person with Down syndrome, it takes only a few hours for him to forget what happened in his day. Whether exciting or traumatic, if enough time goes by, these experiences are not shared with me. By the time I got home from work, Matt had forgotten the incident and had no idea I knew about it. When he welcomed me with his usual smile and "Hi, Mom," I lovingly returned the hello and asked how his day was. "Good," he responded, still no hint of the day's adventure in his tone.

I signaled my husband to the other room, where we could talk. "Do you know what he did today?" I whispered to John. "He pulled a five-finger discount on his teacher."

I caught him up on the details, and he agreed we needed to address this. Matt had no idea of the storm coming his way. John and I instructed him to get his shoes and get in the car because we were going for a ride.

"Okay," he said as he jumped up, happy to be going out.

John, who was as nervous as I was, drove to our destination, which happened to be the same store where we did most of our shopping, which made a crappy situation even crappier. I hoped I wasn't going to have to find a new place to shop.

About halfway there, I could no longer withhold. I needed to prepare my son. "Matt, I understand you stole something from the store today," I said, my voice full of disappointment. His happy disposition faded, and I could see he remembered.

He knew he was in trouble. In a nervous voice, he responded, "I sorry, Mom."

"I've explained to you that stealing is wrong. You know better, bud. Now we have to do the right thing and go tell the store what you've done." His lower lip quivered. *Don't do it!* I quickly turned away before I could see his baby blues flood with tears. I hate it when he cries.

When we arrived, John and I led the way while Matt followed like a sloth, his head hung low. It sucks to take the walk of shame, especially when you're not the guilty party but gave birth to him.

We went directly to customer service, where I sought out the store manager. She greeted us with a smile and immediately recognized Matt. "I know you from the school," she said, but he didn't lift his head to acknowledge her. He was already ashamed, and we hadn't even begun the process of his "freetail" therapy yet.

I pulled her aside and told her what happened earlier that afternoon, explaining that the magazine had been discarded at the school. She looked back at him and smiled tenderly.

"Thanks for letting me know. It's okay. He's okay."

What! NO!

She'd given him that free pass he tends to get too easily. That doggone extra chromosome! I don't care how handsome and fun Matt is, having Down syndrome does not excuse him from making bad decisions. Or does it? I don't know, maybe it does. Maybe next time I

110

should give him a shopping list and have him wear the shorts with the biggest pockets. Wouldn't that be a sight—to see him walking out of the store with a gallon of milk in one and a loaf of bread in the other?

I did my best to give my nice-mom stink eye to the manager and quietly whispered, "Um, I appreciate your kindness, but it really isn't okay. We are trying to teach him a lesson, and I could use your help."

She caught on and said, "Follow me," then took us to a back room where there were several monitors on an L-shaped table. These screens showed images of every section of the store. We waited for what came next.

She had us sit down while she made a quick call. I continued to watch the monitors, feeling slightly guilty as I spied on clueless shoppers. A few minutes later, a security guard joined us. He looked intimidating all decked out in his police uniform, gun on his hip and badge on his chest. As soon as Matt saw him, Matt's leg started to twitch, and his foot began bouncing on the floor. He does this whenever he gets nervous. For a split second, I started to feel bad for taking it to this extreme, but I realized I needed to stand firm as a lesson was taught. Sadly, this has been the best way for Matt to learn.

This gentleman knew what we were trying to do and did a good of job scaring our son in the nicest way.

"So, you took something from us today . . ." he began in an authoritative voice. "You know you can go to jail for stealing?" Before Matt could respond, the officer followed up with, "And you know your parents could get in trouble as well?"

Matt looked at him fearfully, then at John and me. His voice squeaked out a faint, "Yes."

"Is that what you want?" he asked.

Matt's leg bounced faster as he shook his head. He began to blink more rapidly; I knew what that meant. His eyes began to fill with tears. It wouldn't be long before they overflowed.

Matt got the message loud and clear. I looked at the security guard and shook my head slightly, a signal that it had worked and he could stop.

"Okay, I'm going to let you go this time, but please don't let it happen again." His voice grew softer and kinder.

Matt nodded. "I . . . I sorry," he whimpered as a tear rolled down his cheek.

Have I said how I hate it when he cries? My heart aches when my man-boy is upset. My parents used to say, "This is harder on me than it is on you," and, at this moment, I understood it. Teaching our children hard lessons may be the hardest part of parenting.

The value of this magazine was twenty dollars and, initially, I thought it might be good for Matt to work it off. I asked the manager and security guard if they had any work he could do. I suggested spending time bringing the grocery carts in from outside. We volunteered to chaperone Matt as he worked so there would be no safety risk. The manager said she would look into it and get back to us.

She called the next day and shared that Matt needed to be an employee to do any work, or it could be a liability if he got hurt. This meant that, unfortunately, they had no jobs for him. We offered to come back and pay for the magazine (Why hadn't I thought of that while we were there?), but she refused. She appreciated the steps we had taken to teach Matt a lesson.

Before the call ended, the manager added, "Ms. Hooton, I watched the security footage from the afternoon of the incident and saw where Matt put the magazine in his pocket, but there's something else." *Uh-oh, what else did he do?* She went on. "I saw him kneeling on the floor and had to zoom in to see what he was doing. As I got a closer look, I saw him scrubbing scuff marks off our floor. He found the wipes we provide to wipe down the carts and used them to clean up the mess."

A lump formed in my throat.

"He may have made one bad decision, but you have a good son, Ms. Hooton. He's always so pleasant when he comes into our store."

Who had the big alligator tears now? I croaked out a thank-you before hanging up to let the waterworks begin.

My son, cleaning one minute, stealing the next. At least if I'm a mom of a thief, it's a clean thief. This is typical of my life, reprimanding him and praising him in the same sentence.

This could be a good place to end this story, but to do so would leave out the inspiration for this chapter's title.

After talking with John, I called Ash to see if he would like to join us in this teaching opportunity. He replied that he would, but he had a dilemma. His daughter, Matt's younger sister, had decided to take a pack of bubble gum earlier that day at another location in the same grocery chain. Her mom had received the same call I had, and she needed his help with that situation. Torn between which of his children to help, he decided on little sister since I had John to support me.

You hear stories about twins feeling and doing the same things even when apart. These two siblings are hardly twins as there is a fifteen-year age difference between them, but for whatever reason, they both had the same idea on the same day. My husband and I joked that they must have communicated telepathically as they committed their crimes, similar to the children's movie about the brother-sister duo who could speak to each other this way. Whether Matt and his sister have this ability or not, I find it ironic that on the same day, around the same time, at the same grocery chain, these two siblings turned that Wednesday into a "thriller" for their parents.

It has been twelve years, and, thanks to a team effort, I haven't been faced with this issue again. South Valley helps teach the life structure those with special needs can use when they age out of the school system. I will forever be grateful for the additional education and lasting friendships we took with us when Matt graduated.

Lessons Learned
- No cargo shorts for Matt on Wednesdays
- Your child will steal, even if it's the hearts of others.

"Wanna piece of me?"

CHAPTER 10

Down Syndrome in the Dojo

What you can plan for:
Your child can and will exceed your expectations.

If you still own a Blockbuster membership card, I know a place you may be able to use it—actually two: one in Bend, Oregon, and the other in a room above a garage on the outskirts of Salt Lake City. This second location is managed by Matt. And he usually goes easy on the late fees.

Movies are one of Matt's favorite pastimes. It takes special skill to be a dedicated movie watcher. He has no problem viewing the same show over and over—and over and over. This means my days are filled with the sounds of princesses in distress and superheroes saving the world.

When he's not watching them, my movie addict is quoting them. It's impossible to be in a bad mood around him. He squashes it right out by reciting witty one-liners. It's the same when listening to the radio. Within the first few notes of the song playing, he will blurt out what soundtrack it belongs to. His ability to remember these things amazes me. He may not be an actor, but he is definitely an entertainer.

I welcome the day he finally tires of the talking animals or villains that have temporarily moved in with us. One can only listen to the voices of singing mermaids or the sounds of crushing buildings for so long. Matt's way of flushing out the monotony is to pick an actor from one of his favorites and watch everything they're featured in. Not an ideal way of switching things up, but it works—until the next go-around.

One of Matt's favorites is *Kung Fu Panda.* And watching shows about karate prompted his aspiration to become a Ninja. I supported this twice: on Halloween, two years in a row, but these one-nighters were not enough for him. We could tell he longed to be like his panda hero by the fake swords he strapped to his back for days after. I didn't know if he would understand the respect this sport required, but I was willing to give him the opportunity to learn. He needed to understand that karate was far more than a cute panda with a belly (that resembled his own), and his brave buddies defending their village.

Getting Matt involved in physical activity is like running into an ice cream truck that only sells vegetables. Yes, it's good for you, but there's nothing sweet about it. We tried several team sports. They didn't work because he either couldn't keep up, had challenges with his lower muscle tone, or we were just plain bored. As cute as it may have been, I could only tolerate watching Matt pick me dandelions, I mean "flowers," in the outfield for so long.

I quickly learned that when I did find an activity he enjoyed, I had to get him involved before he lost interest. If he wanted to try karate, I would make it happen. Martial arts felt perfect! It did not include running or having to worry about being on the defense—or so I thought. Little did I know how much my son's strength and memory would be tested.

Now that I had made the decision to support Matt, then nineteen years old, my hunt for the martial-art style that suited him best began. Who knew there were so many different styles? Skimming through our mail one day, I happened to run across an ad for a karate class at a local rec center. The flyer promoted being fluent in ASL (American Sign Language), which caught my attention.

They must be a part of the special needs community if they know sign language, I thought as I looked at the fine print. We had attended an event for those with special needs at this place once before, so I assumed this would be similar. Anxious to see if this might be a good fit for Matt, I made a call, and they invited us to come and observe the following week.

"I'm going to be like Jackie Chan, Mom," he announced constantly. "Remember, I'm going to be like Jackie Chan!" I took this as an indication that he was excited about the meeting.

The rec center was located in a sketchy part of town and run down like the buildings that surrounded it. As John, Matt, and I pulled into the parking lot, I couldn't help but wonder if this was the reason they offered a defense class. Now I seemed to recall the inside wasn't any more promising. Turns out I was right.

As we walked the halls, I noticed that pieces of white tiles were missing from the scuff-marked floors and that empty soda cans littered dark corners. The bulletin boards lining the brick walls were cluttered with fliers for past and upcoming activities. Matt was oblivious, but John looked at me with concern. This center needed some attention. I began to question my decision.

Like a hound dog on a scent, Matt led the way while I battled my concerns. He picked up his pace when shouts of "Kiai!" echoed through the hallways. I knew we were close when the temperature grew warmer and the smell of stinky feet permeated the air. Matt's sniffer eventually landed us in the right place. We quietly entered the room and took a seat at the back so as not to interrupt.

I counted. There were only six students, ranging in age from early teens to adults. The instructor, a middle-aged, bald man of average height and physique, reminded me of the actor Vin Diesel. He paced in front of them as he called out commands, the students following his directives in almost perfect unison. Obviously, they had practiced for a while. Unlike the class members dressed in white uniforms with differ-ent colored belts, the teacher wore all black. From what I understood, this symbolized his skill in the sport. At least that's what I'd learned from watching *The Karate Kid* and, of course, *Kung Fu Panda* a zillion and one times. As we watched this live demonstration, we learned this was known as Kenpo karate.

Unaware of anything else, Matt focused solely on the class while I became engrossed in studying each student. None appeared to have special needs. Slightly disappointed, I planned to find out if I had mis-understood or if those who had disabilities were absent that evening.

As the class came to an end Matt's enthusiasm grew. Mine did too. Impressed by what I'd seen, I'd forgotten all about the condition of the location.

I leaned into John. "So, what do you think? Should we go for it?"

"Well, I don't know how we couldn't. I mean, look at him!" We both looked at Matt, smiled, and decided we wanted more information. We stayed after to meet the gentleman in charge.

"Hi, I'm Mr. A." I recognized it as the voice I had talked to on the phone.

My husband went in to catch his inviting handshake, but Matt intervened, accepting the offer.

"Hi, I Matt," he said excitedly, wanting to make his presence known. Mr. A smiled at him as he gripped his hand.

From behind them, I introduced myself as the woman who had called the week prior.

"We're interested in hearing more about Kenpo karate," added John. "What's the difference between this and regular karate?" he asked.

"Kenpo focuses more on defense," I thought I heard Mr. A say. To be truthful, I didn't pay attention to these details as I had other questions. Mom questions.

We were having a nice conversation when Mr. A almost immediately agreed to take Matt on as his student. Once again, I misunderstood this as saying there were others who had special needs in his class. Mr. A suggested we bring Matt for the next few weeks to try things out, and if he still showed interest, we would make it official—although Mr. A pretty much made it official when he presented Matt with a white Gi before we left that evening.

Pronounced "ghee," it is the loose-fitting uniform worn in martial arts, and our son was ecstatic. We couldn't turn back now! Still, I wondered how long he would last once he started to feel the physical impact of the sport. I had a feeling when he got kicked in the gut and dropped to the floor, his kung-fu phase would suffer a similar fate.

Before leaving, I asked Mr. A about other students who were differently abled. To my surprise, he said there were none.

I learned a lesson that night. I assumed this was an adaptive program because the instructor could communicate using sign language. You know what they say about assuming. Mr. A shared he had family members who were deaf and that was why he knew how to speak with his hands. He taught me that being deaf did not mean one had disabilities. The tables had turned. Normally, I was the one educating others, but in this case, I became the student.

We attended his class for a month as Mr. A suggested, and Matt showed no signs of retiring his desire to become a ninja. In 2009, he officially joined Jeff Speakman's Kenpo 5.0. Because Mr. A wanted to seal the deal, he instructed Matt to remove the jacket portion of his Gi. Matt looked confused as he did so while eyeing his sensei. Mr. A smiled and held up the official patch. Instantly, Matt grinned like a Cheshire cat. As he handed over the jacket, Mr. A committed to having the patch attached and returned in time for the next class. Matt's fun-loving personality had won over his instructor and peers.

About two months into our karate adventure, the studio moved to a location near our home, making the commute very convenient. It also meant no more gloomy hallways. The taller ceilings allowed us to observe in a cleaner, brighter atmosphere, though it didn't take long before the stench of sweat and stinky feet permeated this place as well.

The new location meant new members, and new people always involved uncertainty. I'd always felt hesitant to involve Matt in typical classes because of the numerous times I had been told, "There are programs out there for people like him." This new group now had ten adults and at least five teenagers. Matt remained the only student who had special needs.

We had already taken the time to establish relationships with the original members at the old location. I didn't want our new friends to be worried that Matt could hold the entire class back. Surely, they had enrolled in this activity as an outlet for themselves and to learn karate. They might be hesitant to work with a student who had different abilities.

But they surprised me. This group was different. In fact, these were the type of people I wanted in Matt's life—nonjudgmental and patient.

Every person treated Matt respectfully. I never sensed any concerns. For practice, participants took turns pairing up with one another. As each paired up with Matt, they took the time to make sure he understood the movements of the routines and did their best to help him perfect his moves. When their turn came to spar against Matt, which is a freeform fight also used for combat training, they did so gently. Honestly, this was against my wishes, as I wanted him to be treated like every other student. I'd seen what he'd experienced in his young life already; he needed to be able to defend himself should he ever be in the position.

It took only one or two sessions before they realized their mistake. Matt did not show them the same mercy! In fact, he didn't always know his own strength. Thankfully, the class didn't take it personally when he attacked them, sometimes injuring them, when they were doing just the opposite. In his defense, I had warned them.

Kenpo karate requires knowing fourteen techniques and several forms and sets to advance from one rank and title to the next (except yellow, which only has ten techniques). The belts go from white to yellow to orange to purple to blue to green to brown to black. To my surprise, Matt stayed through white and yellow, then on into orange and purple. It shocked me even more that as it got tougher, he made it to blue and went as far as green! He advanced through six ranks. He memorized sixty-six techniques, several blocking and striking sets, and many forms. WOW! This was something I never dreamed he would or could accomplish.

It did not come easily and took dedication from all involved to make this happen for Matt. My husband and I, along with Ash, adjusted our schedules to make sure we were able to get him to the practices each week. We also had to stay committed if we were going to make it to the tests.

At times it was painful. Not like getting-thrown-to-the-mat kind of pain but more like being the boss of your spirit and forcing it to do something it didn't want to do. There were days Matt didn't want to go, and sometimes I almost caved. Vegging out in my pj's and watching Saturday morning cartoons or kicking back in my recliner on those Monday nights after a crappy day at work was tempting. We were all learning that in a sport that required discipline, we had to suck it up to help him understand that sacrifice is how we achieve the things we want. In this case, the reward was a rainbow of colored belts—along with bragging rights for Matt and his parents!

As students prepared for each tournament, the studio's red-and-blue throwing mats became saturated with blood, sweat, and tears— DNA from each of them as they showed off their skill sets during intense workouts. Wise guy that I am, I proclaimed after practice about two years in, "You know, I should have a Gi and colored belts too." It seemed only fair since I, too, had shed tears and sweat throughout the years of Matt's practicing—a challenge on my part when surrounded by a gang whose waists boasted their strength.

"You should sign up!" they dared me. While I enjoyed watching them, I had no desire to take a foot to the face or an elbow to the back.

I took no notice. My taunting went on. "I'd hate to make you look bad, being better than ya'll without even using an ounce of physical energy." I loved this group and how well they treated my son. We now considered them extended family, and the bantering told as much. While those mats may not have had my physical blood, sweat, or tears on them, they were covered with my emotional DNA for all involved with my not-so-little ninja.

On test days, in addition to the physical routines, each colored rank had a unique pledge we spent hours rehearsing. Mr. A offered us an out by forgoing this portion of the test, but if I wanted Matt to be treated like the others and this was a requirement, we had to at least try. But I will not lie, it added extra stress and pressure. What was I thinking?

It didn't matter how much we practiced; test days always made me nervous. John and I would get Matt hyped up with "You're so awesome!" and "You've got this!" chants. It worked; he has always been easy to encourage. I, on the other hand, could have used my own chants, or, better yet, a stiff drink.

And mine weren't the only nerves on fire. The studio reeked of anxiety as each participant waited for their turn to show off their new skills. One by one, their names were called. We were like class parents, proudly cheering after everyone performed, praying they all passed. And then the moment for which we were really waiting: Matt's turn. On this day, he was testing for his green belt.

"Matt H., you're up!"

Matt jumped up from the floor, where he patiently waited, and hollered, "Me?" (His response anytime he hears the word *Matt*.) I scooted to the edge of my seat as if that extra inch gave me a better view. Matt then made his way to the middle of the floor, where he stood tall with his arms at his sides, waiting for his sensei to begin.

Mr. A took his position in front of him. As he did so, Matt bowed to him, a sign of respect to his sensei and the Dojo. Mr. A then asked him to recite the green-belt creed. Matt closed his eyes, squeezing them tightly as he concentrated on the words. I mouthed along, knowing how difficult this was for him.

"I pledge a continued effort to sharpen my skills, to increase my knowledge, and to broaden my horizons. I shall obligate myself under the direction of my instructor to learn the skills of a teacher, which will enable me to teach my skills in the prescribed manner outlined by Mr. Ed Parker."

It's a mouthful. Though he was unable to enunciate every letter and remember every word, I couldn't help but be proud. I had a hard time remembering it too.

Mr. A gave him a nod, and Matt stood in the at-ready stance, waiting for his sensei to begin with the technique portion. Since these were two-person attacks and defenses, it required an opponent of higher rank to assist with the testing, this individual joining Matt in the middle of the room.

Mr. A took a deep breath and, then, in an authoritative voice, yelled, "Disappearing Mace!" And Matt's opponent came at him. From out of nowhere, Matt landed a left-hand punch to the groin, spun around, and kicked the guy in the thigh, followed by a ball kick to the stomach. He finalized the technique with a right-hand punch to the jaw, temporarily disabling his attacker. *Take that,* I quietly cheered.

The series of techniques that followed were equally impressive. Thirteen remained, and Mr. A called them out one by one: "Wings of Silk," "Conquering Shield," and "Gift of Destruction," with Matt defending himself against each attack just as he had been taught.

From the edge of my seat, I watched him prance around the room, showing off his skills. The beautiful sounds of him slapping his thighs and his feet hitting the mat filled the silence as he executed each move.

And then they were done. Matt, now dripping with sweat, bowed to his opponent as well as his sensei, who nodded and instructed him to take a knee. I slumped back with relief and let go of the breath I had been holding.

Mr. A called then each participant to join Matt and instructed them to kneel quietly as they waited to hear their results. I tried to read the judges' lips as they whispered amongst themselves, sharing their assessments of each student. I had made it clear I wanted Matt to be treated like the others. Now, I hoped I could handle the repercussions of this request. Beads of sweat dripped down my face, or were those tears? I couldn't tell as I watched and waited for them to complete their evaluation of Matt.

It felt like forever before they called him to come forward for the ceremony. He'd passed! As he stared in the mirror, my heart felt like it would burst. He smiled at my reflection as they performed a sacred ritual that ended with them removing his blue belt and wrapping a green one around him—a beautiful moment between sensei and student and a reward for both after months of hard work.

We went through this process a total of six times.

I was one proud mama of my special karate kid. My thoughts took me back to that physical therapist who sat on my floor and told me my baby might never walk. I KNEW she was wrong. He would walk.

Fast-forward twenty-five years to this moment, and not only did he walk, but he used those legs to carry him all over the floor to perform amazing ninja skills. *Take that and stick it in your things-they-will-never-do file,* I thought as I watched Matt.

It took Matt longer than most to learn and remember each routine, and, as a result, he trailed the class by one belt color. But this didn't bother me because it meant he had earned each of them; they were not participation awards. The instructors took the time he needed and had the same expectations they did for the other students—exactly as I had asked.

Then, one day, we received a special announcement. We were going to have the opportunity to meet the owner of the school, Jeff Speakman, who would be visiting from Las Vegas. He had starred in a few martial-arts movies, and we were elated to think we would be meeting a movie star. Of course, Matt was exceptionally excited, especially after we showed him several clips we found on YouTube.

The number of participants doubled in anticipation of the meeting. If Mr. Speakman could not see it for himself, I planned to sing this school's praises. We couldn't wait for him to meet Matt and, for once, I had no plans of stopping Matt should he go into show-off mode. As routines were performed that day, I watched more intently. This martial-arts expert eyed each student as they traded off with Matt, who, knowing he was being observed, emphasized each move. Mr. Speakman circled them, nodding and smiling as he watched. Excited by this reaction, I elbowed John to make sure he was seeing this. I hoped Mr. Speakman felt Matt represented his school well. We were able to get a photo of him with Matt, the smile on Matt's face mirroring what I felt inside. For this mom, the school did Matt good.

It was cool to later learn that according to the internationally recognized website www.martial-arts-network.com, Mr. Speakman is now voted to be the most popular martial artist in the world. He is the only martial artist rated higher than Bruce Lee, who is second, with Chuck Norris third. He's not only an actor but one cool dude.

It took Matt six years to become our own martial-arts expert, but in those six years, he accomplished more than I ever expected. In fact, he exceeded my expectations. I had underestimated my own son. There were times I wondered if it was time to quit, but Matt persevered. When I wanted to give up, he surprised me and pushed harder.

Sadly, this location eventually closed its doors, but we had more than the multiple-colored accomplishments Matt had earned. We'd formed long-lasting friendships with a group of amazing humans. They'd given our family, specifically Matt, their time and patience, which couldn't have always been an easy task. We had experiences I did not anticipate and will never forget. Matt's success could not have come without his "brothers and sisters" in Mr. A's class. To each, I will be forever grateful.

When Matt heard there would be no more karate, he didn't exactly show emotions of sadness. In fact, the opposite. Practicing two to three times a week for six years is a lot. That said, I think part of him misses it. Every now and then, I will hear the familiar sound of his sticks smacking against each other as he does these routines in his room. Occasionally, as he hops about practicing his kicking formations, he puts the stability of the walls in my living room to the test, all while singing his own praises and making comments about his amazing ninja skills. My son, the humble ninja.

Up till now, there is one term in karate I have not mentioned: "tapping out." It's used when one submits to their opponent. There were times Matt tapped out when sparring, and there were times others had to tap out on him. He still refers to this term when he doesn't want to do something.

Lessons Learned
- For those times in the last thirty years I have wanted to tap out, I'm grateful to those who jumped in and rescued me.
- "Mom, where's my cup?"—a phrase I never imagined my son would use. I'm glad he does, for I'm reminded of his dedication to the sport!

Poonami survivors.

CHAPTER 11
Buy a Dyson—They Suck

What you can plan for:
Cleaning up can get messy.

Who knows what the inside of a bowling ball looks like? Who knows how to get a slice of bread out of a VCR? (Who even knows what a VCR is?) Who knows what a Dyson vacuum looks like completely disassembled? Me! Me! And me!

I doubt I would be able to boast about seeing the guts of these things if it weren't for Matt. I suppose in that aspect he's like any other kid. He is curious, helpful, and sometimes trouble. For this story, I am going to focus on the *helpful,* although a little trouble may come into play.

In our home, an extra chromosome has never been a free pass out of helping around the house—or anywhere else, for that matter. In fact, it may be just the opposite: I may have higher expectations of him—nothing more than he is capable of but more than too many others said he would be able to do. My goal from the moment we left the hospital was to help him become the best version of himself. An extra nudge has been needed here and there, but you know what? Nudging actually works.

I've received disapproving looks from strangers. Evidently, his extra chromosome means he doesn't need to meet the same expectations as children who aren't differently abled. Apparently, this small tweak to his DNA makes it okay for him to act out, be messy, and run away from me in public.

"Aw, come on, Mom," an elderly gentleman said to me as I reprimanded my eight-year-old son one day at a local museum. I'd decided to take him on a date. We were having an enjoyable time until he decided to test me. There were multiple levels at this museum and, for some reason, Matt thought it would be funny to run away from me. Fortunately, this was uncommon behavior for him. I did my best to catch him, but it became a game of cat and mouse. Eventually, the mouse outsmarted the cat, and he lost me.

I went into sheer panic as my mind conjured up every possible scenario. Matt could be an easy target for anyone with ill intentions. I scurried around, quietly calling out to him so as not to bring attention to my situation, but no answer.

After several minutes, I realized I needed assistance, so I sought out an employee. Then I heard it—that familiar giggle. I found my little boy near the Hall of Primates, his favorite section. To say I was upset is an understatement. He's lucky *he* didn't become extinct! Because I feared losing him, I always watched him closely in public. Then, when it happened, I felt horrible! I was terrified he had been kidnapped, was lying hurt somewhere, or, heaven forbid, with a stranger and being taken advantage of.

When I finally found him, it felt like eons when, in fact, it had only been a couple of minutes. I hugged him tightly, relieved, but then he had a lesson to learn. I put a cork on his giggles, and our date ended immediately. No more fun. I escorted him out of the museum and pulled him off to the side to sit on the stairs, where I reprimanded him privately—or so I thought.

I had already learned that it's important to address these issues right away because that's how Matt best comprehends why he is being disciplined. I sobbed as I sternly explained how badly he'd scared me and how important it was for him to stay with his family when in public. His eyes were wide, and his lips quivered as he listened intently.

This was the precise moment when the tall, elderly gentleman decided to interject his "Aw, come on, Mom."

That didn't help at all. *My child needs to understand the difference between right and wrong just like any other child. Just because he is cute and has a loving personality does not mean he should never be disciplined. In fact, his sweet innocence is the very reason it's hard to have these teaching moments, but it's still important that he learn.*

130

I already felt like crap. Moments before, I had been terrified, and now I had a job to do—a painfully hard job. And this fellow may have meant well, but I did not appreciate it.

It is the same when people imply I should relieve my son of tasks, like throwing his trash away at fast-food joints or refrain from requesting homework be sent home—my way of staying involved in what he worked on at school. Another temptation for me and others is to give him money if he's short on funds. What people don't understand is that bailing him out prevents him from learning that we don't get our way all the time. Let's face it—there is not always going to be that stranger who willingly hands him cash when he charms them with his ear-to-ear grin and dazzling blue eyes.

While I appreciate that most people are trying to be kind, my strategy in teaching Matt to become as independent as he can be may be compromised by that kindness. In a way, I think it's possible to show too much compassion. Everything Matt and I do together provides a teaching and learning opportunity for both of us. Stepping in to save the day can undo that. And overlooking unacceptable behavior teaches him it's okay to be disruptive when it's not. That can have terrible long-term consequences.

Someone once asked me what I did to control him when he was running around a restaurant, laughing and causing a ruckus. My response? "Whose son are you referring to? Because mine does not misbehave in public places." Imagine my shock upon learning that, when *not* under my supervision, Matt occasionally exhibited disruptive behavior. When I questioned why they allowed this, they replied, "He has Down syndrome, so it's okay."

It isn't! Down syndrome is not a pass for annoying others when out in the community. In fact, it's just the opposite. I had been working hard to teach Matt how to appropriately behave in public—that it's a privilege to go to special places, like restaurants, where others go to relax and enjoy themselves. Allowing him to act out went against everything I taught him. It disappointed me to hear he was being allowed to behave this way, and it also meant all my efforts to eliminate any negative stigmas associated with Down syndrome were going unnoticed. I wanted Matt to be treated like everyone else, and to receive such treatment, he had to act the same.

In other words, accepting money from strangers so he could make purchases or being obnoxious out in public? No free passes. Being disrespectful? Uh-uh. Bossing others around? Absolutely not. Chores? Again—no free passes.

Speaking of chores—this is what I've been getting to.

I put Matt to work as soon as he could walk, which was around twenty months. His chores consisted of bringing me a diaper, handing me his ointment, and making us a seven-course meal each night for dinner. Some may call it child labor; I like to think of it as promoting independence. You know I'm joking, but, seriously, unlike a lot of kids, including myself as a young girl, Matt has always been willing to help. I hated chores. I would stomp around, cursing my mom or dad under my breath, as I exterminated all the dust bunnies that had taken up residence in our living room. I over-Ajaxed our sink and tub as I cleaned the bathroom of all bodily residue. I did so resentfully because there were many things I'd rather be doing, like gushing over boys with my girlfriends. Now that I'm a parent and have eyes in the back of my head and bionic hearing, I know my folks heard every curse I muttered against them. I'm surprised I didn't spend the majority of those years grounded. And I'm grateful Matt is nothing like me—for the most part.

As Matt got older, around twenty-one months—okay, okay, maybe more like 120 months, we included him in determining what chores he could manage. When I provided a short list for him to choose from, he eagerly chose vacuuming and dusting. Currently, he's in charge of vacuuming the entire house and giving his room a good cleaning once a week, including a good dusting. Believe me, with his extensive collection of superhero action figures, that, in and of itself, is quite the chore!

After he chose what he would be responsible for, we had Vacuuming 101, which included learning that the purpose of a vacuum is to suck all the crap—dirt, crumbs, hair, and any other garbage—off the floor. To make sure he understood, I tossed down some paper scraps so he had a visual and then ran my trusty sucking machine over them to show him how they magically disappeared. He was unduly impressed.

As I gave my demonstration, I reiterated the importance of doing a decent job. "If you are not picking it up, you are not doing good work," I explained. One day he would have a job working for a leader who expected this of him. After a few trial runs, he graduated from V101 and soon became great friends with Dyson.

Matt chose Tuesdays to take care of his weekly responsibilities, which I found fitting. Personally, I've always referenced Tuesdays as Monday's ugly sister—a saying I heard somewhere many years ago.

It changed some when I had the opportunity to observe Matt at it for one week. As I watched, I began to think of them as cheerful chore days. How can cheerful and chores be used in the same sentence, you might ask? It sounds like an oxymoron, right? Well, I'm here to tell you that chores can be cheerful when you live with Matt. He blasts some tunes through our stereo and then loudly sings along over the noise of his cleaning partner. And there you have it—a cheerful chore day.

We recently took a step into the future by making our first robotic purchase, a Roomba. I enjoy listening to the quiet hum of Rosey, the name I borrowed from one of my favorite childhood cartoons, *The Jetsons,* as she makes her way from room to room. It brings me happiness to know my house is being cleaned with no effort on my part.

Matt, however, doesn't appreciate Rosey as much as I do. He refuses to give up this task. Perhaps vacuuming is therapeutic for him, kind of like going to the landfill, another chore he enjoys. There must be something satisfying about standing in the middle of a trailer and chucking junk into the big hole of the unknown. With each toss, Matt yells along with the seagulls screaming overhead.

Maybe it's his opportunity to throw to the wind any frustrations he's unable to communicate.

The good news about how I raised Matt is that his life is very structured, and he follows his daily routines religiously. Unfortunately, he has little flexibility when it comes to making plans. Heaven forbid I try to change things up! Doing so can be like derailing a train, even if the change is something fun. He will even argue and give me a dose of "Mattitude." (This is what I call it in those off times he does get lippy with me.) Yes, this can be frustrating, but in my heart of hearts, I believe structure has helped him retain what he has learned.

Like Matt, my days are structured, but, unlike him, I'm more flexible and will rearrange things, especially if fun is involved. For thirty-five years, I clocked into my nine-to-five job and followed the same routine every day. I envied John's work schedule. He is a tech guy—you know, a brainiac—and worked from home unless he received a request to go out on a call. His flexible work schedule allowed him to be home with Matt and our adorable bichon frise.

Matt was fourteen the year Santa left this little white ball of fur under our tree, and he had the important job of naming his furry sibling. He chose Sugar, which John and I agreed was an appropriate name because she was as white and sweet as the sugary treats that filled our home. We were lucky to be Sugarcoated for seventeen years.

On the occasions John's work took him on a call where he was gone for several hours, our pooch, as sweet as she was, occasionally gifted us with a small poopsicle, though I'm sure she did her best to hold off Mother Nature until we got home. Fortunately, most days were accident-free.

When we came home to little brown-sugar droppings, my husband was responsible for this unpleasant chore. Luckily for me, my gag reflex relieved me of this duty, at least most of the time. On those rare occasions I got stuck with it, I involuntarily showed off the ability I have to dry heave, toot, and pee all at the same time. The jury is still out on whether these are good bragging rights. Although John was kind enough to let me off the hook with this chore, I believe he did so to avoid having to clean up after both female family members.

One afternoon while at work, I finished a conference call in time to wait impatiently for Matt's daily call letting me know he'd made it home from school. We had a rule that he call me even if John was home. The call came at the same time each day unless his bladder or stomach took over, and then it could be just a little later as he relieved himself or grabbed a snack, sometimes both—but not at the same time.

For these reasons, I gave Matt a thirty-minute window before I allowed myself to go into panic mode. On this day, John had gone out on a job, which meant my nineteen-year-old and dog were home alone, nothing to be concerned about—except that my phone never rang. I didn't want to freak out just yet. Since I had a few minutes before my next meeting, I decided to take a quick break and call him. One ring, two rings, three rings. He finally answered, breathing heavily, but I felt relieved as soon as I heard his voice.

"Yeah, yeah, Mom, I home." Panic button disengaged.

"Okay, good. Bud, why haven't you called?" I asked as I doodled on my post-it note pad. "And why are you breathing so hard?"

"Mom, I busy," he said, annoyed I'd interrupted whatever he was doing. His next words paused my doodling.

"Cleaning Sugar's poop!"

Say what? My scribbling came to a halt. He hadn't called because he was cleaning up after his pup. I did my best to remain calm, but in my head surfaced a horrible image. Panic button reengaged.

My mind went into hyperdrive. Although I may not have been in that room, I could feel myself beginning to gag at the possibility of a bigger mess. I learned later that even my overactive mind could not have envisioned the horror that awaited in our kitchen, down the hall, and in our coat closet. Yes, I said the closet! How does one little pile of poop turn into a crime scene of shit?

Mind you, I still had no idea what Matt had done. What I did know was that I could sense the pride in his tone. How could I be mad? I instructed him to go wash his hands immediately and scrub out any brown stuff he could see. Let's face it, he's a boy, so I knew our dog's DNA had landed somewhere on him.

My next instruction sent my son into a fit: leave his phone on the counter so I could sterilize it. Matt was no different from any other teen, possessive of this small piece of technology. You would have thought I'd asked him to cut off a limb. I reassured him I just wanted to make sure there were no germs on it and that he was not being punished because, you know, taking a kid's phone away is the best punishment in the twenty-first century.

"I love you, Matt," I said before we hung up. "You're the best son."

"I love you too, Mom," he said in a not-so-convincing tone, I knew, because I had taken his phone.

My husband then received a call from a raving lunatic—me. He had just pulled into our driveway, so I explained to him what he may be walking into. While we were still on the phone, he opened the door, and I heard him gasp.

"Nope, it's worse."

I panicked. "What do you mean, worse?"

John understood me well enough to know not to share the details. Instead, he said, "Don't worry, honey, I'll take care of this." He told me he needed to go so he could assess the situation and begin damage control.

While John is great with this stuff, the controlling side of me felt restless. I needed to know what he meant, his words looming over me. How could it be worse? I tried to rearrange things at work, but my obligations made it impossible for me to leave early. Maybe it was for the best. I had no choice but to put faith in my man and let him handle what I could not. It felt like forever and a day passed by the time I finally clocked out.

I rushed home. Anxious for an update, I tried to call John on the way, but no answer. If he were in a position to talk, he would have picked up. *Wow! What have my dog and son done?*

When I finally made it home, I grabbed my purse and leapt out of the car. Rushing to the door, I reached for the doorknob but hesitated. Deep breath in and out. No longer able to put off the inevitable, I opened the door, the faint aroma of cinnamon-flavored poop making its way to my nostrils. Yum!

At the time, we lived in a multilevel home. From where I stood in our family room, looking up toward the kitchen, I saw no evidence of any mishap. *Where is my family, and why is it so quiet?* I wondered. I made my way up the three stairs to the kitchen and noticed my husband's lunch box still on the counter, evidence he'd made this cleanup his priority. Before I went any farther, my eyes scanned the floor to make sure it was safe to continue. Phew! Nothing. That was a good sign.

As I rounded the corner, there sat John on the floor of our living room next to a patch of freshly shampooed carpet. In front of him, I recognized the yellow ball of my new Dyson, separated from the base. I may be exaggerating, but John also looked to be surrounded by hundreds of small parts—the guts of my trusted vacuum. *What the—?*

Why in the world had John torn my appliance completely apart? Having grown up with two brothers, I understood men were naturally curious about disassembling things; it's in their DNA to find how objects work. The bigger challenge, of course, is putting it all back together, proving they can do so to themselves and everyone else. But why now? And why my vacuum?

As I looked closer, I could see he had some cleaning supplies and appeared to be meticulously wiping down each of those disassembled pieces. I may be anal (pardon the pun) and like things clean, but I never expected him to disassemble our appliances to get rid of all those nasty germs. Up until now, I had no idea what Matt had done or why my vacuum was involved.

"What are you doing?" I asked.

"Dysons don't pick up poop very well," he said.

"Are you shitting me?" Bless my sweet boy's heart. Matt had taken my instructions literally. I'd taught him vacuums were for picking up crap, and that's exactly what he'd done.

The story goes something like this. Upon arriving home from school, Matt saw the small gift his pooch had left on the kitchen floor. Based on the evidence my husband came home to, the pile had been a fresh one. In an attempt to be helpful, you know, like I taught him, he decided to clean up the mess. Unfortunately, his good deed had turned into poo hell.

If only I had not been a germaphobe and just taught Matt how to clean up after our furry family member, the following would not have taken place.

Matt had remembered that vacuums were meant to pick up crap, so he'd pulled out my new Dyson and began doing just that, cleaning up CRAP. Shame on me for not being more specific.

Can I just say, I loved my brand-new Dyson? The big yellow ball helped it glide smoothly across the floor, making vacuuming an easier and more enjoyable chore, even though it wasn't my job to do. Its smooth, gliding design had apparently helped Matt evenly smear Sugar's number two everywhere, and he'd managed to make a poonami with each back-and-forth motion.

It's too bad our beige-with-caramel-swirling tile hid it so well. What Matt saw was that he had done a wonderful job helping out. And after he'd done his good deed, he did the right but wrong thing and put the Dyson away. He maneuvered it through the kitchen, into the living room, and then to its final resting place, the coat closet. Doing so left a path of dark-brown streaks on my light-colored carpet, bringing new meaning to the term "skid marks." My closet and all its contents now smelled like a porta potty at a sold-out concert in August.

And my poor husband! Matt's intentions were to be helpful with a task not meant for him, and, as a result, John had the grotesque job of cleaning up the cleanup. There was no kicking up his heels after work. Instead, he had to scour and disinfect the kitchen floor, shampoo and deodorize the carpet in the living room and coat closet, and, then, because he's techy and I'm cheap, he'd torn apart our vacuum to sterilize each and every part by hand. John proved me wrong and saved that day in so many ways. I'm blown away not only by his ability to disassemble things without breaking them but put them back in their original state, without having a temper tantrum, no less.

That said, I had no idea of the extent of the damage until years later when John felt safe in sharing the truth. I listened in horror, my face twisting like a dried-up, shriveled apple, grossed out as he shared each detail: how the big yellow ball had turned brown, caked in poo, how every tube was coated in brown guck, and, of course, how the bristles stiffened from the dried-up brown sludge.

Over the years, John has been challenged with disassembling several household items to fix them. Sometimes it's normal wear and tear, sometimes it's Matt repair.

As I watched John clean and received the details of his eventful afternoon, or at least the cliff notes, our little ball of white fur sat snuggled up next to him, oblivious to the havoc she had wreaked upon her people that day. Matt's voice, our background music, sang along to Elton John in one of his favorite jungle movies. "Can you feel the love tonight?" Yes, yes, Matt, as a matter of fact, we could feel the love more than ever. I handed John some Tylenol for the headache my son had caused and thanked him profusely. I also thanked Jesus for letting John get home before me that day.

Lessons Learned

- Shit happens, and when it does, Dyson makes a darn good vacuum (seventeen years and going strong).
- Make sure your child doesn't take you literally.
- Teach your children how to do it all, including cleaning up after your pets.
- My husband is awesome!

"I'm twenty-one. Las Vegas, here I come!"

CHAPTER 12
Boobs, Booze, and a Dragon Tattoo

What you can plan for:
Addressing grown-up needs and wants

One of the challenges with parenting a child with Down syndrome is the difficult decisions you must make as they become adults. How do you treat a person who often desperately yearns to be treated like an adult but is still naïve in many ways? In other words, what should you allow? What do you do to keep them safe while honoring their individuality as the years pass?

Just as with any child, maturity levels among those who have Down syndrome will vary. Some may be childlike; some may be more mature. Matt lives in both worlds. He has adult thoughts and wants. We treat him like an adult, and so do our friends; therefore, it makes sense that he wishes to have the same experiences we do. However, Matt remains childlike in some ways—precious ways. He still enjoys watching children's movies and will even spend his money on toys and coloring books. I honor this in him.

In regard to Matt's other world, John and I and our family work our way through each obstacle as it arises. Instead of controlling him, we assist him in making decisions. I feel that in doing this, we honor him, allowing him to make some decisions on his own while guiding him to make the wisest choices he can.

I don't know if my approach has always been the right one. What I do know is that my son is a decent, loving human, and I am proud of him. As a parent who most often knows your child best, you will experience adventures in learning how to support your child when they come face-to-face with adult circumstances. Just know they will.

Oh no, he's going to be legal! Am I ready for this? These are thoughts I pondered months before Matt turned twenty-one.

There were four things he really wanted for his twenty-first birthday: to drink a beer, get a tattoo, see hot girls, and play poker—a pretty tall order for a mom who didn't want her baby to grow up. Even though he had Down syndrome, I wanted to make this birthday special for him in a semi-grown-up way. John and I went back and forth with ideas and finally succumbed to the suggestion we received to take him to the City of Lights. Las Vegas is the nearby go-to place to celebrate reaching legal age and not too far from us. Here, we could fulfill all his birthday wishes at once. We extended an invitation for a mini vacation to family and friends who wanted to join us. *Look out, Vegas, here comes Matt.*

Initially, my brothers suggested making a boy's trip out of it. They wanted to break their nephew in. I love my two younger siblings, but they are typical brothers—devious mischief-makers. No longer the little boys I helped raise, they both tower over me now. When I am next to them, I swear it feels like they are ten feet tall, making me the little sister. My younger brother has the gorgeous skin tone I always coveted. We call him the beautiful one because he sure is handsome. My middle brother got our mother's lighter complexion. We call him the smart one. Out of the three of us, he's always seemed more reasonable, although he's just as handsome, in my opinion. They grew up to be pretty great men. I'm so proud of both of them. So, of us three musketeers, where does that leave me? Well, I'm the funny one, of course.

Matt loves his uncles! The three of them have fun when they are together, and I enjoy watching their interactions. They treat him like one of the guys—but that's the problem! Treating him like one of the guys means sometimes teaching him, let's just say . . . some less-appropriate guy stuff.

I know it's all in fun and they are just trying to annoy me like they did when we were younger, and sometimes it works. However, there was no way this mama was granting this request to escort him to Las Vegas unchaperoned—a no-go the minute they let it slip that they wanted to take him to see strippers. Things may have gone differently if they had not shared this with me—or not. I couldn't control the short movie clip that played in my mind the minute they suggested it—an image of three grown men, one having an extra chromosome, whistling a barely dressed lady as she danced before them. I couldn't stand the thought of my son getting escorted out of the venue for calling it as he saw it: "Nice boobs, lady." While I'm sure it's par for the course in that profession, I refused to have my son bring in twenty-one being a hoodlum.

My brothers were disappointed. They had obviously been conspiring to show their nephew a fun time, but big, bad sister had ruined their plans. While I do not regret my decision, it was one of the many times I have wanted to allow my son to experience things like other neurotypical kids. I made the easy but difficult decision based on what I thought was best for him. *Please forgive me, brothers.*

So, instead, I planned a family-friend trip. Matt could not wait, his excitement contagious. He loves his birthday so much we've joked it's a national holiday. He and his caravan of party attendees arrived in Sin City on the Friday night after his big day. After all, we had to wait until he was of age. Our rowdy group and my very loud son could be heard whooping and hollering through the hotel lobby as we proceeded to check in. We definitely got the attention of the other guests, or so I worried. As if Vegas is normally a quiet destination.

As soon as we settled in, we made sure Matt had his ID, and then the real shenanigans began.

The first thing on Matt's list was getting a tattoo. I knew very well this would not happen, but it had to be him making the call. We began the hunt for a parlor/studio and didn't have to go far. Only in Vegas. In true Matt style, he barged through the door, announcing his presence, his loud entrance initially catching the guy at the front desk off guard. He appeared to be in his midthirties, his curly, light-brown, shoulder-length hair almost a mullet. Of course, he was covered in tats.

In fact, tattoos were everywhere. Images of the art plastered the dark-gray wall, and a few sample books lay on a red couch to our right. I could only imagine how many fannies had sat on it as they contemplated what design to permanently place on their bodies. This was probably the only way what happened in Vegas *didn't* stay in Vegas.

The first thing Matt noticed was the girl on this dude's forearm. "Heeyyyyy! Nice tattoo! I want that."

The guy looked down at his arm. "Thanks! You like it?"

"Ya!" Matt exclaimed excitedly. "It's my birthday. I twenty-one. I want tattoo my birthday."

"Well, happy birthday," the artist said. "What kind of tattoo do you want?" he asked while looking at me as if questioning whether we were actually going to do this.

"Would you mind telling my son how tattoos are done?" I asked. "And do they hurt at all?" I winked, hoping he took the hint.

He did.

"Yes. It hurts *a lot!*" he emphasized as he grabbed one of their tools to show Matt. "This is a needle, and we have to poke it in your skin over and over with color to make the tattoo. The bigger the design, the more we poke, and the more they *hurt.*"

Matt's face dropped. Part of me felt bad for bursting his bubble. He stood there as if he didn't know what to do now.

"Bud, it's kind of like when you go to the doctor and they give you shots with their needles—only this is a lot more poking. Do you still want to get one?

"No!" Matt exclaimed as he took a step back, waving his hands.

"Okay, thank you for your time," I said as I took hold of Matt's arm and exited the studio. I mouthed, "Thank you" to the nice mullet-guy on my way out. He smiled a kind smile and nodded slightly.

As much as I knew Matt wouldn't want one as soon as he learned how they were done, it took hearing it from a stranger for him to make his decision. I was instantly relieved. I just knew he'd end up with

144

scribbles of dark markings on him if he didn't know how painful it was before moving forward.

A short time later, we took a walk down Crazy—I mean Freemont, Street—the section of Vegas that's so lit up you can't tell whether it's day or night. Matt's eyes sparkled as bright as the lights that lit up this popular tourist attraction as he took in all the chaos. The protective side of me felt the need to grab hold of his arm.

In the center of the area, in between a man painted gold standing in a statuesque form and two shirtless men dressed like Chip and Dale dancers, I noticed a woman doing Henna tattoos. I pointed her out to Matt, who instantly became excited and rushed to her booth and started ogling her work. He came upon a picture of a dragon and lit up with excitement. Since it looked exactly like the tattoo he wanted, I didn't even have to ask. I had him sit down, and she began painting his arm. Several minutes later, Matt proudly showed off the dark-brown image of a dragon making its way up his arm.

Tattoo: check!

We were able to kill two birds with one stone on our visit down this street. Entertainers of all types tried to lure us in with their one-of-a-kind acts. I had a great time watching the birthday boy take it all in. Of course he found the hot girls. They were everywhere—on the posters on the buildings, on billboards that flashed bright lights, and the real "girls" who walked around flaunting their stuff.

Matt eyed each of them, soaking in their beauty, then made a bee-line to two standing not far from us. The red feather headdresses they wore had to be two feet high. I didn't know how their small necks held them up. Their beaded red bikinis covered everything appropriately—including their *man* parts. Yep! My son had no idea the two hot "girls" he begged me to take his picture with were actually guys. I wondered what they said to each other when we walked away. For Matt, some things are just better left unsaid in his happy and innocent world.

Hot girls, part 1: check!

One of our partygoers, a good friend of mine, ShihLan, who has been like a second mother to Matt, stepped inside a nearby casino to try her hand at three-card poker, or three-card stupid, as she calls it. Matt saw this and let go of my arm to follow her. This was his opportunity to check poker off his list. I followed him and watched as he made himself at home in the seat next to her, pulling out his wallet. The heavy smell of cigarette smoke accosted my nostrils. There were four strangers, two men and two women, sitting at the table having a good time, obviously feeling the effects of their adult beverages.

The dealer took one look at Matt and momentarily looked uncertain. She just stood there, holding the cards, unwilling to deal. I knew what was coming and had prepared him ahead of time.

"I need to see your ID," she ordered through her thick accent. *Lady, you better be nice to my boy!*

He proudly pulled it out of his wallet and showed it to her while exclaiming, "It's my birthday. I twenty-one!"

Her expression turned awkward, and she turned to me. "I don't think I can allow him to play."

Uh-oh. Here came mama bear. Nobody discriminated against my cub. "Why? He's twenty-one, and he's got money," I said a little snarkily. She just stood there not knowing what to do, with things getting really uncomfortable at that table.

Suddenly, ShihLan and the four strangers piped up. "Let him play! Let him have fun. We don't have a problem with it."

I thanked them, and the mention of his twenty-first birthday fueled them to put even more pressure on the dealer. I could see her body relax. She even looked relieved once the other players approved and proceeded to deal the cards. I smiled at her, showing my appreciation. I wondered later if she had this reaction on behalf of the others at the table, thinking they wouldn't be okay with my son joining them.

That night, Matt was a confident young man who got to hang out with adults who were not his parents. He enjoyed himself and made sure everyone else did too. In fact, I think every person at that table won. I'd hit the jackpot when four complete strangers came to Matt's defense, refusing to allow discrimination a seat at that table. They've probably never given us another thought, but I will forever be grateful. After all, because of them, Matt got one of his birthday wishes.

I hoped when the dealer's shift ended that she, too, felt like a winner. We taught her that people with Down syndrome can participate in the same activities as those who do not have special needs and that they have a good time doing so. She even had some good laughs with everyone.

ShihLan, who patiently sat with Matt and taught him how to play poker, won bragging rights for teaching Matt to gamble. And, believe it or not, Matt turned his twenty dollars into seventy-five big ones, fair and square.

Playing poker: check!

Wow! All this had already happened, and we had only been celebrating for a few hours. *Only in Vegas can you have a lifetime of experiences in a short time frame,* I thought as we made our way back to the room to crash.

Our second day's plan was to fulfill his wish to see hot girls. It was just a bonus that Matt got to have a sneak preview the night before. He wanted to go to a show to get this birthday wish, but I did not know how to make it happen. To Matt, hot meant cute and even sexy, but he didn't realize that hot in Vegas actually meant nude or topless. I had certain standards. In other words, my son would not be subjected to nudity despite my brothers' conspiring. After all, he was still my little boy.

I did some research before the trip to find something that would be a win/win for Matt, and for me, in this city of sin. Luckily, I found the Coyote Ugly. I recalled seeing the movie and thought if this pub were anything like it, it could be my winner. It may not have been a hot-girl show per se, but it was a place with hot girls whose clothing covered the majority of their sexy parts.

We arrived early to get a table big enough for our party. Imagine our surprise to learn this was a standing-room-only joint. I'd never been to a club that didn't have a place to sit! Standing for long periods is something Matt does not do well due to his lower muscle tone and wide, flat feet. In these circumstances, it's almost a guarantee that not long into the activity, Matt will start to complain, "My feet so tired. Les go home." I felt disappointed as I was sure we would have to cut our evening short.

Nope! I learned that night that there is no time limit for standing when my son has an opportunity to be around cute girls, even when it's not Katy Perry.

Kindness found us yet again. Matt immediately focused on a cute brunette who had been dancing tastefully on the bar. This little hottie immediately caught on to his vibe, heard what we were celebrating, and made him feel special the entire evening. From atop the bar, she called out to her "boyfriend from Salt Lake" as she danced and sang. Matt loved hearing he was someone's boyfriend and, eventually, the whole place played into it. Matt sucked up the attention as if he were a straw trying to get every last drop of a Slurpee. I had never seen him beam with the joy he did that night.

Hot girls: double check!

Matt had one last thing to check off—drinking a beer. For over a year, I had been on the fence about it, not sure how I felt about contributing to his drinking. What kind of mother would I be to give my son an alcoholic drink? Stuck in my head were the voices of family and friends who often referred to Matt as an angel. *People with Down syndrome are angels and shouldn't drink alcohol.* These thoughts had worried me from the moment Matt shared this turning-twenty-one wish. Before this night, I'd consistently tried to brush it off, thinking he would forget about it, but just like Katy Perry, he wouldn't let it go.

On a different trip with my husband, I'd glanced into our hotel's cocktail lounge, which we happened to be passing. I smiled when I spotted a couple of young men who had Down syndrome. This caught my attention and made me think of Matt, who was home with his dad. Then I noticed they were drinking beer. After a few minutes of watching, I realized I was judging the situation. *Shame on you, Wendy!* These young men were old enough, and they were having a good time with each other while enjoying a brewski—just what other adult men liked to do. I had spent Matt's life requesting he be treated like others, so why did I feel I had to exclude drinking as an option?

When I got home, I began to ask other parents in our Down syndrome groups their thoughts. Some didn't allow it because of religious ideals; some had no problem with it—after all, they were adults. After that, I no longer felt guilty and decided that if this was what Matt wanted as a man of age, it would be his decision and my job would simply be to moderate.

So, who bought my son his first alcoholic drink? Of course, it was his uncle, my middle brother. I mentioned he is the smart one, but I think I left out that he is also sly. Matt calls him Uncle Catfish, an appropriate nickname for the brother who is always up to something fishy. Since he lives in Vegas, he joined us at Matt's party and found a way to welcome him into adulthood, after all. I smiled at the memory of me chasing a freckle-faced little boy with strawberry-blond hair, and now, here he was, buying my son his first drink.

To my surprise, Matt didn't like the fruity drink Uncle T chose for him. He didn't even finish it. My relief was short-lived when I realized this only meant he hadn't found his drink of choice.

His favorite beverage of the night was the shot his girlfriend poured directly into his mouth as she stood on top of the bar. I know what you're thinking—so much for the moderator.

Don't judge me. This is how it went down:

I had to go to the restroom, but they were located outside the club and down an escalator—quite the jaunt to go pee. My mistake was leaving Matt alone with the guys.

You can only imagine the look on my face when I returned to a room full of people chanting, "Go! Go! Go!" When I looked up front to see what the commotion was, I saw Matt, back against the bar, head tilted back, while his girlfriend poured a shot directly into his mouth.

AAAAHHH! I screamed inside my head as I pushed forward. John grabbed me by the arm and said, "Honey, it's okay." I had conflicted feelings. I did not enjoy walking into my baby being initiated into adulthood, and yet he was having the time of his life. I took a breath, letting my tension ease. How could I be upset when this young lady treated Matt like she did every other guy—well, sort of. He did get preferential treatment that night.

I may have been a little annoyed at first, but, eventually, I began to get my panties out of a wad and smiled as I watched him have a good time.

I later learned the shot was a liqueur that didn't have much alcohol, which gave me some peace of mind. However, I watched Matt's behavior like a hawk because I worried he wouldn't know what to think of being intoxicated if he did experience it. Due to Matt's happy nature and the fact that he was able to stand without struggling, I don't know if he ever felt it.

All enjoyed that evening, his birthday celebration morphing from a party of ten to a party of one hundred, the entire bar helping us celebrate. They even struck up a happy birthday song for him, which he soaked up like a sponge.

Seven hours. The time I had to stare at the back of my son's head as he enjoyed the music, the dancing, and his new girlfriend who performed just for him on top of the bar all night long. Seven hours of sweat I could see dripping down his back and the sides of his face. The smell of alcohol and body odor started to get to me as I tried not to think about my aching feet.

Guess whose feet were tired? Hint: not Matt's. To my surprise, we opened with the club, and we closed with the club. Yes, clubs in Vegas do close. I know, right?

We were all hung over when we woke up the next morning. However, it wasn't alcohol-related. We could not get over how great the night had been. *Someone get me some Alka-Seltzer and stat!*

Booze: check!

We were at the tail end of our celebration but still enjoying the sights, soaking up all Las Vegas had to offer. Later that afternoon, I got a text from one of our friends Matt referred to as his girlfriend despite the fact that she was married. She shared with me that she had received a random text from him saying she couldn't be his girlfriend anymore because he had a new one.

I laughed so hard. Then I thought, *Well, this is something else I need to teach him; how to properly end a relationship.* Not to worry about there being any serious heartbreak, as this girlfriend was a happily married friend of ours who was great with Matt. She'd always teased that he was her boyfriend, and now she'd literally been written off.

On the drive back to Salt Lake, we enjoyed sharing our favorite moments of the trip. We had done other things, like walking the strip and going to see the new *Twilight* sequel that had just come out. Matt being "Team Jacob" was delighted to see it. Because we'd experienced something amazing each day, I had a difficult time picking a favorite.

Trying to stay serious, I did squeeze in a minute to discuss Matt's break-up message.

"I raised a gentleman, and a real gentleman doesn't ever end a relationship via text. You will always break a girl's heart in person because girls deserve that respect."

"Okay, Mom," he said as he dismissed me and began to talk softly about his "new girlfriend." He got the message, although, sadly, we've never run into that issue, at least in reality. Funny enough, after our return, Matt never talked about what's her name, that girl in Vegas, again. I don't know where she is now, but she left a mark on this mama heart. She made that evening super special for all of us.

We've been back to Vegas several times since, and Matt is happy for every opportunity he gets to see "hot girls." Each time we go, he is older, of course, and John occasionally has to remind him it's okay to have those feelings, but the appropriate thing to do is not speak of them out loud. "We're supposed to keep those thoughts private," he will say.

I just give him my "Thanks, honey" look and know I will forever remember Matt's twenty-first birthday celebration, the year of boobs, booze, and a dragon tattoo.

Lessons Learned
- The biggest wins in Vegas don't always involve money.
- My son, who will always be childlike, also makes a darn good adult.

Love our "son-shine."

CHAPTER 13
Son's Day

What you can plan for:
Creativity in the extra chromosome

Down syndrome and celebrations go together like peanut butter and jelly. And some of our best celebrations have been unexpected. It could be because we successfully cracked an egg without pulverizing it or learned that Axe body spray does not double as an alternative deodorant when sensitive skin is an issue. I celebrated when we mastered the cooking levels on the toaster. I love my house to be filled with nice fragrances, but burnt toast is not one of them.

October is the official month for celebrating Down syndrome. Is it ironic that of the twelve months on the calendar, the one full of scary witches, monsters, and ghosts is the month chosen to bring awareness to an extra chromosome? Receiving the diagnosis may be scary, and the thoughts that race through your head may be scary, but you will also find your bucket full of sweet treats.

Matt lives to party. He turns the calendar in his room from month to month, sharing what celebrations we have to look forward to. In our family, when the celebration revolves around you, you are the boss, and other family members are expected to wait on you, making you feel like royalty. However, to avoid complete misery for those who aren't being celebrated, we have guidelines on what it means to be considered royalty.

On Mother's Day, my day typically begins with my thoughtful boys surprising me with a yummy breakfast. When my belly is full, we get all gussied up to spend a day roaming the local nurseries, where we shop for flowers for my outdoor flowerpots. After carefully selecting a beautiful array of colors and different varieties, we head home to plant them in their spacious new surroundings. It's not Matt's favorite thing to do, but it's my day, and he knows who's in charge, so he keeps his complaints to a minimum. He fakes a smile as he hands me a nice cold Diet Coke to enjoy as I take in the view of our hard work. My excessive thank-yous make it easier for him to treat me like a queen.

Father's Day is similar. On the years Matt's with us, we start the morning off by making breakfast for John, after which he usually chooses something manly, like attending a car show or an action-packed movie. Matt benefits from Father's Day as he enjoys the same outings John does. The only work usually required of him on this day is to keep a cold Pepsi in John's hands. Because Matt has two kings to celebrate, we split the day so he can spend half of it with Ash. However, I have a sneaking suspicion that Matt gets off easy during this portion of the day. In fact, it's possible Ash isn't getting the royal treatment and instead is subject to his son's commands.

When Matt was about twenty-three, Father's Day was half over when my creative son handed John his soda. "So!" he piped up. "When's Son's Day?" Apparently, he'd had enough of Mother's and Father's Days and wanted a piece of the action.

Never in a million years would I have expected to hear him ask this. I had to give him kudos for his creativity. I responded genuinely. "Matt, every day is Son's Day. John and I take care of you all the time, so you don't need a special day."

Unhappy with my answer, he argued, "No! Not fair, Mom!" Clearly, he wanted a day dedicated just to him. He argued with us for several minutes, neither of us backing down, then stormed off in a huff, leaving me chuckling to myself.

Then it hit me. March 21. This is World Down Syndrome Day, and since we already celebrated Matt on this day, why not add Son's Day to the title and call it good?

Note: On this day, events worldwide raise public awareness, promote inclusion, encourage advocacy, and support the well-being of those living with Down syndrome.

This date was selected because March is the third month and the twenty-first signifies the uniqueness of the triplication of the twenty-first chromosome. It's the one day the entire world comes together to create awareness for those like my son.

Proud of myself for coming up with this solution, I shared my idea with John, who agreed it was perfect. We had just long enough to discuss briefly and were patting ourselves on the back when Matt returned to the room, still sulking.

"Hey, Matt!" I said in my proud-mom voice. "I have some exciting news. There *is* a Son's Day"

"What?" he bellowed in his baritone voice. "Me?"

"Yes, Matt, you. From now on, March 21 will be known as Son's Day."

Oblivious to the fact that we were using an existing day and therefore weren't creating a new holiday for him, he threw his arms up as he hollered out in excitement. "Woohoo! Thanks, Mom!"

That's how easy it is to make Matt happy. It's the little things— although a twinge of guilt ran through me. Had I just taken advantage of my son? If my parents had deceived me, I would have known it.

We had almost a year before the official Son's Day would be celebrated, but when March 21 did arrive, Matt greeted the day with great enthusiasm. He had no problem taking full advantage of John and me.

We were about halfway through the day when I overheard him ordering John around. I had to put him in check. *Oh no, he doesn't,* I thought as I marched into the room and gently reminded him that this day meant he got to be boss for the day; it didn't mean he got to be bossy. He heard me loud and clear.

On Son's Day and Christmas, Matt's excitement is contagious, but his favorite day of the year is his birthday. For us, however, it can be exhausting! In a good way.

When he first came into this world, I had no idea of the expectations he would have of me. I didn't know I needed good party-planning skills.

157

I think it's a normal mom thing to reflect on the birth of your child with each birthday. For me it's bittersweet. That day quickly went from excitement to sadness. The memories will always be there, but I try not to focus on them. I force my thoughts to relive when the joy of this sweet baby crept into my heart and the moment I knew his existence deserved to be celebrated. I had been entrusted with this precious gift, and he needed to be honored for all the happiness he brings to others each and every day. So, we celebrate him. Big!

He loves Disney, so it only makes sense to begin his day with homemade Mickey Mouse pancakes. The recipe is easy—a cup of Bisquick, one egg, milk, and vanilla, topped with syrup and whipped cream, and, of course, that special ingredient—a lot of mama love. He looks forward to his special breakfast every year, and I get a not-so-gentle reminder on the eve of his birthday that I need to set my alarm. "You can't sleep in, Mom."

As if unique homemade pancakes weren't enough, at the age of twelve, this crazy mom stepped up her game and came up with the bright idea of making a few of these hotcakes in the shape of his age. *How fun is this?* I thought as I poured a one and a two on the griddle, completely forgetting what the two would look like when I flipped it. *Dang! I should have done that backward.*

In the event you're thinking this is a fun idea, you're right. It is. However, let me point out the cons. Specifically, it takes skill to master backward numbers. Not only is it challenging to pour them in the correct shapes, but flipping them tests your patience as you try to work quickly and not burn them. I can guarantee that a few won't make the cut and will be tossed in the trash.

Another con? Having to structure your morning around pancakes. After that first year, I hoped Matt would forget and let this new tradition slide, but nope! With the memory of an elephant, he now expects pancakes in the shape of his age to go along with the mouse. Like it or not, I'm all in now, and I am NOT a morning person. Once I committed, it meant having to get up earlier to make his breakfast. I can't tell you how relieved I am when his big day falls on a weekend.

Should you heed my advice, here's a tip. When your threes or fives fall apart, it's easy to mash them back together and cover them with a glob of butter. You're welcome!

I barely make it through our big breakfast escapade when Matt begins asking about his party. Every year, he challenges me with his party-theme requests. I don't know where he comes up with a lot of his ideas, but, remember, this mama bear is not one to be easily defeated. Naturally, I cannot simply just host a party. Nope! I have to put pressure on myself to go above and beyond.

We've had a lot of successful celebrations. A few of my favorites:

When he turned twenty, he was going through a *Mama Mia* phase. He's so my boy. He and I watched the movie over and over. When we weren't watching the movie, Abba blared on the radio. It came as no surprise when he requested a *Mama Mia* party. But how does one do that, you ask? Guests were asked to come dressed in the '70s. I bought a psychedelic cake that had quotes written all over it, and we hung a disco ball and danced to the *Mama Mia* soundtrack all night. We had dance-offs and a soul train line. The guests had a great time, and Matt an even greater time. He went to bed exhausted. Score!

We had the Katy Perry party when he turned twenty-two, though, since Katy was his wife, that party got its own chapter.

The year he turned twenty-eight, he requested a *Black Panther* theme, so we made Wakanda glow-in-the-dark drinks, had guests come dressed like they were part of the Panther tribe, put themed decorations everywhere, and created a *Black Panther* photo area.

We celebrated many of his birthdays at Hooters. I think we all know why he requested this. His twenty-fourth birthday was the most memorable. He requested a *Frozen* theme (yes, it's true) but held at Hooters. Only my son would request a princess party at a place known for its . . . ahem, hooters.

159

Several frustrated Hooter patrons expressed their opinions. When I scheduled the big event, I didn't realize we would be interrupting Sunday afternoon football. Their yelling at the referees for stupid calls could barely be heard over our family singing "Let It Go" over and over. My participation in the sing-along may or may not have been directed to our party. Thank heavens all the waitresses were on our side and played into the celebration. Truth be told, I wouldn't be surprised if the other gentleman customers were upset because my son got all the attention from the hot girls.

By far, my favorite party for Matt was his eighteenth. Ash and I knew we had to do something big since you only turn eighteen once. We had been spared the expense of buying Matt a car and all the associated costs. There would be no increase in our auto insurance, no thinning of our wallets when asked to fork over gas money, no having to help with vehicle maintenance, and no worries about Matt being in an accident. We agreed to splurge in other ways, and splurge we did.

Matt, like both his parents, loves music. His dad and I listen to different genres, and, as a result, Matt loves anything with a beat.

Ash plays bass guitar and loves to jam with his longtime friends. He also has connections to a local popular rock band that plays a good mix of older rock music. I'm talking about the greats, like Def Leppard, Kiss, and AC/DC. Of course, the band members loved Matt, so it was a no-brainer when we hired them to be the entertainment for this outrageous shindig we were planning.

We rented a local auditorium and plastered the place with colorful balloons. We lined the walls with streamers and posters made by family and friends and brought in pizza, cake, and other treats. When the time came, the lights went down, and the band's tunes went up. The beat of the drums and the strumming of the guitars invited everyone to get up on their feet, the middle of the floor quickly filling with partygoers, Matt front and center. Everyone bobbed up and down, waving their arms in the air as they sang along. We had our own mini rock concert. It was amazing!

Many of Matt's greatest fans came out to enjoy this rock fest. Several of his classmates showed up, and many of our friends from the Down syndrome community came to celebrate. I think everyone on both sides of our family, young and old, who could physically attend was there.

The music was almost deafening, but nobody cared. I stood back and watched as Matt's grandparents, aunts, uncles, and cousins jammed like they were in a mosh pit. It was a sight to behold. The older generation, more specifically our parents, who often complained about the music we listened to and were always telling us to turn it down, were now shaking their booties to it. Why? Because everyone in our circle will do just about anything for Matt, including letting their hair down and having a good time. I don't think there was a dry armpit in the house.

I never thought I would gain as much and for as long as I do from Matt's birthdays. Never is the gathering just about him. They're celebrations for his tribe.

Lessons Learned
- Equality: All family members should be celebrated equally.
- Simplify: Be careful when considering enhancing traditions.

"Am I doing it right?"

CHAPTER 14

Help! My TV Is Possessed

What you can plan for:
***Raising a genius. Be prepared for your child to possibly
work electronic devices better than you!***

Okay, I'm going to publicly admit something no matter how much shame it brings to our family name. We have an addiction—technology! You name it: TVs, tablets, cell phones, computers, gaming systems, anything that comes with batteries or a cord—we can't get enough. Don't judge me. We cannot be in this club alone.

The real question is, does your family have the same mad skills we do? (At least if that's what you want to call it). John and I especially have the outstanding ability to operate *more than one device at a time.* I never would have thought that one day I would be talented enough to create an impressive vision board on Pinterest, pass a super hard level on *Candy Crush,* and do some quick online shopping to get supplies for a craft I just pinned—all while enjoying family movie night. Like my online game, I have taken my multitasking to a whole new level. In fact, that's how a typical Sunday night goes for me.

But the events of a particular Monday night were anything but typical. Dinner was consumed and the kitchen had been cleaned, so I gladly accepted the invitation my recliner extended, and settled in to make myself comfy. Matt made a quick getaway to his room. At twenty-four, he would much rather do that than hang out with his boring parents. John escaped to the solitude of his office, so I found one of our favorite shows and settled in for some quiet time with just the three of me (me, myself, and I).

I had been browsing the internet on my tablet, enjoying an episode of *Last Man Standing,* laughing at the banter between Tim Allen's character and his television daughters, when suddenly all was silent. I looked up from my tablet to see the TV had turned itself off. Startled, I looked toward the console and noticed the remotes sat where I left them. Then, the television turned itself back on, my jaw dropping at the image that popped up before me.

What the! I whispered to myself as I sat up straighter, eyes bugging out of my head. The loud sounds of drums and cymbals erupted from our soundbar as a young woman with a darker complexion twerked her bouncy buttocks to the music. I didn't get to see much of her face as her booty filled most of our sixty-five-inch TV. Now, let's just say for a moment that I found myself thankful for being blind in one eye and having no depth perception.

Then, as quickly as it came on, it went back off. Perplexed, I just sat there, but only for a moment, because as quickly as she'd disappeared, she returned. I can only imagine my expression as I watched the television do its own version of twerking.

It was possessed. It had to be.

"John!" I hollered out as I lowered my recliner. He knew that tone and came immediately. When he saw the look on my face, he turned toward the loud music coming from our TV.

"What are you watching?" he asked curiously.

"Seriously! You think I'm watching *this?*" I replied sarcastically. Before I had a chance to tell him our TV was possessed, it suddenly went dark again. Being the techy guy that he is, John stood still, a look of surprise on his face. Just as suddenly, the mirage reappeared, along with the loud drumming and sharp ringing.

"What the hell?" he said as he picked up the remotes and started fiddling with them. After a few minutes of trying to make adjustments, he suddenly straightened.

I knew that look; he had processed what he thought might be happening. He glanced toward our son's room and saw that the door was closed. Before I knew it, he'd bolted up the stairs, but quietly, as if he wanted to catch Matt in the act of who knew what. I watched him, confused. Exactly how could Matt be controlling *my* television?

I heard voices but couldn't make out what they were saying. Minutes later, John came downstairs holding Matt's tablet with a smug look. Matt followed reluctantly, muttering something under his breath. Head hung low, he refused to make eye contact with either me or John. Baffled, I watched both, waiting impatiently to know what in the world they knew that I didn't.

When Matt finally reached the bottom of the stairs, his eyes went wide at the image on our television set. I felt my cheeks flush. I wished we had turned off the power so my son wouldn't have seen this woman and her beyond-incredible skills to twerk the way she did. Lord knows I didn't want him to think his mother had made a conscious decision to watch this show—if that's what you wanted to call it.

Just then, John handed me "Matthew's" tablet. (My son is named Matt, generally, but it quickly switches to Matthew whenever he's in trouble, in case you're unclear about that.) I looked down, and my mouth dropped open. Then my head jerked up as I locked eyes with Matt.

"What? What, Mom?" Matt stammered with a shocked look. I must have changed into my crazed-mom expression—you mothers know the one I mean—because his gaze quickly dropped to the floor again. In my lap, I held the same bodacious bottom that had taken over the family-oriented humor Tim Allen had provided just moments before.

Oh, dear. What has he done now?

I swallowed, ready to put on my disciplinary cap, when something stopped me. I paused, torn between being horrified and remembering my son was twenty-four-years-old. Based on conversations with friends both male and female, Matt's showing an interest in this stuff was normal. *Isn't that what I want for my son? As normal as possible?* I reminded myself. I had no idea what to say. It's not like she was naked or we had caught him watching porn. What this woman was doing was actually considered art *cough* in some countries.

Quizzically, I looked over at John, who had sat down next to me. He leaned over and pointed at the screen still on my lap, then explained that Matt had managed to screen cast, or link, YouTube from his tablet to all our television sets.

How lucky for us!

I could barely work the remote, and here my son had figured out how to select what we watched as a family even when we weren't in the same room. It's a mystery how he learned, but I knew one thing for sure—he was a genius!

Normal or not, open or closed-minded, we needed to address this so our younger family members—and anyone else for that matter— would not be subjected to my son's interest in bouncing booties.

John is exceptionally helpful and patient in these circumstances, and I think he could tell I needed help, and a lot of it, with this one. He took over, explaining to Matt in layman's terms how he had changed the station on me. Unlike how I initially reacted, John gave Matt a gentle reminder regarding the rules with electronic devices and that we should be watching more appropriate videos. And for the billionth time, he reminded both Matt and me that he is the only family member authorized to adjust any settings on our electronic equipment. *Hey! How'd I get brought into this?* To be fair, it's a much-needed rule based on the headaches we've caused John. I may not be good at working a remote, but I excel when it comes to messing up all things technical.

As John finished his *Ward Cleaver* lecture, my son responded humbly, "I sorry." He rarely made eye contact during these conversations, but when all got quiet, his baby blues usually sneaked a peek over the top of his glasses as if checking to see if we were still there. He did just that, and his big, sad eyes met mine. I could tell he was embarrassed and understood that what he'd done was wrong. Now I had to look away. *Dammit! Why does he always make me feel bad for him?* I thought.

Meanwhile, the uninvited guest still did her thing. I looked over at John. "You know, the sound is great, and the colors are vibrant on our television, but now that we've solved this mystery, you can shut her down." I motioned toward the television to remind John what we were watching. Had my personal IT guy conveniently forgotten? Or perhaps he was buying a little more time for himself and Matt.

I just wanted to go back to watching my show. By now, I had no idea how the argument had gone between Tim Allen and his girls. Based on their expressions when my wholesome show returned to the screen, I guessed Tim to be in the same doghouse Matt had been in.

Matt is definitely curious. His browser history proves this, and so does the occasional need to reset his phone and tablet. For the most part, he listens and follows our family rules. And I would never tell him so, but he does a lot better than I ever did as a kid. My poor dad!

Lesson Learned

When my baby was born, I just wanted him to be "normal." Guess what? Apparently, he is!

"Silly Mom, he is real."

CHAPTER 15

I Hope You Like Cookies and Milk

What you can plan for:
Christmas will always be magical if you let it.

SPOILER ALERT: If you are reading this and you're between ages seven and ten, I'm flattered! But you will need to skip this chapter. Trust me. I do not want to ruin the magic of Christmas for you. Shoo!

By now, you know the stories of two of the most popular and favored official holidays in our home, Son's Day and Matt's birthday. Now it's time to hear about his third, Christmas. My son is still crazy for Claus—Santa Claus, that is. Only he usually refers to him as "Mr. Claus" or "SC."

Unlike most kids and even some adults, gifts are not the most important part of the holiday for Matt; it's about the celebration. It's about the man in the red suit showing up every December, sneaking into our home, gobbling up the treats left by Matt, playing with our dog, and leaving a special handwritten note for my sweet son. Even though these are the traditions Matt focuses on, SC still leaves presents because Matt would probably notice if he didn't, don't you think?

Matt's childlike love for the holiday has always made me feel like my home should resemble what I imagine Mrs. C. does to the Claus crib. Not that I'm trying to go up against the queen of Christmas, but I do tend to make a big deal of it with all my decorating, traditions, and such. And I do my best to encourage John and Matt to be part of the hoopla. They may go along, but their lack of enthusiasm does not go unnoticed. I know they are just trying to please me. This mama is not satisfied until my home looks like Christmas puked everywhere. In addition, we must enjoy the season to the fullest by taking in all the colored lights and decorations in store windows and attending any

Christmas performances we are able to, never overlooking the reason for the season. My theory? Because it only comes once a year, we've got to do things right.

I have often joked that I'm going to be the oldest living parent who still has to play Santa. Yes, I said, "has to," not "gets to." Still, I know I'm not in this club alone. There are many parents who have differently abled children who are in the same Christmas stockings. I've been considering forming Santa support groups—ones that can help those of us who struggle to come up with ideas for gifts Santa can leave and additional ideas for presents from Mom and Dad. And a group specifically for us older folks who want to go to bed at a decent hour because our bodies don't work like they used to. Staying up late and chasing down carrots at an old age is rather difficult. It's kind of ironic since Santa is portrayed as an old man. How I wish I knew his secret! Is it that special holiday eggnog? Does he bathe in Ben-Gay? Does he sleep for months afterward? Or is he an exercise fanatic?

Each year, I find myself questioning whether this might be the year I tell Matt the truth—if it's the year I crush his spirit—for selfish reasons, of course. Not only do I become older every Christmas, but after an evening of indulging in a few glasses of mama's happy juice and enjoying an abundance of delectable holiday carbs, I want to lay my head down and take a long winter's nap. Instead, I have obligations to my stupid—yet not so stupid—holiday traditions, and my rest gets put on hold.

I don't believe my Christmas Eve obligations are much different than those of most young mothers. There's the obvious one—staying up until after midnight to properly display Santa's loot. Because I'm a perfectionist, the gifts must be arranged just so—you know, for those perfect Christmas-morning photos. Of course, we cannot forget the consumption of the cookies and milk—a midnight snack that's set out by a young man who feels a need to leave goodies in exchange for all the gifts he expects to receive.

Truly, I've tried to talk Matt out of this particular tradition for several years, explaining that Santa is probably full by the time he gets to our house, but Matt won't budge. He's afraid it may upset Mr. Claus if he gets to our house and Matt's left no sweets out. Matt wants to be sure Santa knows he's been thinking of him. How can you argue with that? So, I suck it up, and when it's time, I drink the milk and force down the cookies, leaving only a few crumbs as evidence. Fortunately, I can always use Tums as a chaser; milk after wine will likely curdle one's stomach.

As much as I am tempted to blow the cover on this whole Santa gig, I keep it up. I fear robbing my son of the magic of Christmas, making it impossible for me to surrender the man in the red suit.

To this day, I still remember the heartbreak Billy caused when he told me Santa wasn't real. We were in second grade and were able to go outside for recess since it wasn't too cold. My girlfriend and I were perched on top of the tricky bars, safe from getting cooties from the boys. Most of them were out playing tag, but not Billy, probably because he had a crush on one of us. We screamed at him in our sassy little-girl voices that he better leave us alone or we were going to tell. He hissed back, "I'm not afraid of you" through his devious grin.

Oh yeah? Well, I had a bigger card up my sleeve. I sat up taller and, while pointing my finger, yelled, "It isn't me you should be scared of. Santa is watching you!" I used this on my brothers all season. Surely this threat would send Billy on his way.

Nope. It backfired. Billy came at me with an unexpected response. "Oh yeah? There is no Santa! Your mom and dad lie to you. *They* are Santa."

I instantly lost my sass (and almost that thing that rhymes with it). I found myself tongue-tied. I had no comeback. He'd just murdered Christmas with his mean tattle-tale, no good, very bad spoiler alert. Satisfied that he got me good, he laughed as he ran off to join the other boys. I felt like I had the wind knocked out of me—only not like the time when I fell off the playground jungle gym. I remained frozen to the bars.

171

My friend and I sat there in silence as the cool winter breeze kissed our tiny, rosy cheeks. I was not the only shell-shocked one. For once, two normally chatty girls had nothing to say. The bell rang, signaling us to return to class. We couldn't be late.

My head now filled with questions, I couldn't concentrate on my schoolwork for the rest of the day. I didn't want it to be true. I didn't want my parents to be liars, so it took a few days of stewing before I finally mustered up the nerve and asked if Billy had told the truth. Sure enough, he had. My parents were liars! It crushed me. I could sense it upset my mom, having to reveal this secret she did not want to give up so soon. She and my dad told me that if I wanted to believe, Santa would visit me. Of course, I still wanted presents, so I chose to stay in the game. Even though I knew, I did not want to ruin it for others, especially my little brothers, so I never spoke of it again.

That day, I learned that my parents, along with every other Santa out there, lied out of love to make the Christmas holiday magical for us children. And it worked. Christmas was magical to me. Even after that, I chose for it to be so.

My gut told me my parents may have had words with Billy's parents as from that day forward, he left us alone at recess. I later learned that his family were Jehovah's Witnesses, meaning they didn't celebrate Christmas. That was different from my family's beliefs, and I never held anything like that against anybody. Still, Billy took pleasure in ruining Christmas not only for me but for others.

A part of me was scarred that day, it's true. And so I cannot bring myself to tell my son, who will forever be my little boy at heart.

To be honest, I'm not so sure he would believe me if I did try to force the truth on him. One year, my husband and I decided to test the waters.

We happened to be talking about Mr. Claus one night, and I said, "Matt, there may come a time when Santa can't come anymore because he is old, and it may be too hard. He may have to save his energy for younger kids." We even used ourselves as an example, pointing out the things that are harder on us because we are older.

Matt refused to entertain the thought. "Mom! Stop telling stories. Mr. Clause loves me."

Well, how could one argue with that? We decided not to force the issue and not to be Billy and ruin the magic.

Still, every holiday season, I find myself joking with relatives and friends about how jealous I am of the people my age who get to go to bed at a reasonable hour on Christmas Eve. I usually receive responses such as, "No. You don't know how lucky you are. I wish my kids still believed" and "I miss playing Santa now that our kids are all grown."

Okay, I admit it. In my heart, I know I am fortunate, and I'm happy Matt still believes because of just how much I loved Christmas as a child. Every year, I find myself reminiscing about a white-bearded man entering our home as we slept, leaving all those presents for my brothers and me, presents wrapped in red Santa paper and placed perfectly around our tree. Each gift had our name written neatly in black Sharpie (coincidently, similar to my dad's handwriting) so there would be no confusion as to whose gift was whose. Our nana's handmade stockings, which had been filled with candy and other small gifts, could no longer be hung on the fireplace because they were too heavy. My young imagination also had reindeer calmly waiting on top of our home for the man in red to finish his job before getting back in his sleigh and flying on to the next house. Yup. Until Billy ruined it for me, my mom and dad had done a wonderful job of making Christmas magical.

As if strategically arranging the gifts and eating the milk and cookies wasn't enough, each year, Matt brainstormed new ideas, including how to make our home more inviting for his holiday heroes. I could not fault him since I enjoyed doing the same for our family.

Have I mentioned I'm getting older and I'm tired?

Matt surprised me and John the year he decided to change up our usual Christmas Eve routine. That night, our guests had gone home to start their own traditions, so I began to clean up what food had managed to escape our ravenous appetites. I heard someone rummaging through the fridge and looked over to see Matt going through the contents on each shelf, determined to find what he needed, looking harder than when I asked him to get something for me.

"Matt, what are you doing?" I asked.

"I need carrots," he said as he opened the cheese drawer.

"Wrong drawer, bud. What do you need carrots for?"

"The reindeer. I need feed Santa's reindeer."

"What? Since when do we feed the reindeer?" I asked, annoyed that my fridge now looked like someone had torn it apart looking for carrots.

"Mommmmmmmmm, I need to!"

How is it we managed to put off worrying about Santa's nine furry drivers for well over a decade, and now suddenly this is important too?

How could I refuse Matt's selfless act of making sure they got a snack as well?

"Okay, okay," I said gently as I showed him where we stored the veggies. He dumped nine out on the counter and handed the bag to me. He then rushed down the stairs to our family room, where he opened the door to the backyard and left them in a neat pile on the patio. I smiled as I watched. *How'd I get so lucky? Santa better be good to you this year.*

Satisfied he had done a good thing, Matt left me so he could get ready for bed. When John and I were sure he was asleep, we took care of our Santa obligations and headed to bed. I had dragged myself halfway up the stairs when I remembered. Those darn carrots. I quickly ran down to the back patio and grabbed the evidence. The weather in Utah is unpredictable. Thank heaven we hardly had any snow that year and retrieving the carrots went smoothly. Pleased it looked like Rudolph and the gang had consumed their special treat, I proceeded to bed, hoping to at least get a few hours of sleep before being awakened by a cheerful "Merry Christmas!" as one excited boy danced in my doorway.

That Christmas morning, Matt gave up on waiting for us and sneaked down the stairs for a peek. I always found joy in his reactions, so as soon as I heard the creak of the stairs, I looked at the clock: 6:00 a.m. *Ugh! It's too freakin' early!* I thought as I woke John. Nevertheless, we dragged ourselves out of bed and joined Matt. I turned the Christmas music on before taking my place by the tree. Matt always made sure the cookies and milk were gone (curdled stomach for the win!). He giggled with his low-pitched, contagious giggle when he saw the empty cup and crumbs. Suddenly, his eyes lit up and he rushed to the sliding door, excited to see that the pile of little orange veggies had disappeared. This new tradition wasn't difficult to start, and it made me proud that my boy cared more for our special visitors than the gifts under the tree.

The following year, Matt asked for carrots to feed the reindeer again. Remembering how happy this new tradition made him, I offered nine orange nibbles for the mystical creatures that would soon be on our roof. However, Matt's choice on how to feed them this year shocked us. John and I watched in horror as he went to the back yard and hurled each one in a different direction. Naturally, this would be the year we were hit with a harsh snowstorm. I looked at John and mouthed, "We're in sooooo much trouble."

The good thing about all this snow? There were divots where those carrots landed. The bad thing about all the snow? How were we going to get to them without leaving human footprints everywhere?

We knew that first thing in the morning, Matt would check the status of the cookies and then the carrots. *Or would he? Could we risk it?* We had a dilemma.

I made a decision I had not yet shared with John. We would skip this part and wing the conversation with Matt. Then we would remove any that remained when the snow melted. Yes, that would work. But John had other plans. I am not sure how many men would do what came next, but that evening proved I'd chosen the perfect man to be in our lives.

After Matt went to bed, I choked down the cookies and milk, followed by Tums. Yes, Mrs. Claus had been into the wine again. I heard the door open and felt a gust of cold air. I turned to see John dressed in his winter gear.

I whispered, "What are you doing?"

"I'm going to see what it feels like to be a reindeer." And the next thing I knew, he was leaping through the cold, deep snow on his toes, trying to mimic reindeer hooves. As he reached each area, he carefully bent over and picked up the carrot without falling over and disrupting the snow. He reminded me of children playing hopscotch.

From the comfort of the warm house, I watched through the sliding door in disbelief. Then I began to laugh. The wine must have kicked in because I laughed harder. John heard me from outside and looked over at me. He stood on one leg like a flamingo, causing me to laugh so hard I nearly peed my pants. I snorted and shoved my hand over my mouth so as not to make too much noise. Then I snorted some more as this grown man hopped through the unmarked snow using the light of the moon and succeeding to make it look like reindeer had walked around our yard eating the snacks Matt had so generously left them. From where I sat and laughed so hysterically, I prayed he only hit the divots that contained the orange carrots and not any brown ones.

It's a good thing he went to this extent because the next morning, Matt rushed to the door to check on the carrots and giggled with delight when he saw the reindeer footprints. I grinned at John.

My son's reactions to our traditions remind me of that magical feeling I remember as a small child—that magical feeling that little punk stole from me all those years ago.

Even though I may complain every Christmas Eve, I will keep doing it as long as my aging body allows me to because of how wonderful it makes me feel when I watch Matt. It's similar to the joy on my parents' faces when they shared stories with my brothers and me about how they had just barely gotten to bed when we woke up, excited and anxious to open our gifts. Or how my dad struggled to get our bikes put together before we could catch him in the act. I treasure the images I have of them. I feel sad when I allow myself to think I will never be able to share these stories with Matt. He will never be able to share in the images of John hopping around the yard or me setting out all his presents or drinking milk after too much wine.

In a way, I'm envious that Matt will forever be blessed with the magic of believing in an old man in a red suit with a long white beard sneaking around his home as he sleeps—a mythical being who leaves presents and plays with his dog as he enjoys the cookies Matt left out, all while his sleigh and reindeer wait patiently atop our roof.

I enjoy sharing these stories with family and friends and people who come into my life. However, I often forget that new acquaintances don't always know about my son, and so I've found myself in awkward situations where I'm asked, "How old is your son?" I've learned to reply by sharing his diagnosis first; otherwise, the looks I receive are priceless as my audience wonders why I still play Santa to my adult child.

Each of these conversations inevitably turns into an enjoyable visit, with much more than funny Santa stories. They also give me an opportunity to raise awareness for the Down syndrome community. Even though October is Down syndrome–awareness month, because I have a strong interest in this subject, I will seize any opportunity to spread awareness. For our family, every month is Down syndrome awareness *and* Christmas because Matt is the gift that keeps on giving.

Matt keeps me young as my body tries to get old. Because of him, I don't have to. I *get* to be Mrs. Claus.

Lesson Learned

Playing Santa is worth losing sleep over, so stop whining—
and go easy on the wine!

"I can't take this kid anywhere!"

CHAPTER 16

The Not-So-Groooovy Mombarrassing Moments

What you can plan for:
Your child will embarrass you!

"Your breath stinks!" Well, those words will silence any adult almost immediately. I love little kids. Really, I do. They are so cute, so honest—and so mean. If you ever want to know if you have a booger, if you're ugly, fat, etc., just seek out the nearest four- or five-year-old, and you'll quite instantly learn these truths—and any other flaws you didn't know you had—within minutes!

Most of the time, their honesty, so innocent and so sweet, cracks me up. They can get away with it, and we laugh, mostly. These adorable little munchkins also have no problem showing public affection and will express just about anywhere how much they love you, that you are their favorite, and so on.

Individuals with Down syndrome are somewhat similar, at least from what I've experienced. Similar to a small child, Matt has no filter. He's loving but brutally honest and tells it as he sees it. My sweet man-boy has caused me *many* embarrassing moments, or, as I've come to call them, "mombarrassing moments" This chapter contains a greatest-hits list in order of mombarrassments. Here we go!

The first time I remember truly being mombarrassed was the year Matt started junior high. The mama bear in me worried that the kids would be mean, that he would get lost, and that he wouldn't adjust well. In hopes of avoiding any or all of this, I took him to the building a few days before school started to help him find his locker and classrooms.

As we walked the halls, we ran into the custodian, who had been working on some small repairs. The man's dark hair had gray flecks in it, hinting he might be in his fifties. He saw us coming and smiled and waved. Blue coveralls a little too short for his taller stature fit his thicker torso quite snugly. I noticed immediately that he had no left arm and that the empty sleeve was rolled up and secured to his shoulder.

I quickly glanced at Matt because I knew it wouldn't be long before he noticed and would have something to say about it. Sure enough, his confused facial expression confirmed my suspicion.

Being the friendly person he is, Matt walked right up to the guy and said, "Hi, I Matt. Where's you arm?" He looked at the spot where his arm should have been and even peered behind the man's back as if he thought he had it hidden. I could feel my face going red.

The gentleman chuckled. "I don't have an arm."

"Why? Where'd it go?" I could tell Matt thought this man was teasing him.

"I just don't," he responded politely. He had a reason, but I could tell by his body language that he didn't want to go into detail. I don't know why, but I felt a need to save him before my child got persistent with his twenty questions, making things more uncomfortable. With an apologetic glance, I grabbed Matt's hand and began to lead him away so we could continue our tour. Of course, he had to get the last word in. Before we rounded the corner, Matt turned back and called, "See ya!"

As we ate dinner that evening, Matt brought it up. I did my best to explain how everybody is different and that we are friends with every-one no matter what. I reminded him of his extra chromosome (Matt knows this means he has Down syndrome and it makes him different). I pointed out the different characteristics some of our friends and family had. These simple conversations work and are all Matt generally needs. He still calls it as he sees it, gets his explanation, and then it's as if he is blind to it. Matt became fast friends with this gentleman, which was no surprise. And he never mentioned the arm again.

180

Fortunately, most of these types of interactions are taken with a grain of salt, but we don't always encounter forgiving people.

Not long after this, when Matt was around twelve, a good friend of mine gifted me two tickets to see *Seussical the Musical.* Dr. Seuss may as well have been a member of our family. I'd read the books so many times I had them memorized—in fact, I think I still do. Matt's favorite was *Green Eggs and Ham,* which may have been because of my animated reading. When he heard we were going to see the play, he was thrilled. I could not wait to dress up for an exciting evening with my little man on our first formal date.

Finally, the night came. Crowds of people milled about, indicating a sold-out performance. The seats in this venue were uncomfortably close to one another. If you have longer legs or wider hips, the show can feel excessively long. I secretly hoped the person next to us would be a no-show and we'd have a little extra room. Also, as much as we enjoy attending events like this, due to some awkward situations John and I have been in with our precious boy, we have learned to plan our seating strategically, sacrificing the coveted aisle seat for Matt or having him sit between us if the three of us are in attendance.

While he can be fun and entertaining, he can also be that annoying person we've all been stuck sitting next to. Yep, he can be *that* one. He will start a conversation with his neighbors about his family or superheroes. He is very observant and may comment on something he notices about them, he breathes and chews loudly, and, unfortunately, he's the one that when you hear "excuse me," an undeniable smell follows. While the majority of these people are pleasant, I can always tell those who are annoyed, so I do my best to intervene. The last thing I want is for Matt to be disruptive to those trying to enjoy an evening out.

For this special date, Matt and I were alone. As we followed the usher, I was happy to see we were at the back of a section that offered a little more legroom, and we also had an aisle seat.

In his excitement, Matt pushed his way in front of me, putting himself between me and the usher. Before I had a chance to tell him where to sit, he plopped himself in seat two, right next to the woman who had arrived before us.

And then he did it.

I had not had a chance to seat myself when he mombarrassed me by loudly proclaiming to this stranger, "Geeze, why you so fat?"

I stood there mortified. She was as well, and understandably so. Here she had been quietly reading her program, minding her own business, when from out of nowhere came a rude little human. She didn't laugh or show any sign of forgiveness. I did not blame her. Being a curvy girl myself, I know how sensitive of an issue one's weight can be.

She wasn't the only one who heard, and the tension grew as thick as my thighs. When I shot Matt *that look,* all the excitement disappeared from his face.

He instantly knew he'd done something wrong. "What, Mom?" he asked as I grabbed him by the arm. I made him stand and sat his little fanny in the aisle seat, where it should have been in the first place. He questioned me until I hushed him and explained that he'd made this woman feel bad. As I sat down, I looked at my neighbor, trying to make eye contact, and apologized profusely, hoping she felt my sincerity. Honestly, I couldn't wait for the lights to go down so the darkness would shield me from my embarrassment.

I am sure my "angel" ruined her evening before it even started. I definitely had a hard time enjoying myself. Not Matt. As soon as the curtain went up and the singing began, he became completely oblivious to the trouble he'd caused. Eyes glued to the stage the entire time, he laughed and enjoyed what the two women beside him could not.

As soon as the lights went up, I grabbed Matt and began to shove him through the crowd as we high-tailed it toward the exit. I couldn't escape the venue fast enough.

The show was over.

We could finally split.

I did not like the tension.

Not one little bit.

To this day, I am still mortified.

You may have figured out by now that our family experiences are anything but boring. We laugh a lot! We tease each other—all in fun, of course. However, I've learned that Matt is impressionable. It's challenging to have a child who, while he's technically an adult and wants to be treated as such, is still childlike in so many ways. What I'm still learning is where to draw the line.

Our family loves the *Austin Powers* movies. I know the dry, sometimes stupid, and slightly crude humor isn't for everyone, but it is one of the things that drew me to John. He has my same silly sense of humor.

These movies have the best one-liners—at least we think they do—and we will often blurt them out to one another. We find them "groovy, baby." To avoid being judged because I allow my son to watch what may be considered smut by some, we have a family rule to hide our big, bad secret. We are only allowed to quote these films when at home. But just like any other rule with Matt, it sometimes gets broken.

One day, when Matt was about fourteen, I took him grocery shopping. I like these kinds of excursions, which provide an opportunity to teach him the skills of the sport: price matching, couponing, and staying within budget. On this occasion, I needed to make a quick stop at a store near our home to pick up a few items for dinner that evening. Just as I'd hoped, we were able to find what we needed and quickly headed to the checkout.

Matt stood at the end, ready to assist with bagging if necessary. I watched as the cashier rang up each of my items, price-checking to make sure they were catching the sale prices in their ad. I could hear Matt talking, but because I was preoccupied, I didn't pay much attention. Then I heard it. "Mole. Mole. Mole." I recognized this from our favorite movie and turned and shushed him, giving him my you-know-better stink eye.

I went back to watching the checkout screen when he began again. "Guaca mooooley . . . moly, moly, moly."

What! I turned to him again and mouthed for him to stop. I did not have time for this, though I made a mental note to remind him of the family rule the minute we were out of the store.

I reached for my wallet, turned to give my coupons to the cashier, and froze. Suddenly I grasped specifically why Matt had insisted on being disruptive—and why he continued to giggle even after I had threatened him.

The cashier—a shorter Polynesian lady with dark hair—had a huge, dark mole just above her upper lip. When I say huge, it looked as though a kiwi had taken residence on this poor lady's face. Okay, that may be slightly exaggerated, but only slightly. Clearly, she had been listening to Matt. As she took my coupons, I got my own dose of stink eye.

Here we were again, with Matt calling it as he saw it and mombarrassing me as a result. Surprisingly, this woman did not take anything she may have been feeling out on my bread, and, to my amazement, my eggs were intact when I got home. I had a hard time with this one because deep down, I wanted to giggle too. Only my son would dare to do what anyone who has seen those movies thinks. Of course, I didn't laugh while Matt was around, instead reminding him of our rule, then grounding him from watching those movies—for a while, anyway.

I couldn't bear to show my face in that grocery store for a while, so either John did our shopping or we went elsewhere—at least until I could get Matt to "behave, yeah, baby. Zip it. Zip it good!"

These circumstances are nothing compared to my most mombarrassing moment when Matt was just seven years old and we were on one of our mother-son excursions to one of my favorite family parks. We did not live close to this park, but we visited it regularly, weather permitting. I had spent a lot of time there with my family as a young girl and had a lot of great memories, so I loved taking Matt there to create our own.

You could buy ice cream cones or other snacks at the concession stands inside the park, but we preferred the Slurpees at the 7-11 across from the entrance, enjoying them as we strolled through the park. On this specific day, they had our favorite flavors—cherry and cola. I had learned how to perfectly pack both flavors in, filling the cups to the brim so we got as much of the icy sweetness as possible.

Slurpees in hand, I headed to the counter to pay, Matt following closely and licking the sides of his cup to stop any drips from spilling to the floor. We had never seen this cashier before. He looked like he may be twentyish and greeted us with a friendly hello as we set our delicious treats down for him to scan the codes on the cups.

"Do you like Slurpees?" he asked, directing the question to Matt, who lights up like a firecracker when anyone talks to him.

He replied excitedly, "Yep." And then his next words made me freeze—just like my cup of cherry ice.

"Hey, dude, you so black."

In sheer mombarrassment, I looked up from my wallet and locked eyes with this young man. Speechless, I just stood there.

He winked and gave me the biggest, most radiant grin, like a mouth full of sunshine. He then said to me, "Mom, don't worry about it. It's all good."

Relieved, I relaxed and smiled back at him, hoping he felt my gratitude for not getting offended by my son's sweet innocence. I proceeded to open my wallet while asking how much I owed when suddenly we were interrupted again.

"I mean, dude, you soooooooooooo black!" boomed a loud voice.

I whipped around and gave my boy the biggest stink eye I could muster. *Where is this coming from?* I wondered. Matt had never said anything like this before. Mortified, I could barely turn back around to face my son's victim. "I'm so sorry" were the only words I could come up with. I had no idea what else to say about my son's behavior.

Do you know what that kind soul did? He laughed! A genuine, from-the-gut laugh. However, I didn't know if he laughed at Matt's behavior or the reaction of a mother who had been put in one of her most horrifying situations.

Then, as if things couldn't get any worse, my oh-so-sweet son did something so uncharacteristic of him that I came close to stepping down as his mother. Are you ready?

Matt took a giant step back to give himself plenty of room and then began to dance in a circle while chanting, "Ooga-booga-ooga, ooga-booga-ooga."

Clean up on aisle one—someone wipe this mother's chin off the floor! I wanted to burrow through their Nestlé display and hide there. Then fear took over; I couldn't even look up. I laid a twenty-dollar bill on the counter, much more than the cost of two Slurpees, then grabbed my wallet, my icy treat, and made a beeline for the door. "Oh, my gosh. I can't believe he did that," I muttered through clenched teeth as I headed for the car.

As I unlocked the car door, I realized that in my shame-filled haste to escape, I had forgotten my son. I'd left my kid in the store—saying who knows what else to this stranger—and couldn't bring myself to go back in. I just stood there and waited. And waited.

As I worked up the courage to face "so black dude" again, Matt suddenly came around the corner with a big smile on his face. In one hand he had his Slurpee. In the other he clutched the change from the purchase. Can you believe it? The guy had given me my change!

I stood there in shock, while Matt, oblivious to what he had just done to his mother, said excitedly, "Let's go park now, Mom." As he opened his door to climb in, I didn't know if I should reprimand him or cry. I may have done both.

To this day, I have no idea what happened in those long moments after I left him in the store with that kind and understanding cashier.

Needless to say, our tradition of visiting that particular 7-11 before our trips to that park ended, allowing that poor guy some level of self-respect and me some relief about being left shocked and speechless. Instead, we now supported the park concession stands by purchasing ice cream cones.

Traumatized, I tried to put it out of my mind. After all, we live in Utah, and at that time, it was a mostly white population, so my son had very little exposure to other ethnicities.

A few weeks later, as I folded laundry in my room, I heard a familiar sound coming from the television in Matt's room. It sounded like that chant he had performed for the 7-11 clerk: *Ooga-booga-ooga, ooga booga* . . .

I rushed toward the noise, anxious to discover the source of my son's inappropriate behavior. Matt had a movie in, his favorite at the time. The scene playing happened to be one where a man learns he has a son who's been raised by an Indian tribe in the Venezuelan jungle. They were performing a tribal ritual that involved a chant and dancing around a fire. My son, the movie buff, had only been acting out a scene from a movie.

Wahoo! Mystery solved. I smiled, grabbed my son's cheek, then gave him a big smooch and went back to my laundry.

The whole time I was folding, I marveled at how that young man could have easily been angered by Matt's actions. He had every right to be offended, and I'm grateful he wasn't. I will forever appreciate that he chose the opposite. He chose to show my son kindness—well, at least up until the chant because, to be honest, I don't know what happened after that.

The honesty I love in younger children is the experience I continue to have in raising a person with Down syndrome. I don't always love it. Honesty is not always well-received *when coming from an adult who exhibits childlike behavior.*

If you ever find yourself in a situation where you're getting direct feedback from someone who has special needs, whether you asked for it or not, please know the parents are more than likely dying inside. My son does not have a malicious bone in his body, and he truly means no harm when he's upfront with people.

On the other hand, if you find yourselves in the opposite situation, where your child may be staring, hiding behind you, or asking loudly when they see someone like Matt, "Mommy, what's wrong with that man?" Please know it's okay.

We get it.

We are living in often oversensitive times. In my opinion, we could be seizing these opportunities and using them to learn or teach. Things might be less awkward if we led by example and did something as simple as our friend at "the Sev" and showed some kindness. Personally, I love to answer questions; after all, there's no hiding in my world. I would rather help educate any day.

In the meantime, apparently I need to shower. As I'm listening to my son in the next room, I overhear him saying, "Mom needs shower. Her butt stinks." How rude! Who's kid is he?

Lessons Learned

- For the times when you'll need to make a quick getaway, invest in a decent pair of sneakers.
- Slurpees aren't that good anyway. Okay, well, that's a lie, as my pocketbook can attest.

You can never have too much *Hairspray.*

CHAPTER 17

Late-Night Highs

What you can plan for:
Your child will be structured. Remember that!

I have excellent communication skills. Just ask me. In fact, I may tend to over-communicate. The verdict is still out on whether that's a good or bad thing. Sadly, I fell short in this area on one important topic, and, needless to say, I paid the price.

Anytime you have a child who has special needs, caring for them requires extra doctor visits. I have always been upfront and honest with Matt when he has an appointment, doing my best to make sure he understands that medical clinics are a safe place and that it's our job to keep him healthy. As he's gotten older and is more aware, I have made it a point to explain what may happen during each visit. For instance, before we arrive, he knows whether he'll be getting X-rays, hearing tests, or drops put in his eyes. He doesn't like that they may make it really bright and hard for him to see. He also knows whether they'll be drawing his blood or he'll need immunizations or shots for any other reason.

Matt's a champ! He's either really brave or has a high pain threshold. His veins, however, like to play hide-and-seek from the nurses. It's uncomfortable as they poke and prod around his arms, searching, but he does so well to remain calm. Me, on the other hand? Not so much, but I do my best to cheer him on from the sidelines. "You've got this, Matt. You're so brave," I say while I look away so he can't see the fear on my face. I hate needles, but this is one truth I don't want him to know about.

I have found that providing as much information as possible is vital, especially if we are going for a full physical. Why? Because I've taught him only two people are allowed to touch his private areas, and that is him and his doctor and nobody else—not even his parents. I needed to somehow protect him against creeps who should ever try to take advantage of him. It made it easier for me to explain and for him to comprehend when there were fewer people who had rights to his body.

It's always been important that he trust me, and at the same time that I give him a chance to mentally prepare himself for these visits. I like to think being honest with him has worked. Well, it's either that or me bribing him with a strawberry shake afterward—a tactic I'm not so sure his dentist would approve of.

In addition to the actual appointments, I also try to make sure Matt understands any medications he may be prescribed, explaining what they are for and how they may make him feel. I'd always done a great job with these explanations, or so I thought. After one particular visit to see a specialist, I learned this was an area I needed to work on. My large, opalescent awesome-communicator bubble burst, big and mighty, spewing bubble guck everywhere. It was that bad, at least to me.

Around age twenty-four, Matt's comprehension appeared to be declining, and we were concerned. Long story short, we noticed him acting confused when asked questions he had always been able to answer, such as reciting his address or saying his ABCs.

Anyway, after visiting with countless doctors to get to the root of the issue, we learned several things, one being that Matt had severe sleep apnea. Starting immediately, he needed to sleep with a CPAP machine. Fortunately, he was easily convinced to wear his mask when we made a big deal of how he looked like Darth Vader. Our good nights now ended with, "Hey, Mom, I am your son."

In addition to the peace of mind that he would not stop breathing during the night, we hoped by him getting a better night's rest, the CPAP would help with the comprehension issues. John and I monitored this for a few months, and while he did well with the machine, we didn't notice an improvement in his cognition. So I scheduled a follow-up discussion with his physician, and she had one last suggestion—we temporarily put him on a stimulant to boost his energy and clear up his brain fog.

I have always been hesitant about putting Matt on a new drug. Because he has never communicated to me how pills make him feel, I usually have to monitor him and watch for changes in his behavior. With this specific medication, I worried about side effects, like feeling odd or loopy. Having had my own experiences with medicine, I knew this could confuse him, and he might not understand that he should share any strange feelings with me. I did my best to explain what the doctor's intentions were and how these pills were supposed to work.

I also tried to share what the side effects might feel like, going into enough detail to help him understand but at the same time not scaring or overwhelming him. However, my excellent communication skills forgot one itty-bitty detail—an important one. I would give this to him once a day, in the morning, with breakfast. Not in the afternoon, not after school, and definitely not before bed. You see where I'm going, don't you?

Fast forward a couple of weeks. Matt, the structured individual he is, knew he needed to take his pill every day. Every morning at breakfast, if I didn't remember first, he reminded me. A reminder I appreciated, specifically on those days I ran around like a crazy lady trying to get us out the door.

It didn't take long before I noticed a difference in Matt. He did not seem so tired, and he definitely had more energy. He was bouncing back! He was more attentive when carrying on a conversation, even initiating them at times. I also noticed an improvement when we asked for his help. Hallelujah! The recommendation appeared to be working.

Then it happened. We were having one of our hectic mornings, and in my haste to get breakfast in his belly and get us both out of the house, I forgot to give Matt his pill. Surprisingly, he forgot to remind me. As soon as he got to school, he texted me to let me know we'd forgotten this part of our morning routine. *Uh-oh,* I thought, *but one day shouldn't hurt.* I replied to his text, "It's okay, Matt. You'll be okay. I'll give it to you tomorrow." I thought it sounded reassuring.

I went about my workday, not giving it another thought—until that afternoon when he called me, as he did every day, to let me know he had arrived home safely from the adult day program he attended.

"Hi, Mom. I home." He said, sounding more excited than usual.

"Hey, bud, did you have a good day?" I asked, despite the fact that the joy in his voice indicated he had.

"Yes, Mom. Had a good day" and then in his proudest voice, he added, "and, Mom, I took my pill." Confused at first, I didn't know what he was talking about. Then BAM! Like a bird flying into a freshly washed window, it hit me. I whirled my chair around to look at the clock at the back of the room and saw the time in big red numbers: 4:00. My adrenaline surged. He should not have taken this pill at this hour. I would be spending the evening with the Energizer Bunny. I jumped up from my desk and darted over to a conference room, where I could continue a private conversation with him. I needed to know if I'd heard him correctly.

"Bud, You took a pill. Do you mean your white pill?"

"Yes, Mom!" he replied proudly, but I wasn't confident he'd understood my question. Matt had a habit of replying yes to questions he didn't always understand. I hoped and prayed this was one of those times and asked again, trying to be more specific.

"Matthew," I said slowly because serious conversations always called for his full name. "You took the tiny white pill, the one you take at breakfast?" Stupid question, I know. He had no other pills.

"Yes, Mom. Yes, yes, yes."

I sensed frustration in his voice.

Then my husband yelled out in the background. "Yes, honey, you heard right. He took his pill."

Oy vey! I played out the scenario in my mind. It began with Matt opening what was supposed to be a childproof bottle and ended with a crazed kid who would be bouncing off the walls that night. *I know better,* I scolded myself. I knew I had to be specific with him. How had I, the perfect communicator, overlooked this?

We hung up, and I went back to my desk, where I plopped back in my chair, momentarily stunned. *Well, crap! Now what?* I thought to myself. I had planned to finish out my day, but the chaos in my mind made it impossible for me to focus, so I shut down and clocked out early, then tried to prepare myself for what was sure to be an eventful evening. As luck would have it, I got stuck in rush-hour traffic. In an attempt to quiet the noise in my head, I turned up the radio. It didn't work, not even my favorite catchy tunes. After what felt like forever, I finally made it home. As I walked through the door, all seemed well . . . so far.

Just like every other day, my boys gave me a warm welcome, as did the smell of seasoned taco meat. John had dinner almost ready, and Matt had the table set. The salsa and sour cream on the counter reminded me it was Taco Tuesday, one of Matt's favorites. The meal itself was no different from any other night. Matt had his head down, nose in his plate, and was snarfing down his tacos as fast as he could, behavior not related to the medication. When it comes to meals, he eats like each is his last. I observed him as I ate and thought, *Maybe the medication didn't have that kind of effect on him.* Perhaps I've been overreacting.

As we finished and began to clean up the dinner mess, we talked about the live version of *Hairspray*, scheduled to air on TV that night. Matt and I enjoy musicals and really liked the 2007 movie version with John Travolta and Christopher Walken. We were looking forward to watching it live to see how it compared.

Matt had cozied up in his recliner, and I listened to the show as I sat at the table making some Christmas crafts. We were about half-way through when Matt suddenly blurted out, "That's my mom," and started to laugh. Seconds later, his chuckle turned hysterical. I looked up from my project to see what all the chaos was about. On the screen, I noticed the scene where Tracy Turnblad's parents sing and dance to "You're Timeless to Me." I chuckled. Because I'm known to sing and dance around the house, I assumed this to be the reason for his outburst.

My husband walked in just then to share some information, and when he heard Matt laughing, he asked, "What's so funny?" to which Matt replied, "That's my mom," throwing him into uncontrollable fits of laughter again. Between breaths, he managed to get out, "She has big boobs just like my mom!"

He'd caught both of us off guard with this answer. John and I looked at the TV, and for a millisecond stood there, mouths agape. Then, before we knew it, we'd joined him in his fit of laughter. After all, he was right.

The important thing to note here is that two of us were not on speed, and two of us eventually stopped laughing. One did not. This could only mean one thing.

I looked up at Matt and smiled. He seemed to be enjoying the show we were watching. Bless the innocence of his extra chromosome. My son has never been shy in telling me how much he loves boobs.

Around 10 p.m., Matt, who was usually sawing logs by this time, showed no sign of winding down. We were discussing this version of *Hairspray* we had just watched when suddenly my pumped-up boy jumped up from his chair and started dancing. I'm not a country girl, but it appeared to be a Western line dance. He hopped around, laughing and stepping from side to side while slapping his knee.

My husband looked at me with an evil grin and said, "Well, he's all yours. I've got to get up early for work." And with that, he left me to enjoy the events of an evening with Matt.

Eventful it was. Matt went into giggle fits, laughing at the most random things, most of them not making any sense. At one point, he ran off to his room, surprising me as he danced down the stairs holding his bedazzled microphone and loudly singing along to "Like a good neighbor, State Farm is there." I just sat back, shaking my head, laughing with him, or more like at him.

"No, Jake, I don't need insurance, but thanks for serenading me."

It made me wonder if he behaved like this at school once the medicine kicked in. I imagined it had to be disruptive and made a mental note to speak to his teacher about it. After all, I needed him to be energized, not obnoxious.

Around 11 p.m., Matt's enthusiasm began to peter out and fatigue finally started to set in. I had expected our night to go on a lot longer, so this pleased me. His yawns became contagious, and I could barely keep my own eyes open, so I told him to go get ready for bed. I made sure he hooked himself up to Lord Vader, and within minutes, he fell asleep. I tucked myself in and dozed off as images of my night replayed in my head.

Earlier in the evening, just after I got home from work, John and I had a window of time before all the silliness began for an in-depth conversation with Matt regarding this medication and when it should be taken. I learned an important lesson that day in being crystal clear in every single aspect when Matt's prescribed anything. I've had no issues since, and fingers and toes crossed, we will never run into this again. If so, I know one vitally important thing: we will not be watching *Hairspray* that night.

Lessons Learned
- Don't be fooled by the communication barrier. Our children are smart.
- Be thankful to the men who can confirm normal behaviors.
- Teach Matt that there are *some* good secrets to have.
- Keep all medication out of the reach of children—for real!

Yes, you are, Matt!

CHAPTER 18

No Need to Apologize

What you can plan for:
Apologies—and how to respond to them

I'm sorry is a powerful phrase in any language, impactful when used appropriately; meaningless, confusing, and even disempowering when used incorrectly.

What is it about this small phrase that can sometimes make it so hard to say? I will blame it on pride. At times, words and egos can be like a fighting match. "Pride and apologies to your corner!" DING! DING! Who will win?

A proud military guy, my dad rarely apologized. You know the type, a tough exterior but at times a soft-and-gooey center. I will forever cherish the memory of the day he let me skip school and took me shopping for my first prom dress. He beamed with pride—the good kind—as he walked with me through the mall from store to store to find a dress, shoes, and accessories.

On the other hand, I will never forget the day he embarrassed me after my very first date. I'd arrived home two and a half hours past my curfew, and he had no problem spewing curses at the guy for not bringing his daughter home on time. Never mind that the poor guy didn't know I even had a curfew. Ugh! That one was on me. Most days, I lived with the rough-and-tough Dad, and so, in those rare times he did say he was sorry, I knew he meant it.

Unlike my father, I overused this expression, particularly in my early teens. I lacked confidence and just wanted to fit in. Anytime I said or did something I considered dumb, an apology followed. If I told a joke or made a comment I thought was funny but nobody else did, I apologized. If friends had get-togethers and I wasn't invited, I felt bad for whatever I had done to be excluded—and apologized. Clueless to how often I said it, I misused the term altogether.

One afternoon after school, my best friend brought this part of me to an abrupt halt. She and I were doing homework while listening to records in her room. We giggled as we talked about the cute boys we were crushing on, focusing more on this than equations and variables. I made a comment that didn't get the reaction I'd hoped for, and, in true Wendy fashion, I stopped laughing and said, "I'm sorry."

Suddenly she blurted out, "Stop apologizing all the time!"

Her callous tone caught me by surprise. Since we rarely argued, this hurt my tender teenage feelings. Confused by her sudden outburst, I fought back the tears. I opened my mouth but quickly closed it, nearly choking on the two words that were again trying to escape. She saw my struggle and gave me a look that said, "Don't you dare!"

The anger in her eyes quickly turned into regret, and she followed up with, "I don't know why you have to say that after everything you say."

Not . . . everything, I wanted to argue back.

Her eyes continued to soften as she suddenly pretended to be interested in her math book. "It just gets old."

Embarrassed, I rushed to the bathroom to "pee," but, in truth, I felt inadequate and had a private mini meltdown. I had a hunch this may have been something she'd wanted to say to me for a long time but had been holding back until she snapped.

My best friend hurt my feelings that day, but she also did me a favor. When I tried to stop using my useless "I'm sorry's," I quickly realized how annoying it must have been. She'd handled me a lot longer than I could handle myself.

On the one hand, I'm happy to report that I improved. Interestingly enough, on the other hand, I went from a teenager who overused this phrase to an adult who occasionally needed a dose of paregoric to spit it out. I've been to the corner a few times with pride, but eventually, I win. When I'm wrong, I'm wrong, and if I hurt or offend, I want to rectify the situation. But dang it can be hard—like trying-to-go-to-the-bathroom-when-constipated hard.

So why do I feel the need to do a chapter about apologies? It's not because I just messed up my online grocery order and had to put my tail between my legs and call the store to apologize. It's not because I want the world to know about my teenage problem. It may teeter somewhat on how this gracious phrase made its way back to me thanks to my son and this crazy ship of life I'm sailing on. At times, that phrase has been my lifesaver when I'm drowning in a sea of embarrassment.

Mainly, this chapter has been inspired by the number of adult Wendy's I've encountered—those who have expressed countless unnecessary apologies when I've shared that my son has Down syndrome.

Telling others about your child's medical diagnosis is not an easy thing to do. After learning of my baby's diagnosis, the thought of having to tell others terrified me, so I never brought it up. I feared the reactions I would get. I never knew what questions would come next or how I would respond during the awkward silences and blank stares. It happened. A lot! I received the reactions I feared I would. Facial expressions either changed to looks of confusion or silence that spoke a thousand words. These moments made me feel uncomfortable and forced me to hurry and change the subject.

However, now that Matt is older and I have shared our story a gazillion times, I'm a pro and will take any opportunity to talk about my son and Down syndrome. Most of the time, they are productive and meaningful conversations. However, there was one response I received that initially put the brakes on my sharing as if I'd hit a speedbump at full speed.

"I'm sorry."

I'd expressed sorrow to God for whatever I did to deserve this, and I'd expressed sorrow to my baby for whatever I did to cause this. I now understand that punishment and Down syndrome don't belong in the same sentence. So why were others apologizing to me?

The definition of sorry is "feeling sorrow or regret." Were they feeling remorse or regretting that my baby had an extra chromosome? Did they think his life had less value? Did they think he would have a bad life? Or were their apologies for me?

As time went on, I beefed up my inner strength, building up the guts of Popeye to help defeat those ideas and people who challenged me.

One day while at work, I felt the force of this strength during a conversation with one of our executives, a gentleman in his sixties who still had a full head of black hair. We were both early to a scheduled meeting. As usual, I doodled on my notepad to avoid eye contact as being alone with the big wigs always intimidated me, especially this guy. He had the reputation of being bold with a dash of cockiness.

The silence in the boardroom felt really loud, but I wasn't the only one feeling it. In an attempt to make small talk, he asked, "Do you have children?" I stopped doodling but kept my eyes on the paper. The company we worked for had over a thousand employees, and gossip spread fast. I thought for sure he knew my story, especially after the carpet-glue incident! We had both been with the company for several years, so how could he not know?

Oh, wait, he's a guy, and if he's anything like John, he'll participate in workplace chatter but certainly not remember this nineteen years later.

"Yes, I have one son," I responded as I finally looked up.

"Oh, really? How old is he?"

Here we go. "He's nineteen." Since most kids have graduated from high school at this age, there are always two follow-up questions: "Is he going to college?" and "Is he working?"

The other meeting attendees still had not arrived, so I took a chance that we had a couple more minutes. I followed up with, "My son has Down syndrome," but before I could share that Matt attended an after-high-school program where they taught him further life skills and provided job-coaching opportunities, he interrupted.

"Oh, I'm sorry."

My mouth worked faster than my brain and, for some reason, I asked, "Why?"

I felt uneasy as we sat there looking at each other for what felt like an eternity. Every day we were faced with difficult conversations with our clients, moments where we had to come up with quick answers to challenging questions. For some reason, this moment made my subconscious want to challenge this, but I immediately regretted it.

That meeting room always felt like an igloo, but it suddenly felt colder than usual. I could tell he felt uncomfortable too. Certainly, I had not intended to put one of my leaders on the spot, but for nineteen years I had genuinely wanted to know what people were sorry *for.*

He answered, but there was no way I could have prepared myself for his next words, which mortified me. "Well, he won't live very long."

As if that conference room wasn't cold enough. *I could sure use some earmuffs to prevent me from hearing anything else he might say and a scarf to cover my mouth to keep it from spitting ice cubes for words. Where in the hell is everybody? Somebody please, please come save me from this uncomfortable moment!*

Not many things leave me tongue-tied, but mine managed to end up in a square knot. As I looked at the clock, I knew where my son was at that precise moment. An image of my healthy nineteen-year-old baby at the theater with his job coach, having a good time and making others laugh as he wiped down the theater seats, popped into my head. And here I sat, in this room, freezing! And don't forget, with a man sitting across from me and boldly telling me my son was going to die. At least that's what I heard. *Deep breath in, deep breath out.*

He was right. Matt was going to die. And so was I, and so was he. After all, death is inevitable.

At that moment, I had two choices: get defensive, which is how I felt, or educate him, which is what I chose.

Deep breath again. Here I go.

I shifted in my seat and cleared my throat. "Actually, the life span of these individuals has increased dramatically from what you may have heard. They are no longer being institutionalized, and their lives are viewed as *valued,* so they are becoming productive members of society." Pause, deep breath, and resume. "They have jobs and college opportunities, and if they are lucky enough to find true love, they even marry."

I could tell I had his attention, so I continued. "A lot more is available to assist with their medical needs than even a few decades ago. You may be surprised to learn that these amazing humans are now living well into their sixties." I then shared that one of our very own work colleagues had an aunt with Down syndrome who was in her seventies. Feeling proud of how I had just handled the situation, I relaxed back in my chair. I had nothing more to say.

"Wow. I did not know."

From the look on his face, I knew I had surprised him, and it felt good to have corrected his misconceptions. I hoped my response spared another mother from going through what I just did. The other meeting attendees finally started to arrive, saving us both from further awkwardness. *Finally!*

However, in true Wendy style, I found myself overanalyzing the conversation. Instead of being "sorry," however, I wondered how I could prepare myself for similar conversations. For one thing, I wanted to continue to educate but also feel more empowered. This individual continued to contaminate my thoughts with the length—or lack thereof—of my son's lifespan. I found myself avoiding the exec whenever possible. The irony is that this man passed away a few years later, well before his time.

My takeaway to this day is that I want to be upbeat and come from a place of love. From that moment forward, I formulated a response that goes something like this: "Thanks, but you know what? There is no reason to be sorry. I am lucky, *lucky* to have a child who loves unconditionally and teaches me to appreciate my abilities. He has no agenda and brings joy wherever he goes. Our family is happy to have him in our lives, and I hope you get to meet him one day!"

Lesson Learned

Arm yourself with *productive* replies for the awkward situations that will inevitably come, and always keep a sweater close should conversations turn chilly.

"I've got your back, bud—forever."

CHAPTER 19

Oh No. You Didn't Just. Say. That.

What you can plan for:
Growing a thick skin while mending a wounded heart

Can you believe the absurd things some people have the gall to say? The words that just spill out of their mouths? I mean, the *nerve* of some people, right?

Now, I'm going to invite you to think back to a time when you were that person, guilty of hurting or deeply offending someone with something you said or did. If we're honest, we've all done it—open mouth, insert foot, leg, and hindquarter.

I'm not proud to say it's happened to me several times over the last thirty-plus years. Memories suppressed deep within me have reared their ugly heads, requiring me to ask forgiveness for something I did decades ago, sometimes to a person I find hasn't given it an ounce of thought since. Although sometimes I find a grateful acknowledgment. Recently, these flashbacks were triggered when I was in the middle of one of these jaw-dropping conversations.

As a mother of a child with special needs, believe me, I have experienced some very awkward conversations. Oh yeah. Certain discussions have caused my mind to come to a screeching halt, leaving skid marks across the inside of my skull!

With that, my intent with this chapter is to let you know that if you have a loved one with an extra chromosome, you might need to remember as awkward conversations come up that we are all human. Unfortunately, as humans, we sometimes suffer from conversation regurgitation, resulting in the utterance of ignorant things. The question for our community is do we laugh or cry? Hopefully, by now, you're beginning to realize that you will do both—and it's okay. Just know there will be a lot of laughter in between these times.

Matt and his unpredictable antics have always provided me with great material for when a good laugh is needed. One day while out to lunch with several friends, I shared a story of some silly thing Matt had done the day prior. As usual, we roared with laughter, tears rolling down our cheeks, which ached from the pain of laughing so hard.

Suddenly, a member of my round-table audience gathered her composure and surprised us all with a question from out of the blue.

"So, are pugs Down syndrome dogs?"

To hide the fact that my chin had dropped, I brought the napkin I had been using to dab moments-ago-joyful tears up to hide said open mouth.

Did she really just say that? No. I heard that wrong, didn't I?

"I mean," she continued, "do animals have Down syndrome, and, if so, are pugs the breed that does? They look like Down syndrome kids to me."

It wasn't just me. The laughter at the table stopped as suddenly as it had started, and all heads whipped around to see how I would respond.

At first, I couldn't. I didn't know how to. When I finally found my voice, I grimaced as I said something like, "Well, that's not nice. Pugs are ugly. To answer your question, they are not genetically like humans, so, no, there are no dogs that have Down syndrome."

I will admit there may have been a sharp tone to my voice, which I regretted immediately. I really didn't think pugs were ugly, and I cared for this dear friend. I knew in my heart of hearts that she meant no harm. Like most parents do, I reacted in defense of my son, and it was not the first time, nor would it be the last.

Thank heavens for the person at our table who was able to think quickly. "Wendy, so what did Matt do when you . . ." And she took us all back to moments ago when we had been laughing like a pack of hyenas. Fortunately, we finished our meal in peace and left the table as friends. It could have gotten ugly, but it didn't, thank heaven. Do you know what *is* ugly? An experience I had with a stranger when Matt was twelve. I wouldn't call that man a gentleman because he was anything but. I'm pretty sure our interaction landed him in the doghouse.

Matt, a mutual friend, and I had gone to see *I Am Sam,* an inspiring movie about a mentally challenged father raising his daughter with the help of a group of friends who were also differently abled. Matt enjoys these movies as much as I do because he recognizes those who are like him.

We had just taken our seats when my bladder made itself known, so I decided I had best take care of business before the movie started. I tried to exit the theater, but a middle-aged couple in a heated argument blocked the doors. I didn't hear what the woman said, but the man retorted with a comment that made my ears perk up, my feet stop, and my body feel like it was going to combust internally.

"I don't want to see a movie about a bunch of retards!" he snarled, his voice hateful.

"Shhhh!" his wife whispered as she glanced worriedly at me, then looked away as she stepped closer to him to allow me out. "You don't know who can hear you."

It didn't matter that I had one arm on the door, about to exit. I couldn't help myself. I looked directly at him and, with the most kindness I could muster, I said, "She's right, you know. *I* heard you. My son has Down syndrome, a condition that happens at conception. He didn't ask for this life, nor did I, but it is what it is, and guess what? It's pretty great."

He scowled at me. I grinned as my bladder reminded me why I was there. I needed to hurry on my merry way, but I hoped I'd left him with something to think about.

When I returned a few minutes later, they were still going at it, only this time just outside the theater. The woman appeared to be losing the battle with this stubborn man. Mr. Not So Nice Guy gave me a smug look, then suddenly placed his foot against the door, holding it closed so I couldn't get back in. As if this would stop me!

"Excuse me," I said, irritated as hell but keeping my tone as polite as possible. He didn't budge, just glared at me, a look that only fueled my fire. By now, I had no choice. I gave the handle a good, hard yank, and as the door flew open, he lost his grip on the large tub of popcorn he held.

All three of us watched in shock and a bit of horror as the entire bucket of yellow puffs of salty goodness flew everywhere. In an instant, he went from angry to furious, his scowl something that would scare Michael Myers.

He didn't scare me.

"Well, was it worth it?" I asked and strode past him, back to my seat. Matt, completely unaware of what I had just experienced, welcomed me back with one of his infectious smiles. I could feel my adrenaline kicking in as I sat down. I don't like confrontation and did not understand why this had to happen. However, I did feel an element of satisfaction. There's a woman you may have heard of who goes by the name of Karma. She invited herself to join me at the movie that day, and I welcomed her company.

Within minutes of this great film beginning, my rivers of tears began to flow. What I realized as I sniffled my way out of my seat over two hours later was that my experience that afternoon paled in comparison to what those who are differently abled are faced with every day of their lives—ridicule, scorn, fear, ignorance, and ostra-cization. The difference? I've noticed these souls operate on a sweet frequency, higher than that of any jerk they may encounter. That guy wasn't just a jerk, he was a bully!

As I left our aisle and turned to walk toward the exit, I noticed the woman who had been arguing with the bully sitting directly behind us, crying, no sign of Mr. Charming. She looked at me, her puffy eyes full of sorrow and regret. I gave her a sympathetic smile, hoping she read it encouragingly as I respected her decision to stand her ground.

Two strangers, both crying, my tears of love and compassion. I imagined hers included tears of turmoil.

Unfortunately, you will run into situations like these, among other things. So take a minute to think through the possibilities. For instance, how do you respond to a person who asks why you bother putting braces on your son? "It's not really a wise use of your money, is it?" Or the person who has the nerve to express their laziness about putting their grocery cart back in the cart return. "I don't do it because that's what retarded people are employed for." Yes, you read that right. People really say those things.

For the most part, I have been able to keep my composure in these situations, meaning I don't always cry or lose it. But it's not always the case. There was one scenario I still struggle with. Being hurt by *that* word? This is a big one for me.

I had a serious debate with myself on whether I should write this chapter. Initially, I did not intend to, but I've got these loud and obnoxious voices that fill my head at times. This time they screamed, *Remember, you are Matt's advocate! And he's not the only one out there.* Obviously, the voices won again!

Here goes, and to all who know me, please know how difficult this has been for me.

"You're beautiful!" I heard a sweet, soft voice from behind me as I wrote the check to pay for Matt's adult day program. I looked up to see a cute young lady leaning on the counter, her irises sparkling as she made eye contact. Her short blonde hair was cut in a bob, and her smile was contagious. "And I like your shirt," she added before I had time to thank her for her first compliment.

I had decided to go au naturel that day, with no makeup, and I had styled my hair just enough to poof up my bedhead. Prior to the pandemic, I never left the house until my hair and makeup were done, but on my new journey, I dare to be my natural self most days, even when I probably shouldn't.

"Thank you. You are so kind!" I said as I returned her smile. "I think you are very pretty, and I like your shirt too. It's so sparkly." She looked down at all the sequins on her shirt and flashed a big smile.

"I love this shirt. I got it for Christmas."

My new friend had Down syndrome. She saw something beautiful in me on a day I felt so blah, and she made sure she told me. This sweet girl exuded a radiant spirit that shone so brightly it could cast a shadow over the sun on its brightest day.

As I drove home that afternoon, I couldn't help but think of this authentic young lady and her sincere compliment. I glanced in the rearview mirror, trying to see what she saw. I did not feel beautiful in the least. Still, I smiled. Then it hit me. My fifty-sixth birthday was just a few weeks away, and we were planning to celebrate with a movie, a comedy I had been dying to see. I now knew how I would give back on my big day. I wanted someone to feel as valued and significant as she had made me feel. I wanted to make people smile.

The day I celebrate when I first graced this earth with my presence finally arrived. I awoke feeling spectacular, which surprised me. After all, I was a year older. I looked forward to spending the day enjoying my boys' carefully thought-out plans. Secretly, I couldn't wait for the grand finale when I unleashed the dragon on my favorite dessert, white cake.

As we stood in line to buy popcorn at the movie, I noticed three much older women in the line next to us. They were obviously enjoying each other's company as they laughed, occasionally grabbing one another's arms, I assumed to keep from falling over and breaking one of their delicate hips. I observed them for a few minutes and smiled as I imagined myself with my friends at their age. I loved watching their interactions.

Moments later, I walked over and caught them off guard when I asked if I could buy their snacks. I then handed them a gift card and told them to enjoy their movie. For a moment, they stood speechless but then burst out with immense, surprised appreciation. They couldn't believe I wanted to do this for them. They thanked me as I walked away, their smiles and gratitude filling my heart with so much joy. Ironically, they ended up in the same movie as us. I smiled as I watched them carefully walk up the stairs, carrying a huge bucket of popcorn and their large drinks, then take their seats two rows ahead of us.

My entire day felt just like that, like three senior women happy to be together enjoying each other's company. It had been full of laughter and love as the sweet men in my life made sure we spent it doing exactly what I wanted—of course, being kind to strangers along the way.

And then . . .

In true "Chapooton" style (the nickname we have given to our household—a combination of John's, mine, and Matt's names), we capped off the day in our customary way by going to dinner at my favorite Mexican restaurant. My mouth watered for their chips and salsa long before we arrived. Once we were seated, those chips didn't stand a chance. We talked and laughed as we devoured them while waiting for our main course.

The hostess seated a youngish couple about Matt's age, along with an older mother figure right behind us. The younger female spoke a lot, no problem with that, "hello pot," but she was also rather loud, so I couldn't help but overhear some of what she said. Busy with my own family chatter, I didn't really hear her until she started talking about how special she was.

"We had this activity, and I was cleaning up the mess, and Dan said to me, 'Sheila, you are pretty special, you know that?' Then Michelle, who was helping us, said, 'Dan's right, you are special. How do you do all this? You are so good.' And just then, Alice walked around the corner and joined Dan and Michelle by saying, 'Sheila, they are right. You really are a special person.' I couldn't believe it. They kept saying how 'special' I was, and all I kept thinking was how I wished they would just stop because it made me feel like I was retarded."

The young woman laughed while I choked on a chip.

She continued. "I mean, seriously, they wouldn't stop telling me how special I was, and I just thought, *Geez, I'm not a retard, so you can stop saying that.* I don't want to be special if it makes me feel retarded!"

She laughed again, and I could barely breathe.

Matt sat across from me, enjoying every last bite of his street tacos, oblivious to what was going on behind me. My sweet boy, full of unconditional love and life.

Secretly, I wanted something to shut this young woman up! Especially when she proceeded to talk about a lesson she would be teaching in church the following weekend. I hated that I could hear her. *You could sure use a lesson on speaking in a more Christlike way,* I wanted to turn around and say.

To tell you the truth, I was dumbfounded. I'm into this journey thirty-two years, and my heart still hurts when I hear people use *that* word. The way this woman used it is exactly the reason the Down syndrome community is putting so much focus on *not* using it!

This girl could not have been much older than my son, which surprised me even more. *How can she speak this way? Doesn't she know better?* There is more awareness, interaction, and exposure to people with Down syndrome than ever. I tried without much success to forgive her. Someone had failed on educating her on this, but who?

I couldn't finish my meal. I needed to get out of there. I was torn between wanting to introduce my "special" son to her and wanting to politely stuff a tortilla between her lips to silence her. I did neither, however, and her husband, a man who looked like he wasn't afraid to fight, made eye contact with me. As I helped my son get his coat on, I engaged him in a heated stare-down. He noticed Matt, but I could tell by his "I don't care about you" expression that he was unmindful of my son or the tears I fought to hold back. I wished his wife would look up from her mess of an enchilada for just one second so I could include her in our ocular discussion. She never did.

I didn't even make it out of the restaurant before I started to cry, mad at myself for not taking a moment to educate her, for not standing up for my son. I had failed Matthew, my sweet gift from God.

Later that evening when we were back home, my white cake tasted like dried tears, and sadly, when Matt sang my birthday song, it

214

fell on deaf ears—which is normally difficult to do with Matt's explosive voice. I felt relieved that he couldn't tell I was miserable.

I had been so excited for my day and the request I had assigned my tribe—to make a stranger smile—but instead, a stranger's words at the end of the day, *my* day, had brought me to tears.

You see, *that* word is not **just** a word. That word hurts people in the worst place—the heart.

I lived in massive regret that night. There's not a lot that gets me tongue-tied, especially when it comes to my son, yet I've come to realize that this stranger's words left me speechless for a reason—so I could share this with you.

The R-word. What does it mean?

As I prepared to write this chapter, I decided to look up the definition. To my surprise, I found it has been changed.

retarded...
1 dated, now offensive : affected by intellectual disability:
<u>**INTELLECTUALLY DISABLED**</u>

> NOTE: The term *retarded* is increasingly considered offensive. The use of *intellectually disabled* is now preferred over *retarded* in medical, educational, and regulatory contexts, as well as in general use.[1]

Hallelujah! Thank you, Webster! I sat back in my chair and soaked up all the feel goods flooding my body.

To be fair to this discussion, I'm going to be genuine and raw.

Prior to my son's birth, *I* used this word regularly. In fact, I even know of two times during my pregnancy that I used it, my exact words: "I wouldn't be surprised if God sent me a retarded child to teach me patience." I know, right? At the time, I even laughed at my remark. Honestly, I meant no harm. Now, these are unpleasant, uncomfortable memories. In fact, I hated putting that in writing just now.

Then I gave birth to my son, and the word escaped through my lips once, which I shared at the beginning of this book, but I removed it from my vocabulary when Matt was a day old. I broke the habit that quickly.

"What's the big deal?" you might ask. You can learn more about it on the Spread the Word: Inclusion website:

> The thing is, when you use the R-word as slang, you really are hurting people with intellectual disabilities because of the negative connotation of your comment. The R-word has been associated with people with intellectual and developmental disabilities since its inception, so when you use the word in a negative context, you're putting down people with intellectual disabilities, regardless of if you mean to or not. (March 2023) (2)

What took place on my fifty-sixth birthday left me feeling like I failed as Matt's advocate on this topic. This is why I've decided to address it from a place of love, including difficult but loving conversations on hard topics. I've shared these difficult scenarios because I believe there is a silver lining in all things, including what happened at the restaurant. It has sparked some difficult conversations and some great ideas.

For one, I was able to write this chapter—a chapter I originally did not intend to put in my book. Matt's unconditional love, compassion, and forgiveness gave me the strength and courage to do it.

Secondly, a dear friend of ours, Amber, who adores Matt, heard the story. She instantly put her artistic abilities to work and designed a small notecard that includes an illustration of Super Matt on the cover with a short blurb on the R-word. She surprised us with a handful of these personalized notes to keep in my purse to hand out anytime I'm in these uncomfortable situations or find myself tongue-tied. What an angel!

Third, it resulted in an inspiring project Matt and I will be working on together—owning our voices and providing folks access to Matt in a remarkable way that may counter some of the ugly stereotypes out there. I can't wait to bring this vision to life.

In an ideal world, it would be great if everyone made a more conscious effort to avoid saying *anything* hurtful, if everyone realized how much our words matter. That said, I also want to make sure you are prepared to know that for every person who hurts us, angels often appear on the scene as well.

Lessons Learned
- There are times you will feel defeated, but in the end, you will be the victor.
- My son is not the only angel in my life.
- There's not a Band-Aid big enough to fix the heart of anyone who's been hurt by another's words. We must educate.

[1] https://www.merriam-webster.com/dictionary/retarded
[2] https://www.spreadtheword.global/resource-archive/scenario-1

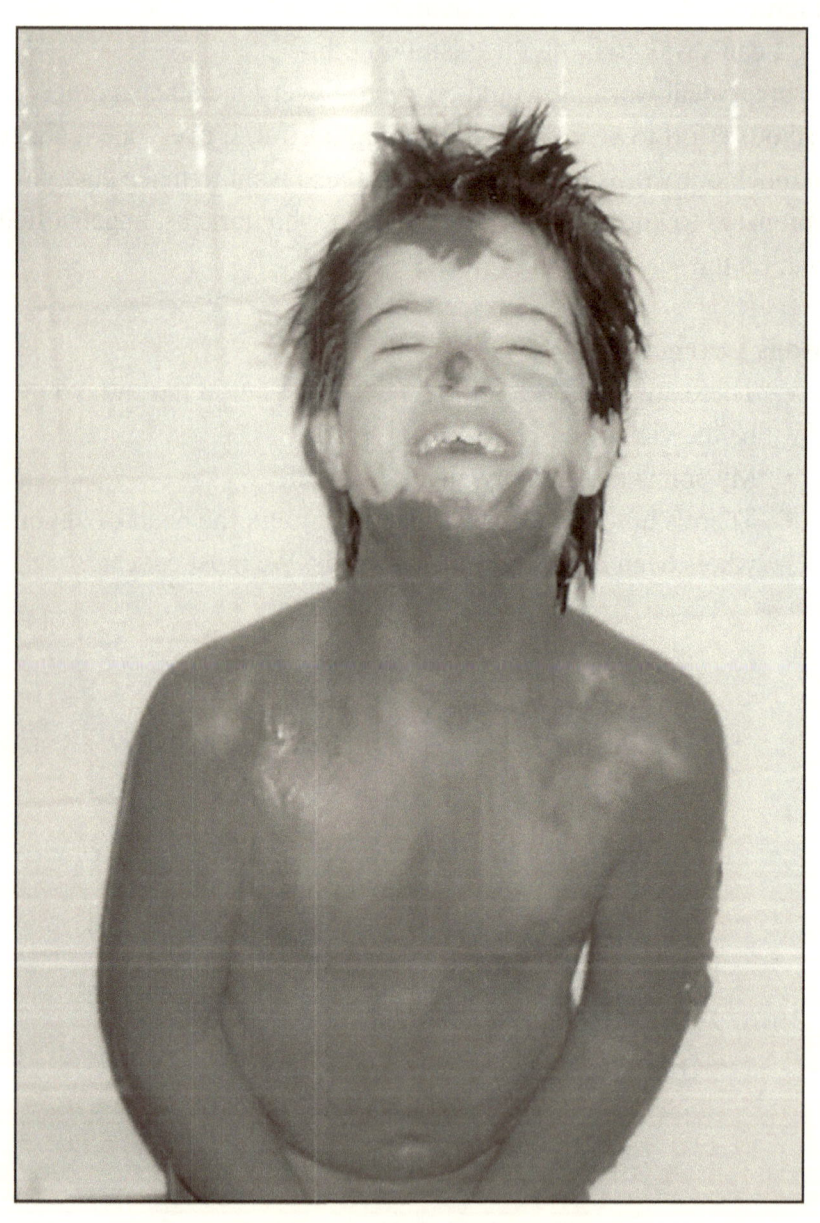

This is how you become Mother of the Year.

CHAPTER 20
Bathroom Etiquette Fails

What you can plan for:
A modestly immodest child

As I looked through my window at the freshly fallen snow, I was blinded by a shimmering blanket of tiny diamonds that peeked through the fine powder. Each took its turn to sparkle brighter as it caught the sun's rays. Just last week, I'd worn flip-flops, and while my toes were excited to get a taste of spring, I couldn't help but soak in the beauty of the undisturbed snow. Still pure. Still white. An invitation of peace.

While admiring this beautiful scene, I couldn't help but think of the twinkle in my son's crystal-blue eyes. As Matt got older, he struggled to make eye contact, but when he did, it was next to impossible to miss that incredible sparkle.

At birth, Matt's eye color surprised me (along with everything else) since his dad had green eyes and mine teetered on gold and hazel. I was glad his turned blue because it's like looking into a pool of happiness—*my* pool of happiness.

Speaking of pools and blue made me remember an unforgettable story that involved root beer, Smurfs, and two "home teachers," courtesy of The Church of Jesus Christ of Latter-day Saints. Home teachers were members who visited various families each month to check on their welfare.

As a young boy, Matt loved nightly bath time. I would barely get the tub filled with warm water and bubble bath and he'd be stripped naked, waiting impatiently for me to move aside so he could jump in. He loved to splash around on his belly while dunking his bath toys in and out of the bubbles, chattering to himself the entire time. "More bubbles, peas," he'd beg because I never seemed to put in enough to satisfy his desire to swim in a sea of suds.

Matt could entertain himself for hours if I let him, but, of course, that never happened. Bath time was over when his fingers resembled raisins and the soap suds dissipated. Occasionally, he would whine, sometimes even splashing me if he didn't want to get out when mean ol' mom came for him with his favorite dalmatian-covered towel.

Determined in my duty but hugging him tightly, I kept him warm as I dried him off, taking in the smell of his freshly washed hair as his baby teeth chattered. Okay, okay, there *were* times I couldn't resist his adorable "pleas" for more tub time, and I would add warm water and bubbles and let him play for "just a little longer." Like a sponge, I soaked up his ear-to-ear grin of excitement—a look that made me feel like I'd just been nominated mommy of the year.

When he was around age nine, Matt had just stepped into the tub when I heard my doorbell ring. I glanced at my watch. Who could be stopping by at this hour of the evening? I tossed him a washcloth, smashing the mounds of bubbles he had just scooped together. "I'll be back, bud," I said, needing a break from all the steam and heat anyway. Our front door was at the bottom of the stairs just outside his bathroom, and I wouldn't be long.

Through the peephole, I saw two familiar faces. I opened the door to greet my home teachers, who stood on my porch dressed in their Sunday best. They had been visiting my neighbor and decided to stop by, something they did monthly, to check on me and Matt. They were always ready to lend a hand to a single mother who worked full-time and sometimes needed help with simple projects, like changing the battery in a smoke detector on a vaulted ceiling or putting up a fence in the backyard. I welcomed their visits; I felt they genuinely cared about me and Matt.

I invited them in, but I did not want to leave Matt fully unattended in the bath, so I plopped myself in the chair next to the stairs. From here, I could listen to the bubbly bantering just feet away.

We had only been visiting for a few minutes when I heard, "Hi, Mom" and caught a flash of vibrant blue out of the corner of my eye.

220

I had to do a double take at the sight that beckoned to me from the top of the stairs. My son giggled as he stood there, buck naked and blue as a jaybird from his neck to his feet. I gasped before catapulting myself up the stairs, but not fast enough as our friends caught a glimpse of me shooing an overgrown Smurf back into the bathroom. They started to chuckle.

"Just a moment!" I hollered down the stairs as I slammed the door behind us.

My nostrils were hit with the sweet smell of root beer, and the walls of the bathtub shone with a blindingly bright blue. In between my son's giggles and my shrieks, I frantically tried to figure out just what he had done. I knew better than to keep any cleaning supplies in this room, and I saw no evidence of markers or fingerpaints.

Then I saw it, floating semi-camouflaged by the bubbles that surprisingly still filled the tub: the now-empty container of root beer–scented bath wash he had received as a gift. Don't ask me why the color was blue, but regardless, my little stinker had decided to use the entire container to paint every square inch of himself! As far as soap goes, he had done a fantastic job applying it. He looked like an oversized blueberry. Actually, to give you a more vivid picture, he looked exactly like one of the characters in *Avatar,* a movie that hadn't even been dreamt up at the time.

I hollered down the stairs, "Um, guys, I have a situation! I need to take care of it, so it will be a few minutes. You're welcome to come back another time if you prefer."

They were more than okay to wait. Having caught a glimpse of Matt and hearing all the commotion, they wanted the scoop.

Matt laughed uncontrollably as he stared at himself in the mirror. I happened to catch a glimpse of him and could tell he was proud of himself for pulling this on his mom. "You couldn't have done this at a more inconvenient time, dude," I said as I ushered him into the tub so I could hose him down.

Then I couldn't hold back anymore, laughing as I tried to find my son under all that blue. Inch by inch, his true color emerged. As he turned around and I rinsed his backside, I chuckled at my own funny thoughts. *Sure, my visitors decide to drop in on a night my son pulls this stunt—something that happens once in a blue moon, literally.*

Despite frequent unexpected circumstances at our residence, our friends continued visiting us each month.

It feels like eons have passed since that Smurf-streaking night, but it doesn't stop them from bringing it up whenever I run into them—how the smell of root beer permeated my home and how a young mother tried desperately to keep her "little boy blue" from being seen. Of course, from that moment forward, I did not leave the bath wash within reach, nor did I ever answer the doorbell if Matt was in the tub. Eventually, bath time ended whenever the water got cold. Period. Well, most of the time.

Speaking of cold water, my sweet and innocent son, you know the one, picked up some not-so-funny humor having to do with the "little boy's room." I think this room may have earned its name because of circumstances that bring out the little boy in grown men.

I've done my best to teach Matt proper toileting etiquette. However, out in public, because this is the one room his mother is not allowed to enter, I'm at the mercy of others. Thank heaven for John! In my stead, he has relentlessly taught Matt the unspoken rules of the men's room. He still has had to remind Matt that urinals are not an appropriate location for chit-chatting with random people. It took some time, but eventually Matt got it—for the most part.

Imagine how frustrating it is when it doesn't take much to undo all our hard work.

One Sunday afternoon, we decided to join some of our good friends, ShihLan and Brad, at a matinee. We have known this couple since before Matt blessed the earth with his presence. Brad, who is one of John's good friends, has always treated Matt like one of the guys. In fact, at times, he has instigated behavior that, in this mother's opinion, has tainted Matt's innocence. Brad is twice Matt's age and is known for being a jokester. You never know what's going to come out of his mouth. What I do know is that if his lips are moving, be ready for a tall tale or joke only he finds funny. Still, you can't help but love Braaaaad.

As we watched the movie, a story about superheroes saving the world, of course, we worked up an appetite. It's hard work cheering the victor on from the comfort of a movie-theater recliner. Apparently, the large tub of popcorn we consumed could hardly be considered a meal and our ravenous stomach's began to attack our innards like intestinal villains.

We all agreed: we needed some real food. However, before heading to the restaurant, another internal organ, our bladders, took rank. Should they not be drained soon, none of us would be going anywhere except home to change our pants. So, skip to the loo we did.

The guys took Matt into the men's room. They were the only three in there. This meant that strangers were not standing on either side of my son—and thankfully! Still, in that one visit, everything John had taught Matt to do and not do went down the drain. Matt was initiated as one of the guys.

"Boy, that water sure is cold," Brad said as he laughed at his own joke. My husband chuckled at the reference. Matt followed suit and laughed, too, completely oblivious to what this meant. (Think looong on that one, folks.) At the time, we were unaware that Matt understood this as normal commode chat, so we, I mean John, didn't think to prepare for future possibilities.

No thanks to our friend and his dumb comment, my husband one day found himself in an uncomfortable situation when Matt decided to experiment with said remark. To John's dismay, Matt randomly announced the water temperature as he relieved himself amongst a crowd of men. As expected, this caught others off guard, especially John.

Now, I know it's inappropriate to laugh, but I'm a visual person, so when I heard this, into my mind flashed the image of a row of strangers standing at the urinal and the one least expected to make this type of comment, the young man with Down syndrome, is the one who surprises all by boasting, in a roundabout way, of being well endowed. My sweet boy, clueless as to what he had been bragging about, laughed at himself. Thanks, Brad! But seriously, we love you.

Speaking of boasting, my office is located just outside Matt's bathroom. I spend most of my days locked away either working or doing research, aka shopping on Amazon, getting online organization tips, and writing this book. Depending on which activity I'm engaged in, it's either distracting or entertaining when my son talks or sings to himself as he does his daily grooming. Not that I am bragging, but, when needed, I have mastered the ability to tune him out so I can focus on work.

Some days, I must admit, are more difficult than others. This depends on how loud and entertaining he is or what kind of attention he's seeking.

Part of his daily ritual includes opening the door once he's dressed, taking one step out, and turning quietly in my direction, where he will stand statue-like until I look up. His point in doing this is to get attention for the shirt he's selected, fishing for a compliment or approval. He continues getting ready once he's satisfied with my response.

One morning, the sun's rays bounced off my blinds, nearly blinding me, but not as badly as the outfit Matt chose that day. Coming from the bathroom were the usual sounds of running water, his electric razor, and drawers slamming shut as he finished brushing his hair and teeth. But this morning, the sound of uncontrollable giggles joined the usual sounds coming from the other side of his door. The giggling got louder and louder, turning into a machine gun of giggles. *What is he doing in there?* I wondered, because no matter how hard I tried, I could not tune the ruckus out.

Then his door flew open, and he made his grand appearance, the color of flesh taking space in my peripheral vision. When I looked up, Matt, age twenty-five, five feet eight inches, two hundred pounds, and smelling of freshly applied deodorant and hair gel, stood before me in nothing but his socks and underwear. I nearly spit out my coffee. Yep! That's right! My grown son stood before me with his man-boy chest puffed out in a super-hero stance, his hands placed on his hips, awaiting my reaction.

While he did his best to stay in character and remain serious, I did my best to hold in my laughter. Before I had a chance to scold him for his lack of clothing, he exclaimed, "I'm a sexy beast, right, Mom?"

I could no longer hold it in, and I started to laugh; in fact, I threw in a few snorts. He fell out of character and joined me. We laughed hysterically for several minutes. He definitely got the reaction he'd hoped for and then some. I pulled myself together, put on my mom cap, and sat back in my chair.

"Dude, I'm your mom. You don't ask me if I think you're a sexy beast. The answer is no! I don't think you're sexy, but if you will close the door and finish getting dressed, I'll tell you how handsome you are when you reappear."

"Okay, okay," he said as he walked back into the bathroom, clos-ing the door behind him. He began talking to himself, I'm sure while looking in the mirror because he's obsessed with mirrors. "My mom thinks I funny!" He continued to laugh as I ran to my own bathroom. His unexpected surprise had almost caused his mother to pee her pants.

When he reappeared minutes later, fully dressed, I told him how handsome he looked, as promised.

As a young boy, Matt did something similar. He would call to me after he showered, and when I would round the corner, he'd be standing at the top of the stairs with his hands placed on his hips in his little superhero underwear. It happened frequently enough that I began calling him Super Underwear Boy! It may have been cute back then, but not so much now that he was older and hairier. We tease him that he is part gorilla, which is fitting because he loves all monkeys. But, man, does he need to shave. He gets that from his dad. (Sorry, Ash.)

Speaking of shaving, Matt does well with his face but not so well with his bum. What? You mean you don't shave your behind? Butt seriously . . .

225

You would've thought I'd learned my lesson with the blueberry incident. You know, the lesson where moms make sure the bathroom is free of anything that could potentially be dangerous or spark curiosity. I had done my best to childproof the rest of our house too. I'm not sure how I managed to miss *my* bathroom, except for Matt never used it. When he did around age five, I learned this lesson the hard way.

Matt had asked to shower in my bathroom. Several minutes into his shower, I heard him whimper. I opened the door to a blast of steam. "Are you okay, Matt?"

His sweet, small voice replied in a panic, "Mom, blood!" My son has always hated the sight of blood. Even the smallest drops still scare him. Initially, I had no concerns. What could have possibly happened in the shower that resulted in blood? Especially since I knew he hadn't fallen.

I walked in, and as I pulled back the shower curtain, I gasped. A pool of bright red filled the bottom of the tub, eventually swirling down the drain. Shocked, I quickly examined Matt to see where it was coming from. It only took a moment before I found an area on his bottom that looked to be the culprit. I grabbed the handheld showerhead to rinse it off and analyze the situation. As I did this, I glanced around to try to find the enemy, or weapon. Then I saw it—atop the soap dish instead of in its normal place sat my razor, evidence of fresh blood from a little boy's bum on it.

"Matt, did you touch this?" I asked as I pointed toward the razor.

"No, Mom. I didn't!"

"Are you lying?" I asked sternly.

"I'm not," he answered less confidently. He knew I had busted him.

I needed to focus more on the damage than a scolding, and, technically, this was my fault as I hadn't taught razor safety yet.

I applied some pressure, and, after a few minutes, the bleeding stopped. I checked his wound. Phew! We were going to be okay, no stitches needed—although we all know a tiny cut from shaving can sometimes look like a crime scene, which is what happened when Matt took my razor to his fanny.

The wound went vertically, of all things. I couldn't get Matt to tell me why or show me exactly what he did, so I could only speculate. Perhaps he had a better grip or it was just a better angle. He had never watched me shave, thank heavens—or his poor, small shin may have looked like he had taken a cheese grater to it.

Thankfully, he survived that incident with about a one-inch scar on his backside. I survived *butt* felt like I failed my son. I did an audit of my bathroom after that and made sure I had it childproofed. We also talked about shaving, although, in reality, the site of blood taught him more than I ever could have. To this day, Matt uses an electric razor, and, to my honest, cross-my-heart knowledge, it is only used on his face.

Razor: one. Matt: zero. Mom: minus ten.

Lesson Learned

The bathroom is the one room that has provided countless opportunities for learning, teaching, and good storytelling. Knowing my kid, I have a gut feeling there will be more to come.

Overcoming obstacles one at a time.

CHAPTER 21

Super Matt

What you can plan for:
You will parent a superhero.

Most people swaddle their babies in blankets. I swaddled mine in a cape. Why? Because I gave birth to a superhero. I began calling him Super Matt at a young age, not only because he was my very own superhero but because, in my opinion, he has several great qualities that make him a mighty wonder! Coincidentally, it's a nickname he earned from Ash as well, so it must be true. He's the hero of our family.

Unlike most caped crusaders, Matt has no idea of the powers he possesses or how fitting it is that he chose Marvel and DC Comics as the theme for his bedroom. His love for heroes like Captain America, Aquaman, and Wonder Woman is obvious the moment you enter his headquarters. Be warned, if you aren't careful, you may be hit with a surge of the awesomeness his 21' x 12' space contains.

Most superheroes do everything they can to keep their true identity a secret, not wanting the world to know who they are. It's the opposite for Matt. The world can see his true identity—but it is hidden from him. He is clueless about the effect he has on other humans and that his special abilities hardly differ from the heroes he's attracted to.

Just like in the comic books, Matt has been blessed with out-of-this-world strengths to help save those around him.

Let me build his hero character for you.

Matt has the strength of the Hulk. He isn't just physically strong. He can lift others when they need lifting, but his unpredictable sense of humor can make you laugh when you want to cry. His skin radiates yellow from the sunshine that glows from within him, drawing away nearly any disturbances in one's personal storm. When a person is acting crabby (possibly me) he will smash those nasty crabs, sending them scurrying back to whence they came. And do you know what's really frustrating? When you're trying to give someone the cold shoulder (Who, me?), and the Hulk steps in and squashes it! He ruins every bad mood simply by being who he is.

For example, he enjoys singing, which always makes me smile, and he knows it. Do you know how many times I get serenaded? If only we could all be more like this—imagine the peace the world would feel. Although, we also know who could use singing lessons, so it may not be that peaceful.

Matt has the vision of Hawkeye. He sees the good in everyone and everything. And he is unable to see our bad qualities or characteristics. The only thing blocked from his vision is seeing when someone is cruel to him.

Matt's senses are comparable to Spider-Man's. However, Matt's are not limited to the five we are born with. He has an extraordinary sense, and that is he knows when someone needs emotional help. If he randomly asks, "You okay?" you know he has recognized that you may be having a bad day. It does not take physical tears for Matt to know when someone needs a hug or a hand-drawn picture, which is his way of showing he sees and hears you. I have a box full of hand-drawn pictures equaling the countless times Matt saw the heartaches and physical pains I've experienced. My son's unwavering love is the best unconventional medicine. He is a natural healer.

I wish I could say he had the ability to move fast like The Flash. Unfortunately, I think the only thing fast about him is his bowels, which digest his food quickly and at times cause some real inconveniences.

When I watch him eat meals, I know how far we can venture off afterward by the amount he eats and how fast he eats it. Yes, his digestive system controls whether we can leave the house right away, or, if we're out in public, if we need to stay in the vicinity of a restroom for a bit.

We once made a big mistake when visiting Yellowstone National Park. John, Matt, and I were on a short getaway and had enjoyed a day of breathtaking landscapes and wild animals in their natural habitats. We finished by getting some grub at one of the restaurants in town. As usual, Matt devoured his food like a wildcat after its kill, protective of it.

Once our bellies were fed and happy, we loaded the car and hit the road. We were on the highway in the middle of nowhere when all of a sudden from behind us, John and I heard Matt mutter, "Ummm, why my belly squishy?"

We looked at each other in panic, immediately realizing our mistake. In our excitement to be on the last leg of our trip, we forgot to have Matt take care of business before leaving the restaurant. We glanced around at the desolate surroundings outside our car, looking for a sign for the nearest town or rest stop. We knew we could possibly be facing punishment for our hasty decision and began relying heavily on the strength and discipline of Matt's sphincter. *Please, please!* I begged, *Do not fill the back seat of my car with your chocolate surprise.*

John and I sprang into action. It may not have been legal or safe, but desperate times called for desperate measures. John pressed the pedal to the metal, and I turned in my seat and said, "Bud, I need you to undo your belt and unbutton your shorts right now."

He looked at me, confused, and shook his head like he thought I was crazy. Having pants that were unbuttoned anywhere but in the bathroom was unfamiliar to him.

"Please do it, Matt. Trust me." I needed any and all pressure against his stomach to be released—and stat. I explained how this would help.

I turned back around and found a good song on the radio for us to sing to, hoping to distract him. Listen, at this point, I was desperate and would try just about anything. I'm not so sure it worked for the occupant squirming around in the back seat, but it kept my mind busy. Oh, who am I kidding? Fortunately, we came upon a sign that said we were about ten minutes from safety, four with John's driving. We made it, barely. It was John who turned into The Flash as he rushed to Matt's side of the car, nearly causing him to fall out when he opened the door. I tried not to laugh as I watched Matt scurry after John, doing his best to keep his unbuttoned britches from falling to the ground. I prayed I would not see a trail of brown sludge as they made their way to the restroom.

It's a good thing we arrived when we did. John barely got him to the stall in time, and all the chaos had thrown my own bowels into an uproar. The second greatest thing about finding a toilet in time? Seeing a large roll of toilet paper ready to be put to use.

We got so lucky. This girl didn't need to worry about someone sparing a square, and my son didn't have to leave his underwear in the garbage at that rest stop.

I've saved Matt's strongest and most impressive superpower for last. Matt has the endurance of Superman. How lucky am I to have given birth to the greatest of all superheroes? I have my very own Super Matt!

Just like Superman, Super Matt can withstand afflictions most of us cannot. I've often wondered if he has immunity to certain kinds of pain. Somehow, he can remain calm, like the seas before a storm, even when it comes to bodily harm. I've always been in awe of this ability— but also confused and concerned. I've explained to him that it's okay if he hurts. He can tell me because we all go through it, and as his mom, it's my job to take care of him. Still, he rarely complains.

For instance, he handles blood draws like a champ. This does not mean it doesn't hurt him; it means he behaves differently than his mother does when he falls victim to the phlebotomists and their tiny instruments of torture. Unfortunately for Matt, they always have a difficult time finding his veins. He will watch intently as the tiny metal snake glides around under his skin, looking for the perfect spot to strike. The lack of sobs or whimpering from him may be a sign of courage, but eventually his face will say what his lips do not. (Tip: Hydrate your child with lots of water before going to these appointments. I've been told being well-hydrated helps bring the veins to the surface).

Believe it or not, despite our love of ice cream and Slurpees, Matt has never, ever had a brain freeze. The roof of his mouth is so deep it helps protect him from these fierce attacks. However, when he sees the rest of us suffering, he doesn't want to be left out—so he pretends, holding his head and howling right alongside us! As you're likely painfully aware, a brain freeze is not something that can be faked, but we laugh at Super Matt's exaggerated attempts. I just know that if I were to sign him up for an ice-cream-eating contest, we'd win, hands down.

When Matt was around five or six, I experienced what I felt was a huge mom-fail. We were coming home from one of our dates—the usual, a night out for ice cream. Of course, I experienced a case of brain freeze, and Matt pretended to. After that, we sang to the radio, our banana-split sugar rush enhancing our singing skills. I pulled into the garage just as one of our favorite songs ended.

Matt loved to jump out of the car to try to beat me to the door. But on this night, instead of hearing him rushing behind me, I suddenly heard "Ow! Ow! Ow!" I looked back toward the car and noticed him standing still, a look of horror on his chocolate-stained face. I dropped everything. Rushing over to see what was happening, to my horror, I saw that the door of our green Beretta was shut, painfully holding his thumb hostage.

I panicked and quickly opened the door, setting his flattened thumb free. Then I grabbed it, ready to smother it with mommy kisses and hoping to get it to puff back up into its normal shape. Going in for the kiss, I noticed just one tiny cut through all the smashed skin. Surprisingly, the attack required only one stitch. I was sure the bone was broken as tightly as our car held him captive, but, fortunately, no. Still, had this happened to any other child or even me, there is no doubt there would have been window-shattering shrieks. I'm surprised I even heard the ow's coming from young Super Matt.

The thing is, Matt can selectively ignore pain under the right circumstances. Any Disney lover knows that when you visit the parks, your feet are sore after walking and waiting in lines all day. Unlike me and John, Matt never complains. In fact, he denies the pain, even when it's obvious he's hurting. "Matt, do your feet hurt?"

"No, no, NO!" he'll insist as he tosses his shoes to the floor while falling back on the bed, fiercely massaging his toes. Just like at the Coyote Ugly bar, it's almost as if he thinks the fun will end if we know he's in pain. Rather than ask, I've learned to give him a dose of ibuprofen when I'm taking care of John and myself. For someone who isn't hurting, Matt consumes them like candy, and only a bit later I hear him sighing in relief.

And his resilience regarding pain doesn't stop there. Because people with Down syndrome are born with tiny ear canals, they are more prone to ear infections. Matt has suffered from them most of his life. I've never had one, but my younger brother gets them frequently and has shared how painful they are. Just another thing Super Matt never complains about. I've had to be on alert for the nasty green slime oozing down the side of his face or constant tugging on his ear to know something needs my attention.

Around age twenty-five, we learned Matt had an antagonist—a villain so unexpected we didn't know what to do about it at first. Those nasty infections caused him to experience some hearing loss. We immediately got him hooked up with hearing aids. He entered that appointment as Matt but was so excited to leave as Green Lantern, the super "hear-o."

However, it was too good to last. The hearing aids fit so snugly in his small canals that they acted more like plugs, stopping any airflow. As a result, the ear infections came back with a vengeance.

Eventually, we succumbed to the idea that Matt's Green Lantern superpowers were starting to fail him. Matt's ear, nose, and throat specialist suggested a cochlear bone implant. The surgeon implanted a processor under the skin behind Matt's ear so a receiver could be attached to a small bolt. It worked like an outer hearing aid. And so Bolt Man was born. Matt's super "hear-o" name for his new device.

The surgery was a success but came with challenges. The device had to be attached and removed daily. Matt's skin tried to reject it, which is a common side effect. What was not common were the three additional procedures he needed as a result. I had my worst experience ever with my son when he ended up back in the hospital. *Infection, swelling, bleeding, redness—surely my sweet boy has to be hurting. He needs me.* Yet, still no complaints!

"Does your head hurt, Matt?" I asked.

Matt actually said, "My head feels weeeowd."

I couldn't let him down! I borrowed his cape and did my best to swoop in and save the day—as (trumpets blaring) Supermom.

During one intensive, in-office procedure, Matt tensed up and began to whine. I could see the pain on his face as he tried to fight it.

"Does he need more numbing?" I cried out, unable to bear the thought of my son feeling this horrific procedure as well as the large needle used to numb the side of his head. My heart broke as I watched a single tear roll down his cheek, my insides screaming for him.

Then, just like that, the doctor finished. "I'm done," he said as he put down his tools and disposed of his surgical gloves. He put out a hand to high-five my son.

"I okay," Matt said as he bolted out of the chair, anxious to make a run for it. He high-fived the doctor, and we high-tailed it to the car. *How? How does he do it?* I wondered, a bit envious of his pain tolerance.

Lost in thought, I started the engine, pausing to think about how Matt had to endure these uncomfortable situations. I found myself getting angry. *This is not fair to him!* These thoughts were interrupted when the speakers began booming with "Rock and Roll All Nite" by Kiss. I looked over to see my son's oversized tongue hanging out of his mouth, hands in the air flashing the rocker sign, and his head, wrapped in gauze, banging along to the music.

In spite of my trauma, I found myself chuckling. *Well, I guess he's going to be okay.* I watched him laugh at himself in the side mirror. No longer needed, the tears that had been about to overflow evaporated. We headed to his favorite, Chick-fil-A, or, as he calls it, "Chick Café" to get his strawberry shake, his go-to reward for bravery.

Is the inability to feel most pain a superpower? I have had the opportunity to talk with other moms of children with Down syndrome who have also wondered about their child's pain tolerance. It remains a mystery.

Still, way beyond this are the incredible superpowers that amaze anyone who gives themselves an opportunity to meet him. I love Super Matt and all his superhero qualities, from his tender, Hulk-like strength to his Hawkeye and Spiderman super sensitivities for the feelings of others. And while his Superman qualities sometimes act like kryptonite, his selfless desire to save the planet—one smile or giggle at a time—is my ultimate favorite. These help him to conquer any villains who try to take him down.

Lesson Learned

Superpowers are not limited to fictitious characters in comic books or movies.

"The most important lesson you taught me, Mom."

CHAPTER 22

Big People Don't Pee In The Park

What you can plan for:
When they gotta go, they gotta go!

When the weather called for it, a day at the park was a must for me and Matt. From an ocean-blue sky, the warm sun called, not just for us but for everyone, to come out and play. Those were the days worth a drive to a favorite hangout. For me, it's always been Liberty Park in downtown Salt Lake City.

Located on eighty beautiful acres, it's full of ginormous trees that have to be hundreds of years old. The park was built in 1852. These incredible trees provide great shade on scorching summer days. In the middle of them sits a large pond you could call beautiful were it not for the hundreds of annoying ducks and seagulls that have taken up residence, doing their thing and always looking for free handouts.

At one time, there were paddle boats you could rent and take out on the pond. As a young girl, I always wanted to try it, but the fear of being attacked by the ducks or falling into the murky water kept me at bay. They've since removed the boats. It's just as well as the stench of stale water and layers of slime are not very inviting.

But there are plenty of other enjoyable ways to stay entertained at this park. Years ago, when Matt and I frequently visited the park, several playgrounds provided hours of fun. Matt loved the aviary, which housed several different species of our winged friends. Their squawking was obnoxious as they conversed with one another, especially as you walked through their territory. Matt enjoyed collecting the loose feathers scattered across the ground while I worried about him catching the bird flu from his filthy souvenirs.

Next to the aviary were several carnival rides intended for younger children, some having been there since I was a child. In fact, I have pictures of my mother holding me as I sat on top of one of the brightly colored horses, the colors having since faded.

I've spent a lot of days at Liberty Park and continue to have the best memories of it. In my childhood, we had several family reunions there. We'd show up with our buckets of chicken or packages of hot dogs to roast over the built-in barbeques and, of course, a deliciously sweet watermelon. It was the perfect place to meet up to watch the parade every July 24th, our state holiday. My cousins and I had a tradition of plastering the older family members with water balloons. When they retaliated, we would squeal as we ran away. We played badminton, horseshoes, and perfected the skill of throwing a frisbee. These experiences are what continued to bring me back as an adult, wanting to create new memories with my son.

The park had undergone several changes since my younger days. Most of the carnival rides were removed and replaced with a large climbing structure and play equipment.

In 1993, my employer, who loved fountains, graciously donated a unique water feature that mimicked seven of our state canyons. Water flowed down each one, forming a small wading pool at the bottom. This addition made it a more appealing place to take kids on those hot days. After playing and before heading home, we would take off our shoes and wade through one of the many streams, giggling as we splashed each other with our feet.

We didn't just go in the summer months, though. You could get as much satisfaction on the cooler days of spring and fall, especially if you were feeling a bit gloomy and needed to get out.

One year, in late September, when Matt was about ten, I found myself bored and itching to go for a drive. Sunday mornings usually did that to me. We were in the midst of fall, the colors in all their splendor. Going for car rides during this time of year has always brought me

240

joy. There is something about the deep reds, oranges, and yellows that brightens my soul.

As if on autopilot, my car magically found its way to my favorite park. As Matt and I pulled in, I noticed that the summer crowds had disappeared; however, several people had the same idea I did. Some were having picnics, bicyclists zoomed past, and dogs barked at one another as their owners took them for a walk.

Matt and I hopped out of the car and let our feet be our guides. As usual, I walked slightly ahead of him because I tend to be a fast walker. But he does well to keep up, considering that his lower muscle tone makes it twice as hard for him.

He magically sped up when he spotted a playground ahead. He giggled as he ran past me and noticed there were kids around his age. He had no problem approaching the other children, who were having fun. They, on the other hand, were skeptical of this boy who joyfully approached, a boy they could scarcely comprehend and who seemed different.

I watched the familiar pattern play out: some were friendly and accepting, but most moved to another area in an attempt to exclude him. It always broke my heart, and I was grateful he could not see what I saw. Oblivious, Matt did what they were doing—even when they tried to lose him! If they decided to go down the slide, he was right behind them. If they moved to the swings, so did he. They were playing a game with him and didn't even realize it.

On this day, one by one, each child ran off to their mother when called, leaving Matt to play on his own.

We had been there for about an hour when he ran over to me. "Mom, I need go bafroom!"

He began to do the potty dance, a sign that, as usual, he had waited until the last minute.

"Okay, let's go find one." I directed him to the closest restroom I knew of, fortunately not far from the playground, only to realize my worst nightmare. The doors were locked! Panicked, I peered around, trying to remember where the next closest bathroom was. I felt relief when I spotted one a short distance away. *Please, please, PLEASE don't be locked!*

I turned to Matt to lead him in that direction and gasped at what I saw. It was small and white and had a crack in it. Staring me in my face was my son's bum. Apparently, he had taken matters into his own hands and decided to water the bushes, which were as bare as his bottom. With the change of seasons, the leaves had all fallen and the trees were of no help in providing any privacy.

Mombarrassed, I quickly did my best to fan myself out like a curtain to shield him. I then "yespered" (that's yelling while whispering), "Matthew! What are you doing? Big people don't pee in the park!"

"I sorry, Mom. I have pee!" he yespered back.

Well, I certainly couldn't stop him now. The floodgates had been opened. As he continued to relieve himself right there in plain sight, my head bobbed around like an owl, praying nobody could see beyond me. For once, I found myself appreciating my voluptuousness, and, for once, I found myself wishing I were slightly larger! The last thing I needed was for my ten-year-old to get arrested for indecent exposure. I sure as heck wasn't going down for this! After all, my pants weren't the ones on the ground.

I was as relieved as his bladder that the park had fewer people that day. Otherwise, I don't know what I would have done. Needless to say, our playdate ended. I didn't want to run into anyone who may have seen my boy sprinkling sunshine.

Back at work the next day, I replayed the scene with my dear friend and leader, Mary, in her office. The scenario was definitely funnier after the fact. We laughed until our cheeks hurt. We laughed even harder when the company teammates who sat outside her office became curious. One by one, they stood up in their cubicles, like a pack of prairie dogs.

We finally got a hold of ourselves, and when our laughing subsided, we both had an aha moment. My retelling of yespering to Matt that "Big people don't pee in the park!" felt catchy. Mary, who knew I had plans to write a book, said, "Wouldn't that make a great title for your book?"

Yes, Mary, it would!

Sharing my story has been cathartic, but it took years before I found the courage to make myself vulnerable enough to share my truth with anyone who may need it.

Lessons Learned
- You'll find humor in a lot of the things you go through—after the fact. Perspective is everything.
- When you gotta go, you gotta go, even if it is not the most convenient time or place.
- I hold the key to the fountain of youth. It has a name. Matt

We are still on this journey. Still learning,
still growing, still having fun.

CHAPTER 23

Still On the Journey

What you can plan for:
An extra chromosome is like that person who shows up to your party uninvited… but then ends up being the life of the party.

My fingers have spent countless hours trying to keep up with my supersonic thoughts as I've selectively chosen how to articulate each of my stories. However, a year into creating my masterpiece, Down syndrome tried to beat me again.

What in the world do you think you are doing? it hollered one day. *How can you help other parents when you can't help yourself?* I allowed doubt and fear to squeeze their way into my head. I almost let them beat me, and the creation of my book almost came to a halt.

You see, I'm still on this journey of being a mom of a child with Down syndrome, which means I still have hard days. When I open my eyes each morning, it's a mystery whether my day will be one of blessings or lessons. Even now, I occasionally experience defeat. Can you believe I actually thought life would get easier as Matt got older? *Now, why would you think that, Wendy?* Exactly! My son is still growing; therefore, I am.

Still, for years, I let things hold me back. *I'm not an expert. I'm just a mom.*

I've made many trips to my laundry room where the water runs, but not always from my Maytag. I find it ironic that this is the room I've chosen to allow my feelings of despair to overcome me, feelings that I'm not qualified for the job. But I'm thirty-two years into this journey, and I sure as hell know that's not true. So, I give my soul a good cleansing, then put it through the rinse cycle before drying off and moving on.

On more than one occasion, I've been able to use my tears as fuel to rev my engine and navigate myself out of a situation. My destination? Opportunities to grow and be creative. Regardless of how amazing Matt is, the inevitable challenges force me to step up my game.

In the end, I won't let a tiny extra chromosome get the best of me.

While doubt may have crept in, almost causing me to give up on this book, the one thing I will never give up on is my son. A fierce fire burns within me. I am Wendy the Warrior, armed and ready to take on anything that tries to get in our way. Mom to Super Matt, always ready with waterproof mascara and tissues in hand as I receive the rewards the Universe has prepared for us, rewards that continue to come.

For this reason and for all you may face as a parent, I want to share one last and recent celebratory moment that came in the form of an experience—a once-in-a-lifetime, drop-to-your-knees, overcome-with-gratitude experience.

I received a call from a stranger in Denver Colorado, a kind woman who wanted to extend an invitation to Matt to attend The Best Buddies Gala they were hosting in the fall of 2022. Best Buddies is an international organization dedicated to establishing a global volunteer movement that creates opportunities for one-to-one friendships for individuals with intellectual and developmental disabilities. I stumbled across this program as I researched opportunities for Matt just after the pandemic. Best Buddies paired my son with a young man Matt enjoyed hanging around with. His peer buddy has taken him to a movie, to hang out and play video games, and bowling on several occasions. Matt got excited each time he got a chance to hang out with his new friend.

"If you accept," she said, "your son, Matt, and his buddy are to be honored as Champions of the Year, representing the state of Utah."

"What! Are you serious?" I exclaimed when she finished her speech—as if she really needed to sell me on this opportunity. No way would I, could I, say no to this invitation!

Giddy with anticipation, I waited impatiently for John to get home from work so I could share the news. Naturally, he was thrilled, and he immediately contacted his boss to make sure he would be able to get work off.

Two days prior to the gala, we would be celebrating a national holiday, otherwise known as Matt's birthday. John and I decided to add his birthday celebration to the weekend to make it even more memorable. We couldn't tell Matt because he would talk nonstop about how his weekend would be all about him, driving everyone crazy until the day finally got here.

The event was at the Ritz Carlton in Denver on Saturday evening, but we arrived a day early to get the party started. First, Matt's stomach was our compass to good food, then we were fortunate enough to get into the Meow Wolf Museum, thanks to a nice member of the staff. (Note: This museum contains fun and psychedelic art from different dimensions, which was right up Matt's alley.) After a day of fun, we headed back to the hotel to get all gussied up for Matt's big night. I will never tire of watching John help Matt get ready for formal events—the way they laugh and tease each other as John ties Matt's tie and splashes him with just enough cologne because a little goes a long way and when Matt applies it, it goes a long, long, long way.

Since the gala was black-tie, the men were decked out in nice suits, some in tuxedos, and the women wore long evening dresses with matching shoes and clutches. Meanwhile, our humble little family dressed our best. I wore my fancy dress slacks (because this girl doesn't wear dresses) and what I thought was a gala-appropriate black silk blouse, complete with my bunion-unfriendly shoes and matching pocketbook.

John was pleasing to the eye in his dress pants, white button-down shirt, and new silk tie. He looked quite dapper considering his usual attire is jeans and a Utah Utes shirt. Although, did I mention his new silk tie may have had the Utes logo on it—a tribute to one of the big games they were having on the same night?

During cocktail hour, the room buzzed with excitement as servers dressed in pressed shirts and pants walked around with silver serving trays, offering up light appetizers and glasses of champagne. This definitely was not In-N-Out. John and I did our best to try to fit in, while Matt, oblivious to the different lifestyles, was at the height of his glory and had no problem commingling. My boy sure looked handsome in his black, two-piece suit and the new black silk tie he had picked out specifically for this event.

After an hour or so of enjoying the cocktails, the event hosts called the champions and their buddies to the ballroom for dinner. A sea of tables with formal place settings, enough to seat the hundreds of excited celebrants representing the West Coast, greeted us.

The emcee introduced each champion and their buddy while we were served a nice meal of chicken or salmon and roasted vegetables. I was proud of John, who ate his veggies with minimal complaining. I do think he may have been confused when he saw all the different pieces of silverware laid out at each place setting. Not Matt. A fork is a fork. Just give him something to shovel it all in. But seriously, I watched proudly as he used his best table manners to consume his fancy feast.

When it came time for Matt's peer buddy to be recognized, he had Matt stand with him, refusing to accept the glory without his reason for being involved in the program. This small gesture impressed my mama heart. Their budding friendship was less than a year old, but you wouldn't know it by their strong connection. My cheeks began to burn from my ear-to-ear grin as I watched these two young men, arms around each other's shoulders, accepting the award together. When they were done acknowledging Matt's buddy, they did a small intro to Matt, announcing his birthday, which had taken place a few days prior. This, of course, caused him to stand abruptly and throw his hands in the air while shouting in his loud baritone, "Me? Me?" while turning to look at each of the guests. He about knocked over the poor waiter who had stepped in to fill our wine glasses. In true Matt style, he had the crowd's attention, and they laughed and clapped loudly for him. Not quite the response his buddy had received; it appeared Matt's lack of humility had won over the room of raving supporters.

As the evening went on, we heard the stories of those involved in the program and enjoyed a performance by a group of special little dancers. I had to grab a tissue as I watched the many differently abled children perform for an audience who could barely keep their emotions in check. I thought my heart would burst.

Suddenly, Kool and the Gang's "Celebration" exploded from the speakers in the DJ booth. Matt, who is no stranger to this song, bolted toward the dance floor with his companion in tow. My young dancing machine would not be missing out on this opportunity. Matt's buddy, on the other hand, claimed to have two left feet and abandoned Matt when he pulled out his exaggerated Gangnam-style and sprinkler dance moves. You know you're at the perfect dance party when there's no personal space. You could barely see the floor through all the feet dressed in their Sunday best. But the crowd didn't intimidate Matt. He nearly bumped into those who danced next to him as he busted out his moves. Can I just say, my boy can dance! I stood off to the side, laughing and cheering and, of course, taking a ton of pictures of my young John Travolta. It was all I could do to keep from jumping in and showing off my mad dancing skills. I refrained, though. After all, this was not my night.

My baby is now a man, and, each day, he continues to surprise me as we are given memorable opportunities. I will never forget him on that dance floor, Gangnam style, tearing it up.

To say my life has been amazing is an understatement. When I think back on that young mom who spent those first few days crying and grieving, it saddens me. And yet it was what it was—a young mom scared for the future of her child. Here's the thing: had I only known how wonderful our journey was going to be, I don't think the tears would have flowed as hotly.

Everyone has moments when they wish they could look into a crystal ball and know what the future holds. The purpose of this book is to be that crystal ball for you and anyone who may need it, early on or later, to help dry up some of your tears and bring you peace. To help you see a future of unconditional love and happiness. No one will ever have another Matt, but *your* child will be unique and beautiful and super in their own way as they create their story with you.

And so, ladies and gentlemen, as you can see, I have not been defeated by the challenges of my journey. I have not allowed one tiny chromosome to beat me, for here I am, the captain of my soul, and **this** is my master-PEACE.

The Final Lesson Learned, at Least for Now

Now it's your turn. What will you choose to do with this one beautiful, amazing unknown with your child? I have learned this: you are the expert; you are the parent.

A Note to the Reader

I see you. I feel your heart. We are intrinsically linked. Ours is a journey of healing, hope, and humor.

I am committed to helping you and the loved ones who depend on you to not just survive but thrive together. I invite you to stay connected with me and to please allow me to help you however I can. If you have found value here, please share my message and find me on my website, wendylhooton.com, through my speaking on podcasts and radio, and via my consulting. You deserve a positive, uplifting, supportive community, and together we create that.

You are officially now part of the club of miracles.

The Special Child

Fifteen years ago,
A "special" babe was born.
"You must be special people,"
We were told on the next morn.

We were a young couple,
Your average man and wife.
Then suddenly, one November day,
We were given a "special" life.

Well, believe it or not,
I'm ashamed to admit,
We didn't want to be "special,"
Not one extra chromosomal bit.

Where's the baby we expected—
The son we waited for?
That baby didn't arrive;
We've been given so much more.

My eyes have been opened,
But it took a little time
To understand what "special" meant,
And I am proud he's mine.

Maybe the "special" as they meant it
Was not because we're great.
Maybe the special they talked about
Was to help us before it was too late.

Now our child has grown.
He's turned into a fine young man.
Our "special" babe came to us
To help us be all we can.

I don't feel I am special.
I believe he's a message from above
To help us to stay focused.
We were sent a child of pure love.

I'm going to say Matt's special,
A "savior," you could say,
To help his earthly parents
Be their best each day.

Wendy Hooton
June 16, 2006

Our beginning.

Then.

Now.

Becoming a big brother.

Forever fun,
forever playful.

Forever playful,
forever fun.

Making space for medals.

Best Buddies - 2022 Champion of the Year Gala.

Me and my boys.

Acknowledgments

Dreams can come true! I am humbled by the author's journey I have been on. I firmly feel I have been guided—whether by the Universe or my Creator—from the time I made the decision to retire until the present. I remained open to faith and trust, and here I am.

My success as a mom and an author is not mine alone. The success of my story as I have lived it and written about it could not have been possible without the love of the many important people who've supported me and my son from the sidelines.

First, to my Creator, thank you for trusting me with this beautiful soul I get to call my son and for knowing I needed him more than he needed me.

To my parents, although I wish you were here to experience this dream with me, I KNOW you have been guiding me along this journey. I love and miss you.

To my knight in shining armor, Sir Jonathon, thank you for swooping in and rescuing this damsel in distress and her little prince too. You have been a rock-solid pillar of strength. Thank you for giving the best hugs, for the endless laughs, for helping me to see a different perspective on how to resolve things, and for always wearing shirts with sleeves soft enough to dry my tears. Thank you for all your help and support with this lengthy and occasionally difficult project, for cooking our dinners, for doing the laundry when I forgot, and for keeping Matt quiet as he kicked your butt playing video games whenever I was on one of my many calls. Thank you for not letting me give up when I almost did. I love you!

To the smart one and the beautiful one, I am lucky and proud to be your big sister. Thank you for believing in me and supporting me when I shared this idea with you. Thanks for giving me the best sisters, niece, and nephew, each of whom I'm so proud of. To Ryan and Kiera, here it is—you're in a book. I love you more than you love sprinkles on donuts and Nutella.

To Cuz, thanks for the endless love and support and for always being honest and saying and suggesting exactly what I need to hear. Thanks to you, I now own a blazer. XO

A special thank-you to ShihLan. From the time he was our little Buddha baby, you have been like a second mother to Matt. My boy will never starve as long as you're around.

Thank you to Mary Jensen Smith, my director-turned-mentor-turned-cherished-friend. Thank you for challenging me, empowering me, and believing in me. Get the beast charged up because I'm going to need your help carrying all my books.

I have been blessed with an abundance of amazing people I call friends, aka citizens of my city. Initially, I began addressing each of you individually because you deserve personal acknowledgment. However, I changed my mind when this began to look like the final credits of a *Star Wars* movie. That and my menopause brain put me at risk of overlooking someone. ALL of you accepted my son from the moment you met him. You've supported us in our numerous fundraising events, cheered Matt on at the Special Olympics, worn your crazy socks, and have been a sounding board when I needed it. You have helped dry many tears and at times cried with me. Thank you for reminding me that, more often than not, my sweet boy was no different than your children. You are more than just friends; you are a part of our family.

To my incredible mentors: without you, my master-PEACE would still be a dream stuck in my head. Bridget Cook-Burch, I wouldn't be me without you. Thank you for inspiring me, for adding your "special sauce" to my book, for knowing when I could do more, and for being the strength I needed when fear and doubt tried to creep in.

To Richard Paul Evans, Debbie Ihler Rasmussen, and the Author Ready Program, it's been an honor to be mentored by one of the best.

The monthly meetings, weekly classes, and Timepiece Ranch have been instrumental parts of my journey.

To my "funtastic" publisher, Rebecca Hall Gruyter, I want to thank you for all the laughs we had together as you so kindly led me on this journey. Thank you to the team and Todd Schofield for bringing my book to life. To Michele Preisendorf, my amazing editor, your attention to detail has made not only my masterpiece but my overall message significantly better.

A special shout-out to my beta readers. You had an important job, and you did it well.

Thank you to the incredible teachers and coaches who helped my son succeed in becoming the person he is today. He has accomplished more than I ever imagined thanks in large part to you.

To my extended family who have cheered me on, thanks, I love you!

Ash, we may not have been able to do marriage right, but we nailed it with our son. Thank you for being a part of the biggest and best gift I've ever received. In addition, I appreciate the love and devotion your family gives Matt.

To Matt's 'little' sister, thanks for filling a role I'm sure may be difficult at times, but a role you carry out so lovingly. I appreciate you!

To all new parents embarking on this journey with an extra chromosome, congratulations! Grab your party hat and prepare yourself for the wonderfully hard and amazing life that lies ahead.

Lastly, thanks to you, dear reader, for taking the time to join me on my journey with an extra chromosome. I hope our stories made you smile and allowed you to see those with extra needs in a different light.

About the Author

Wendy is a Down syndrome advocate, speaker, motivational coach, and best-selling author of Share Your Brilliance. Prior to becoming an author, she spent thirty-five years with a Fortune 500 company, where she helped leaders in megacorporations strengthen their culture through employee recognition. In this position, she received several awards for her performance and ability to manage difficult circumstances.

Wendy also has eighteen years of experience volunteering with a nonprofit organization, where she developed ties with the community while offering support to families. She learned to carefully balance her demanding job responsibilities with the many hours dedicated to helping those in her community, allowing neither to interfere with her most important job of raising her son. However, she does credit both for providing her with the strength to advocate for the special needs community.

In sharing her story, she hopes to offer support to parents experiencing the emotions she did after the surprising diagnosis she received. Through healing, hope, and humor, she plans to share all the amazing "extras" these parents will enjoy because of that extra chromosome.

Wendy lives with her husband and son on the outskirts of Salt Lake City, Utah. When Wendy's not writing, you can find her on road trips with family and friends, vacationing at the beach, attending various cultural events, or driving through the majestic mountains of Utah. Her favorite activity, though, is being entertained by her hilarious son.

Email: whooton@comcast.net
Website: https://www.wendylhooton.com
Facebook: https://www.facebook.com/wendy.lhooton/
LinkedIn: https://www.linkedin.com/in/wendy-hooton-1bb072148/
Instagram: https://www.instagram.com/peaceowendy/?hl=en

Scan the QR Code below to go directly to my website

Reviews

"Big People Don't Pee in the Park: A Mother and Son's Journey with Down Syndrome is an inspirational and moving story written with great heart and honesty. The radical authenticity makes it a compelling and amusing read perfect for anyone whose life is touched by Down syndrome."
  -*Richard Paul Evans, #1 New York Times bestselling author*

"Big People Don't Pee in the Park is full of honesty, humor, and so much love! Wendy Hooton writes from her heart as she shares about "her person with Down syndrome" and you can't help but smile, laugh, and see the world as a better place. Wendy brings comfort and light into some of her darkest moments, in the hope her words might help others. One extra chromosome has given her son superpowers and she is training him to become a hero!"
  -*Tiffani Freckleton, NICU RN, bestselling author of My NICU Story: Written with Love and Letters to a Future Nurse*

"Super Matt's mom, Wendy, is a superhero! She is super: humble, funny, relatable, authentic, and funny. Did I mention funny? Humor is her secret weapon for sharing the important lessons every parent needs to master. Wendy's heartwarming book, *Big People Don't Pee in the Park*, made me laugh and cry and laugh until I cried. This book will make you feel as if you have a new BFF. And doesn't everyone need a superhero friend?"
  -*Roni S. Miller, mother of three young men, including Remington, who has learning disabilities, librarian, and author of Guy Manzer: The Magician's Reckoning*

267

"As a mother, grandmother, and para-professional working with Special Education students, I encourage all individuals who are blessed with a child with different-abled abilities to read this book. The author is authentic, real, and passionate about educating our community concerning special needs children. Her sense of humor, dedication, love, and determination will give you the tools to better cope with the challenges and joys of being able to associate with such wonderful children. The stories she writes will have you crying from laughter, sadness, and love."

-Jennifer Ann Gillins, author, S.E. paraprofessional

"With brutal honesty and wonderful humor, Wendy lets us glimpse into her journey raising a child with Down's syndrome. This inspiring book is really about being a successful parent and reminding us that all people have value, worth, and are to be respected. Thanks, Wendy."

-Elda Robinson, author of A Simple Cup of Tea and coauthor
of Empowering You, Transforming Lives

"This mother and son journey brilliantly captures the rawest emotions felt when living with someone with Down syndrome.
"My sister, Jenny, made child number ten in a unique yours, mine, and our family. After her condition was explained to us, we felt she wouldn't have a very bright future. I'm happy to say Jenny is a high school graduate, has won awards in the Special Olympics, loves performing in her special needs' groups, and just celebrated her fifty-fifth birthday! Jenny is a continuous source of joy and love for our family. She is the glue that keeps us all connected."

-Mikki Anderson, co-owner Anderson Trucking, sister to an adult
sibling with Down syndrome

"This book captures the reader's attention with the build up from Wendy's early childhood/teenage years to the leap of joining the "club" with her son, Matt, who was born with Down syndrome. She has written, with grace and humor, the true magic and wonder of receiving a gift and blessing. Her writing speaks volumes of wisdom and discovery, in a manner that will help other parents and children who may be embarking on this life journey in this "club." What a beautiful story to honor her adventure with Matt!!!"

   -Rebecca Taylor, MA, Licensed Psychological Associate, RTC Psychological Associates, PLLC

"Wendy Hooton takes you on a journey that is honest, heartfelt, and hilarious. Reading about her finding the strength, voice, and purpose, in an extremely difficult situation as a parent, is beyond inspiring. You will laugh and cry at the same time. A must-read!"

   -Todd Schofield, graphic designer

"Uplifting, funny, and inspiring. Fall in love with Wendy as she shares living life fully with Matthew, the gift of special needs, and the love he brings."

   -Maureen Ryan Blake, Maureen Ryan Blake Media

"A deeply heartwarming, humorous, honest, and personal memoir filled with raw emotions. Not being a parent myself, I felt I highly benefited with reading *Big People Don't Pee in the Park*. I am confident all can benefit from reading this one-of-a-kind storytelling nonfiction. One of the insights I took away, *was how can I be more inclusive to all*. With this, I believe everyone should have a copy. I know it will be one that I will pick up again and again."

   -Laura A. Phillips, Associates of Graphics Design & Commercial Art UVU, retired, dog mom :)

"From heartbreaking surprises to heartwarming blessings, this read will take you on a roller coaster of emotions. After finishing the book, and having the privilege of watching a few of these situations unfold, I found myself improved as a person. I give joyful thanks to Wendy and her son for sharing their story with grace, humor, and truth."

-Mary Jensen Smith, mom to two, wife, business executive (retired), twenty-six year MS Warrior

"In her amazing book, *Big People Don't Pee in the Park: A Mother and Son's Journey with Down Syndrome*, Wendy Hooton does an outstanding job of going through her experiences and sharing insights. Her humor and stories kept me laughing (she's a real hoot ☺) and "making my eyes sweat." I loved every minute of this read. It gave me a better understanding of the lives of my students with special needs outside of my classroom, and most of all, I have a new respect for all of the parents of my students. You are truly my heroes."

-Lena Johnson, Special Education teacher

"Wendy had me at the title of her book, *Big People Don't Pee in the Park*. I laughed out loud because, in seven short words, she encapsulated my experience raising a child with Down syndrome. And it got better. I couldn't put the book down. Wendy opens the door and invites the reader into the challenges and joys that are her life with her son Matt. Although the anecdotes are Wendy's, any parent can relate, not just parents of children with disabilities. This book is a treasure, a delightful and humorous read that I recommend to anyone. It is truly a genre classic that will bless the life of anyone who reads it."

-Gerald Nebeker, PhD, DBH, President, OrangeSocks.org, father to a daughter with Down syndrome

www.ingramcontent.com/pod-product-compliance
Lightning Source LLC
Chambersburg PA
CBHW030409130626
46549CB00004B/1690